DATE DUE

AP 27 06			

DEMCO 38-296

CHINA SUPERPOWER

China Superpower

Requisites for High Growth

Francis A. Lees
Alois J. Theis Professor of Global Finance
College of Business Administration
St John's University
New York

St. Martin's Press
New York

St. Martin's Press, Scholarly and Reference Division,
175 Fifth Avenue, New York, N.Y. 10010

First published in the United States of America in 1997

This book is printed on paper suitable for recycling and
made from fully managed and sustained forest sources.

Printed in Great Britain

ISBN 0–312–16499–8

Library of Congress Cataloging-in-Publication Data
Lees, Francis A.
China superpower : requisites for high growth / Francis A. Lees.
p.   cm.
Includes bibliographical references and index.
ISBN 0–312–16499–8
1. China—Economic conditions—1976–   2. China—Economic
policy—1976–   I. Title.
HC427.92.L433   1996
338.951—dc21   96–39186
                                                          CIP

To my four children, who keep me feeling young

Contents

List of Tables

List of Figures

Preface

Writing a book about China inevitably draws from the author his or her utmost in thought, resourcefulness, and humility. China is contrast, stark differences, filled with the inconsistent. China is changing in a dynamic way, but appears unmoved. The economy is becoming capitalist, but remains a mix of mercantilist and communist regulation.

When I took on the task of studying and writing about China, there was an attitude on my part that this would be just another interesting book. Not so. It is a struggle to reduce this vast country to 200+ pages of simple narrative. As a struggling author I have revised my 'game plan' on this project several times. Hopefully, this is not apparent in the reading.

Lack of clear success in responding to the question 'When will China become a superpower?' compelled me to estimate, decompose, and explain this nation's impressive economic growth. This has become a central aspect of the volume. The first three chapters outline how an economic and political opening took place, and the following two chapters outline the growth rate and its major components. The remaining chapters amplify the sources of economic growth and prospects into the future.

China's opening and development are creating critical geopolitical issues for the world. These are not discussed very closely in the text. There simply is not sufficient space and they are too important issues to be given brief afterthought. But they must be considered and dealt with. The sleeping giant is awake and still growing.

May 1996

1 From Dragon to Superpower

China is rapidly taking on the appearance of a world superpower. This is a vast change from a little over a decade ago, when the nation appeared to be no more than an oversized developing country with little prospect for successful development. Simultaneous with the 'last stretch' to super-power status, the People's Republic of China (PRC) is displaying other visible signs of modernity and vitality. These include a more business-like approach to managing its domestic and external economic affairs. For example, China now makes use of macro-stabilization programs to curb domestic inflation, is building a legal infrastructure with which to protect the rights of foreign and domestic investors, and is improving the balance between the demand and supply of infrastructure services. This leap toward modernity also is reflected by the development of more flexible financial markets that assure foreign investors that in China they will be able to secure needed financial services.

Over the past decade China has been enjoying an economic boom, which is transforming this country into a modern industrial giant. Indications are that China's growth will continue at an impressive rate despite obstacles such as transport bottlenecks, widening class differences, and bursts of inflation.[1] The magnitude of change taking place in China is breathtaking. The economic boom that originally was concentrated in coastal regions is spreading inland to population centers along the Yangtze River valley, and into the vast hinterland. State and local enterprises are transforming themselves into capitalist giants, Chinese-style. Municipalities are selling hundreds of formerly unused factories to foreign investors, and major infrastructure projects are underway or planned for execution in the near future.

THREE VIEWS OF CHINA

China watchers generally lean toward one of three basic views regarding how to evaluate and deal with China as it rapidly expands trade and investment links with the world. The first and probably most naive is to focus on unlimited business opportunities that apparently are available in

1

the PRC. This view was expressed by the chairman of a large American multinational company who said, 'the Chinese market has virtually limitless long-term potential.'[2] The wild-eyed projections of a country with 1 billion consumers do not sound so far-fetched anymore, and companies like Heinz, Procter & Gamble, and Johnson & Johnson are opening more and more plants in northern Chinese cities.[3]

A second view of China is that it is the biggest and most fearsome dragon in Asia. Singapore has given expression to concerns shared throughout Asia, due to China's drive to modernize its armed forces, test nuclear devices, and reassert its claims to areas such as the disputed Spratly Islands.[4] Beijing is on an arms spending binge, and its neighbors are becoming nervous. On the economic side Japanese trade associations are warning their members they should be careful about investing in China. They fear that Japan's domestic industry will be undermined by a shift of production.[5]

A third view is that the PRC is a risky partner, suffering from basic instability in its economic and political systems. China observers raise the question of succession upon the departure of Deng Xiaoping, and note that when the political strongman passes on, it is possible that China will experience collapse, political break-up, and eventually, disintegration.[6] Whoever succeeds Deng is unlikely to enjoy the almost mystical power to lead that he possesses.

A SLEEPING GIANT AWAKENED

China has awakened, and the shape of the world in the 21st century will be determined by how the leading industrial countries respond. In the past, the industrial countries have dominated the world economy. Japan joined the industrial country club when it achieved sustained high economic growth and rose to the rank of a leading producer and exporter. Perhaps the most important change in relative economic position witnessed this century has been Japan's becoming the world's second largest economy.[7] The most important change in the 21st century will be China attaining superpower status and displacing Japan as the second largest economy.

According to a *Financial Times* analysis, China's transformation is not a great leap forward, but more like a great leap outward.[8] In the 1980s Chinese economic growth averaged 9.5 per cent a year, doubling every 7–8 years. The World Bank views a 'Chinese Economic Area' which includes Taiwan and Hong Kong. This 'Greater China' already boasts considerable economic power:

(a) Measured in the standard manner, its GDP was well over $400 billion in 1991, almost half that of France. If measured at common international prices (using Purchasing Power Parity) its GDP now exceeds that of Japan.[9]
(b) Its imports are two-thirds as large as Japan's, and likely will exceed Japanese imports in 8–10 years.

The present rapid expansion phase enjoyed by China has a parallel in US industrial growth between the Civil War and 1913. As a result of this growth, by the eve of World War I the US was generating a third of global industrial output. This created an upheaval in relative economic power. The current expansion of China's economy also will have devastating impacts on the relative power of countries around the globe. These effects will be of a much larger order than those following the achievement of economic hegemony by the US:

1. Relative power is transformed, sometimes leading to armed conflict.
2. The world economy is destabilized. After 1913 the US played the game of international politics by its own rules, leading to a breakdown of the treaty-based commercial policy system of the nineteenth century.
3. Painful economic adjustments are imposed on nations. The ascendancy of Asian economies is likely to create greater difficulties for established powers (the US, UK, Germany) than did the previous shifts of relative power. This will take the form of increased North–South trade in manufactures, and lower demand for manufacturing labor in Northern economies.[10]

A shift in relative power currently is being demonstrated on the economic front by a large flow of competitive exports from China and other Asian countries. This will turn to flood-level proportions as China's industrial and export power mounts. China enjoys substantial labor cost advantages against almost every country in the world (Table 1.1). Discussions of policy responses in industrial countries have focused on protection against imports of labor-intensive manufactured goods. However, the application of protectionist policies against China would create further difficulties. These include failure to restore export markets already lost (unless discriminatory free trade areas are erected against low-cost producers), a need in industrial countries to shift productive resources as trade alters the configuration of what can be produced competitively, a lower aggregate welfare imposed on countries that choose to produce at higher cost rather

Table 1.1   Labor Costs per Hour in Manufacturing, 1993

Germany	$24.87
Netherlands	19.83
Japan	16.91
United States	16.40
France	16.26
United Kingdom	12.37
Taiwan	5.46
Mexico	2.41
Poland	1.40
Thailand	0.71
China	0.44

Source: *Financial Times,* June 28, 1993, p. 13.

than import lower cost manufactured goods, and growing friction between the US and China.

WHOSE CENTURY IN 2001?

The 'American century' is nearing an end, and the big questions are (1) will the US continue to remain dominant into the 21st century? If not, (2) which country can achieve world hegemony in the 21st century? In recent years writers focusing on these questions either declared the 'end of the American century,'[11] or the coming of Japan's century.[12] Events since the 1980s have proven these claims incorrect, or at least much ahead of real world trends.

Since 1979 China has been preparing itself for a global leadership role. In a perceptive analysis, Hamrin has analyzed China's early phases of getting ready. She analyzes two phases of preparation since China's opening.[13]

First Phase (1979–82) – Search For a New Model

In this first phase the Stalinist and Maoist models of economic and political behavior were shelved. Government leaders espoused partial deregulation of the economy and a readjustment of investment priorities. Higher priority was given to investment in agriculture and light industry. As the country experienced a nearly explosive escalation in investment demand, Chinese leaders searched for ways to more efficiently allocate scarce resources. As a result, the government moved toward better methods for preparing the annual economic plan, opened Special Economic Zones (SEZs), allowed joint ventures with foreign participation, and offshore oil exploration with foreign cooperation.

Deng steadfastly insisted on moderate reforms, and realism in planning. He emphasized that China could not expect to leap ahead of other countries, but could gradually narrow the per capita income gap while at the same time developing a more market-oriented socialist economic system.

Second Phase (1983–84) – Ideological Struggle and Breakthrough

In the early years following the opening to the West, China experienced several sharp twists in policy that reflected an unraveling of the 12th Party Congress compromise between moderate and more radical reform. At various points it became necessary for Deng to mediate between hard-line reformers and intractable conservatives. These dialogues led to better understanding of (a) the close connection between ideology, policy, and power politics; and (b) the inevitable linkage between domestic and foreign policy.

Some move toward decentralization of authority was achieved. More cities were given the authority to plan their own economic development under national rather than provincial guidance. At this time Chinese observers were busy studying the global technology revolution and its potential influence on China's ability to develop industries under competitive world conditions. Deng's emphasis on moderation held sway, and the consensus moved toward 'building socialism with Chinese characteristics.'

Broad and ambitious economic targets were adopted, including the quadrupling of per capita GNP by the year 2000. This was to be accomplished by opening the coastal regions and gradually shifting the development–modernization focus westward toward interior regions.

The PRC adopted a more flexible approach toward internal economic development and external political relations. In this regard Beijing espoused peaceful reunification of Hong Kong. Meanwhile, localities were given greater control over the use and development of productive resources. Urban economic centers were offered the opportunity to commercialize activities within an increasingly more market-oriented environment.

Since 1987 the economy of the PRC has performed better than the economies of Germany or Japan when they experienced their own postwar 'economic miracles.' China's growth rate is surging, exports are crowding into world markets, and foreign investment is pouring into China to feed an economy hungry for capital and technology. Foreign multinationals are tripping over one another to get into a market about which they have long fantasized. Not since the heyday of America's infatuation with China in the early 1980s have US corporations been so gung-ho about China as in the period 1992–3, according to a *Business Week* special report.[14]

Talk of China becoming a 21st-century powerhouse, dismissed as naive after the Tiananmen Square massacre in 1989, is credible again. The only thing comparable to what's going on in China is the reconstruction of postwar Europe under the Marshall Plan.

Projecting growth into the early 21st century, a *Business Week* Special Report foresees China more than doubling its production by early next century and firmly establishing itself as one of the world's top economic powers.[15] This new industrial giant will be the world's largest manufacturer, the largest market for a wide range of high-tech manufacturers (telecommunication, aerospace), one of the largest global investors, and one of the world's largest users of capital.[16]

While China will be an economic superpower, it will not compete head-on with US and European technology-based industries as Japan currently does. By contrast, its strength will be light manufacturing and lower-tech heavy manufacturing (including ground-based transportation equipment and ocean-going vessels).

During the 21st century the world economy will be much more focused on developments in the Asia-Pacific region. In this context China's superpower status will provide it with the ability to influence the trend and direction of economic and political events. China's large size and vast potential will give it increasing leverage on world political developments. How China uses this influential status is a critical question for countries currently enjoying a position of world leadership.

SUPERPOWER, FORMERLY DRAGON

How can we designate the PRC a virtual superpower? Only a few years ago this country was regarded as one of the least developed. In 1982 with a reported per capita income of $310, China was in the lowest tier of developing countries. At this time it was perceived that its enormous population and high percentage of workforce employed in agriculture would make it difficult for China to achieve a structural transformation in use of productive resources.[17] Since 1982 China's per capita income has outpaced most other low-income and middle-income developing countries (Table 1.2). To address these questions and issues we analyze recent data concerning China's income growth and income level.

Recent Income Estimates for China

Entering the decade of the 1990s China experienced a surge in its overall economic growth rate. While in the decade of the 1980s China's income grew at an average rate exceeding 9.5 per cent per annum, in 1991–2 the growth rate accelerated to about 13 per cent. In 1993 the Chinese government confirmed that the economy was growing faster than previously expected. In the first quarter of 1993 GNP growth rose to 15.1 per cent,[18] and in the first 9 months grew 11.4 per cent.[19] One factor explaining the sharp surge in growth rate was exceptionally high foreign investment inflows. Over the period 1991–5 real gross domestic product advanced at an average annual rate of 11.7 per cent.[20]

In 1993 the IMF freed China and other developing countries from the 'shackles of the dollar' by using a new way of assessing economic growth.[21] Instead of converting their local currency national income into

Table 1.2   Per Capita Income Level, China Compared with Other Developing Countries, 1982 and 1991 (US $)

	Per Capita Income 1982	Per Capita Income 1991	Percent Change 1982–91
Low Income:			
China	310	370	+18%
Sri Lanka	320	500	+56
Pakistan	380	400	+ 5
Middle Income:			
Bolivia	570	650	+14
Philippines	820	730	−11
Nigeria	860	340	−60
Peru	1310	1070	−18

Source: *World Development Report,* 1984 and 1993.

dollars at market exchange rates, it used purchasing power parities (PPP) which take account of international differences in prices.[22] The result was a jump in the share of world output of developing countries from 18 per cent to 34 per cent. The new IMF figures lift China's share in world output to 6 per cent, three times its previous weight, making China the third largest economy behind the US (22.5 per cent of world total) and Japan (7.6 per cent).[23] The new IMF country weights suggest a Chinese GDP of almost $2000 billion in 1992 ($1700 per capita).

The World Bank also publishes GDP estimates that indicate higher per capita income than the standard figures. These are based on the United Nations International Comparison Program (ICP), which revalued developing country output at international prices. In Table 1.3 we have GDP per capita using the standard method of estimation (based on market exchange rates), and World Bank estimates (using PPP) for a selection of countries in 1992. The World Bank PPP-based estimates place China in second rank (in terms of aggregate GDP); the IMF estimates place China in third rank; and the standard estimates place China in tenth rank.[24]

Table 1.3　Comparison of GDP per Capita, Using Standard Method (Column 1) and New World Bank Method (Column 2)

1992	Developing Countries GDP per capita, $		GDP, $bn Purchasing Power Parity
	Market Exchange Rates	Purchasing Power Parity	
China	370	2460	2870
India	275	1255	1105
Brazil	2525	4940	770
Mexico	3700	6590	590
Indonesia	650	2770	510
South Korea	6790	8635	380
Thailand	1780	5580	320
Pakistan	400	2075	240
Argentina	6870	5930	190
Nigeria	275	1560	190
Egypt	655	3350	180
Philippines	820	2400	155
Malaysia	2980	7110	130

Source: *The Economist*, May 15, 1993, p. 83.

Massive Internal Market

The preceding discussion suggests that the internal market in China for consumer goods may be several times as large as formerly believed. Domestic purchasing power affords Chinese consumers an ability to acquire over $2400 worth of goods yearly on a per capita basis (Table 1.3). Large US companies are making investment decisions that support the view that the purchasing power of Chinese income is several times larger than indicated by standard measures. Motorola started assembling pagers in China in 1992. Motorola is being pushed along by China's surprisingly strong internal markets.[25] China is Motorola's biggest market for cellular phones outside the US. Other companies reflect this view of a huge and growing market. Chinese airlines are expected to buy 500 wide-body jet aircraft over the next decade. Companies like Procter & Gamble and H.J. Heinz are opening additional plants in Chinese cities. DuPont is shifting the bulk of its new investment to China, and by the year 2000 investment in the Asia-Pacific region will reach $2 billion. China will have the bulk of this investment.[26] Similarly, Hughes Electronics is ready to pump more investment into China. For Hughes, China is an emerging market growing rapidly from a relatively small base.[27]

2 Political Opening and Economic Reform

At the conclusion of the 1970s China initiated an open policy toward the rest of the world. Politically, closer relations were established with other countries, especially the industrialized nations. In addition, closer ties and membership were initiated vis-à-vis leading international organizations (the World Bank, International Monetary Fund, Asian Development Bank, and the European Community). Economically, China embarked on a program of increasing its foreign trade and investment with all regions of the world. On the trade side this included reducing tariff and other barriers to imports. Also, China embarked on a program of bringing foreign investors into the country, and providing them with assurances of stable operating conditions and better legal protection of property rights. Equally important, China reached out to make strategically important contacts around the globe. These included tapping overseas capital markets to obtain investment funds and foreign exchange, and undertaking overseas investments in selected natural resources and technology enterprises.

The opening of China to the outside world was probably the most significant global event in the final quarter of this century. As a major Asia-Pacific nation, China could not maintain its separation from the outside world. China's leaders recognized that as the Asian region was growing in importance relative to the rest of the world, it would be necessary for the PRC to demonstrate its desire to play a more constructive role in all aspects of international relations.

Over the period 1960–2000 Asia's production relative to the world total has been surging. In 1960 Asia accounted for only 4 per cent of world production. In 1992 Asia produced 25 per cent, and in 2000 Asia will account for 33 per cent. If the 21st century is to be the 'Century of Asian Hegemony,' what problems might face the world if China remains closed, alienated, and a source of potential instability?

A global reordering has been taking place, with Asia growing in importance in world production, and world saving and investment. China has awakened, and over the past 15 years has made up for 'time lost' when it followed autarkic policies. In this chapter we examine China's opening, its need for closer political-economic ties with the industrial world, the gains from China's opening, and the related transition problems.

11

CHINA'S OPENING

Two years after the death of Mao Zedong, the leaders of the People's Republic of China (PRC) initiated a program of economic adjustment and reform. There were two key elements in this program initiated late in 1978: (1) a political opening to the West to facilitate the building of a more modern industrial structure, and (2) reorganization of the domestic economic system. These two elements are interdependent. Success in achieving a political opening to the West can be measured by the extent it contributes to economic restructuring. At the same time the reorganization of the domestic economy requires closer political-economic links with industrial countries that can provide technology, capital, and managerial expertise.

Economic reorganization has included modest decentralization of decision-making to provincial and enterprise levels, and a reorganization of agricultural activity. This reorganization has included the dismantling of peoples' communes, and giving private enterprise motives more leeway in the production and distribution of food products.

Theory and Ideology

In what kind of historical perspective can we fit or 'accommodate' China's opening? Can we reconcile China's opening with socialism, nationalism, or some mixed variant of social-capitalism? It can be argued that China's policies since 1978 are the latest in a long series of attempts to learn selectively from foreign countries.[1] Unfortunately, this statement begs the question regarding the ideology that lies behind China's opening.

National leaders generally affirm that China remains a socialist state. But socialist states have experienced great difficulties in integrating their economies within an increasingly more dynamic and competitive world system. To accomplish this integration socialist aspects of economic and political organization and decision-making have been discarded one by one. This has been necessary to increase efficiency and satisfy the standards of rigorous international credit markets and demanding investors and portfolio managers. As a result, the British have privatized major sectors of their industry, the East Europeans have created laws protecting private property, and many Asian and Latin American nations have lowered tariff duties and undertaken structural reforms.

Foreign economic policies provide a common element in the conversion of socialist states toward capitalism. This applies to China as well. One way to test China's ideological status is to consider foreign economic policy from a conceptual viewpoint. Using Gilpin's three-way analysis, we can consider China's foreign economic policies as (1) liberal, (2) Marxist, or (3) mercantilist.[2] The liberal policy approach adheres to Ricardian laissez-faire doctrines (e.g. free trade), and can be associated with a global viewpoint (Table 2.1). The Marxist view sees class struggle dominating economic relationships, foreign and domestic. In this view foreign capitalists can be expected to exploit host countries. The mercantilist (nationalist) view is suspicious of free international markets, since by definition the state is more limited in using its power to influence trade and investment for national advantage. Unlike the Marxist approach, mercantilist policies support the nation-state as it seeks to exploit other states. By contrast Marxists view different class interests (across all nations) as in conflict.

Where does China fit into this ideological scheme? It is clear that China does not fit the liberal foreign economic policy mold. The opening was limited, foreign investors must negotiate entry under narrowly defined guidelines, and state enterprises continue to be protected and heavily subsidized.

Until the opening in the late 1970s China followed the Marxist pattern. Since the 1970s, government spokesmen continue to express Marxist sentiments, at the same time emphasizing the dangers of economic exploitation or social corruption that can follow from foreign contacts. In their view capitalism is at the root of foreign attempts to exploit China. Criticisms of foreign investment are Marxist-oriented, expressing concern over foreign partners in joint ventures that monopolize markets and seek to control management policy. The Chinese press has frequently referred to foreign capitalists as deceptive and dangerous. The increasing presence of foreign businessmen results in local governments competing with one another to attract investment, offering incentives that offset much of the advantage derived from foreign investment inflows.

While the Chinese express fear of foreign capitalism, they espouse the economic policies followed by Singapore, Japan, South Korea, and Hong Kong. During the 1980s Chinese commentators have applauded the achievements of East Asian capitalist states, and often focus on the successful government intervention practiced by Japan and other Asian countries. In this regard, China's spokesmen have espoused nationalist-mercantilist economic policies. This is reflected in China's analysis of the opening in which the international economic system is described as one of competing states using policies to serve national interests. In this competition, the economic and political opening gives China opportunities to develop its wealth by earning foreign exchange to purchase advanced

Table 2.1 Conceptual Basis for Evaluation of China's Opening

	Liberal	Marxist	Mercantilist
Analytical basis	Free trade and investment lead to international specialization, efficiency, and universally higher welfare.	Capitalists in rich countries use trade and investment to obtain cheap labor and extract profits from poor countries. Developing countries become dependent on rich countries for capital and markets.	National interests should determine state policies. Global conflict operates between all nations, rich or poor.
Policy direction	Pursue free trade and investment, i.e., laissez-faire.	At each stage of history the nation's structure shapes its political relationships. State serves interests of dominant class. Autarkic policies generally result.	Use state powers to regulate and influence trade and investment for national advantage.
Economic focus	Global focus, comparative advantage overcomes national distinctions. Viewpoints of nation states diminish in importance as global economy develops.	Focus on class conflict. Divergent class interests. National economic policies serve class interests.	National focus. Nation state must devote energies to achieve national advantage.

technology. Government agencies employ a mixture of capitalist-mercantilist practices, using foreign exchange resources to acquire owner-ship of overseas enterprises (e.g. Peruvian steel, US timber). The government role is seen as subsidizing industries, engaging in trade pro-tectionism, and importing technology. In contrast to the Marxian dogma that trade results in exploitation of poor nations, Chinese observers express confidence that the developing nations (including China) can negotiate effectively to obtain favorable trade and investment terms.

Pragmatism Behind China's Opening

The opening aimed at achieving concrete improvements in China's economy. Over the past 15 years the government has adopted a pragmatic approach toward its openness to the rest of the world. At times, the gov-ernment has accelerated the pace of opening and modernization. At other times, it has been considered necessary to slow or even reverse the opening process. Nevertheless, China appears to be edging gradually further away from the Marxist paradigm, replacing it with a curious mixture of capitalism and national mercantilism.

After 15 years the political opening and economic reforms can be said to have contributed to impressive changes in China. The following are most noteworthy:

1. Many goods and services are produced according to market forces rather than by arbitrary and bureaucratic government plan. In such cases a profits equal price-minus-cost calculus is the determinant of investment and production decisions.
2. The privately owned industrial sector now accounts for more than half of industrial output.
3. The industrial sector has access to more modern technology, made available by foreign investment and importation of advanced capital goods.
4. Agricultural production has leaped ahead. Increases in agricultural productivity are releasing rural workers for employment in industrial and commercial sectors experiencing dynamic change.
5. A large number of diverse types of banks and financial institutions are being created to support and finance the growing private sector economy.

These successes should not be looked at in isolation. China is a long distance from becoming a free market economy. Large industrial enterprises continue to be owned and controlled by the government, and subsidized to the extent of many billions of dollars each year.[3] Price controls continue to apply to a range of industrial products. Finally, China is a long way from developing a unified national market, due to transport bottlenecks and regional rivalries.

NEED FOR REFORM POLICIES

Over the period 1949–78 the Maoist development model guided the Chinese economy. According to this model centralized planning dominated resource allocation, and a bureaucratic government administration oversaw most aspects of economic decisions relative to production, investment, and prices. Production units in agriculture and industry were given little incentive to improve their economic performance.[4]

The Maoist model proved to be inadequate to China's economic needs, and the economy remained in a state of torpid slumber for several decades. The true potential of China's high growth rates remained concealed. Factor productivity stagnated. In the 10-year period 1966–76 worker productivity in state-owned enterprises rose only 11 per cent.[5] Over a longer period (1950–79) the decline in total factor productivity in industry averaged 2.75 per cent per annum.[6] Dernberger blames this inefficiency on overemphasis on investment in heavy industry, energy shortages, weak infrastructure, and inadequate analysis of demand. The economy was plagued with shortages until and well beyond the opening.[7]

Chinese economists began to assess the inefficiencies created by central planning in the 1970s. According to Rabushka, the severe criticism of central planning by the Chinese Communist Party and government must be interpreted as partly political. It was necessary for the government to justify rejection of old policies and the adoption of new ones.[8]

Even with an increase in the ratio of investment to national income, the overall growth rate declined in the 1960s and 1970s. This can be seen in Table 2.2 where 4-year period growth rates are presented for the industrial and agricultural sectors. The mid-1960s can be characterized as one in which high growth took place in industrial and agricultural production. For the following $1\frac{1}{2}$ decades the growth rate of production declined. However, in the late 1970s China instituted a series of reforms in agriculture, providing strong incentives toward efficiency and entrepreneurial activity. Consequently, agricultural production experienced strong growth over the period 1978–86. Similarly, the political opening to the West and economic reforms introduced in 1978 and after led to an upward shift in

Table 2.2   Growth of Production in China, 1962–90

Period	Growth in Industrial Production	Growth in Agricultural Production
1962–66	98.8%	49.4%
1966–70	45.9	6.0
1970–74	35.4	14.4
1974–78	53.9	10.5
1978–82	33.5	28.4
1982–86	75.4	29.4
1986–90	66.2	21.9

Note: Four-year interval growth rate.
Source: International Monetary Fund, *International Financial Statistics*.

growth in industrial production. Note that in the periods 1982–6 and 1986–90 industrial production expanded by 75 per cent and 66 per cent, respectively.

Several problems persisted under China's economic system prior to 1978. First, the government relied too heavily on large state enterprises to achieve advances in production and technology. There was little opportunity for entrepreneurial incentives to operate. Resource allocation was straitjacketed along the lines of the bureaucratically determined economic plan. Second, China's growth was molded according to an autarkic system. In this system foreign trade was discouraged. Foreign investment and foreign loans were rejected as likely to subject China to undesired external influence and pressures. Finally, ideological attacks were directed at the capitalist world. Chinese scientists and engineers were encouraged to develop an industrial technology suited to the Chinese system and Maoist economic model. Rejection of Western trade, investment, and technology resulted in China falling far behind neighboring Asian countries. It was not until China chose to develop and actively seek economic ties with the West, that it could reap any harvest from economic reform.

REAPING THE HARVEST FROM REFORM

Economic reforms introduced by Deng and his followers over the past decade and a half have aimed at correcting the distortions and improper incentives that prevailed under the Maoist economic planning model.

Beginning in 1978 Chinese leaders agreed on the need to abandon the centralized, autarkic, and rigidly controlled economic model. Interestingly, they have failed to agree on crucial issues such as the pace of price reform, privatization of state enterprises, and the role of market forces in allocating productive resources.[9]

Nevertheless, economic reforms have come about. These have helped to push China in the general direction of a market-oriented economy. Specific measures that have been instrumental in modernizing the Chinese economy are:

1. State enterprises were given greater authority in their management, including retention of a large share of profits.
2. Enterprises were given greater discretion in budgeting, including utilizing retained earnings for capital investment, purchase of equipment, and improved labor compensation.
3. The state's role in financing investment diminished, from two-thirds of fixed investment in 1978 to approximately one quarter in the mid-1980s. More diversified sources of financing are appearing, especially in the Special Economic Zones such as Shenzhen.[10]
4. Prices and costs for many industrial products are arrived at in more flexible markets. Government rules play a lesser role in this area than formerly.
5. New enterprises (private, collective, foreign joint venture) have grown rapidly, both in number and size. The share of industrial output provided by these new enterprises has increased from 14 per cent (1979) to over half (1992).
6. These new enterprises are increasingly supported by new and innovative financing. This includes banks, trust companies, investment companies, farmers' cooperatives, and the issue of bonds or shares of stock. Several new stock markets have been organized in Shanghai and Shenzhen, and other urban centers have requested permission to organize stock markets.
7. An industrial labor market is developing in China. With this, labor mobility is increasing and employment agencies have been established in larger cities.
8. Legal reforms are being initiated to protect property rights, establish reforms in bankruptcy law, and guarantee rights to the foreign investor.
9. Extensive reforms have taken place in agriculture. The communes (resulting from Mao's social experiments) were abolished, and peasant households have been given control over agricultural land.

Direct government intervention in agricultural production is in large part a thing of the past.

The economic reforms and related upsurge in growth have raised per capita income and living standards in the PRC. Between 1978 and 1990 peasant incomes more than tripled, and urban incomes doubled. As a result the rural–urban income gap narrowed.[11] Consumption of durable goods increased. Between 1978 and 1987 the number of television sets per 100 people increased from 0.3 to 10.7, and the number of bicycles per 100 people increased from 7.7 to 27.1.

Despite these improvements in living standards, problems continued to plague the government. In part, these are related to the transition the economy is going through as market forces grow in importance.

PROBLEMS OF A TRANSITION

China's transition from a centrally planned economy to a more dynamic, market-oriented economy has been accompanied by a number of problems. Prominent among these are regional disparities, inflation, corruption, and rising uncertainties related to a difficult to control decentralization of political power.

Regional Disparities

China has been plagued by wide disparities in regional development. This is a result of several factors. First, regional disparities are a legacy of Mao's efforts to provide regional self-sufficiency. Under Mao, provincial governments were encouraged to develop their own comprehensive industrial sectors. As a result, provinces and lower levels of government (prefectures and municipalities) have been engaged in a broad range of business and industrial activity. Many provinces possess their own local fertilizer, steel, textile, and goods processing plants. From the point of view of the provincial and municipal governments this development has been considered attractive. These governments are able to exercise control over industry, investment spending, trade and commerce, and tax revenues.[12]

As the provinces have progressively gained increased authority over their own economic management, they have been able to provide incentives appropriate to their special conditions. In this respect, growing regional authority over economic planning and policy can be considered favorable to the process of reform. The economy can respond more readily and dynamically to opportunities and changing conditions. Nevertheless, regions can become mired in interregional trade wars. Also, intense interprovincial competition bids up prices of relatively scarce inputs (raw materials, capital goods).

Inflation

Early in 1993 China's economy began to show signs of overheating. The annual inflation rate climbed above 20 per cent, the government budget deficit exceeded 5 per cent of GNP for the second consecutive year, and domestic plus foreign investment levels were growing at unsustainable rates. In July 1993 the government appointed Mr Zhu Rongji as Governor of the People's Bank of China, the Central Bank. Along with his other responsibilities (senior vice-premier in charge of the economy) Mr Zhu's overall duties effectively gave him the power of an economic tsar.

When China tried to cool an overheated economy in 1988, the nation experienced a 'hard landing.' The economy stalled for nearly three years. Mr Zhu's efforts in 1993 were more carefully orchestrated to yield gentler results. Initial efforts aimed at restraining inflation via credit controls and a more austere budget. The treatment of cooperatives highlights the softer approach. In 1993 many companies cooperatively owned and operated by small towns and villages were converted into joint stock companies. In such cases stock is issued for modest cash payments by owners. Within seven weeks of introduction of the stabilization policies joint stock conversions were reported to have raised 700 million yuan ($120 million). This contrasts sharply with experience in 1988 when cooperatives were simply eliminated on the grounds that they wasted raw materials and energy.[13]

By the end of September 1993 it was reported that key construction projects remained unaffected by the central government tight money policy. Projects such as the Shanghai–Pudong bridge were continuing toward completion. By contrast, the real estate sector was a prime target on the government's hit list. In the speculative boom of 1992–3 real estate companies borrowed money from financial institutions without offering secure collateral, and realized big profits by quickly reselling land and condominiums. Beijing ordered provincial banks to recall unauthorized loans. As a result inflated prices on real estate properties fell back to more realistic levels.

In addition to the above measures, Chinese government authorities suspended price reforms for the balance of the year. In part this was an attempt to satisfy farmers, who were unhappy over the sharp rise in the cost of fertilizers and pesticides. Also, the government's anti-inflation program should result in redirecting investment toward agriculture, which was starved for funds as 'hot money' poured into industrial development zones and real estate projects in the coastal regions.[14]

Another priority of the government's anti-inflation program was to strengthen the Chinese yuan, which depreciated over 50 per cent against the US dollar on the officially sanctioned currency swap markets in the 12 months prior to July 1993. On several occasions the Central Bank was obliged to intervene to support the yuan at Yn5.7 to the dollar. Closely related is the problem of the foreign trade gap, which recorded a deficit of $3.5 billion in the first half of 1993, compared with a surplus in the previous year. China is trying to avoid direct administrative measures to curb imports, which would be harmful to the country's efforts to gain membership in the World Trade Organization (WTO).

Inflation and the associated currency instability lead to capital flight. As foreign investment pours into China, funds flood back out. Entrepreneurs and public sector managers often are in no hurry to repatriate offshore balances, accumulated in the trade boom of recent years. The main windows used for flight capital are mis-invoicing, understated exports and overstated imports. Flight capital can return to China disguised as foreign investment. Since it is a disguised flow, it is difficult to measure. One set of estimates places the amount between $15–25 billion in 1990, and between $13–28 billion in 1991.[15]

Corruption

By most indications living conditions in China have improved steadily over the past 15 years. However, economic reforms have created sideproblems. Income inequalities have worsened. A new class of rich peasants has been created in rural China. Corruption is widespread among government officials and in the private sector. Allegations of stock market insider trading and share price manipulation led to riots in Shenzhen in 1992. Soon after the government set up a new agency to regulate the country's stock markets.[16] A system of privilege and favoritism has emerged in urban centers. These and other social side-effects of economic change have generated widespread resentment, criticism, and demands for reform.

Seeking reform, many individuals including school-age youth have joined political organizations for this purpose. This democracy movement led to the Tiananmen Square protests in 1989. Since the Tiananmen incident many young Chinese espousing democracy have gone into hiding or have tried to flee abroad.[17]

Taxes, corruption, and the surge in income and wealth in the cities have led to unrest among Chinese peasants. The nightmare of an army of angry peasants marching on the capital has returned to haunt a regime that four decades earlier came to power as a result of similar claims of corruption and unfair treatment. Internal government documents cite hundreds of incidents of peasant uprisings resulting from local officials beating and imprisoning penniless people who failed to pay 'taxes' on existing wealth.[18] Given the new prosperity in the coastal provinces, peasants have witnessed a decisive shift in income and resources. The income gap between peasants and city dwellers widened in the 7-year period since 1985. Other complaints voiced by peasants include the decline in land available for cultivation resulting from speculative real estate development, issuance of IOUs rather than cash for remittances payable to peasants, and rampant black market activity.

The government is not unmindful of the problems of corruption, and has taken steps to deal with it. These measures include arrests and extreme penalties, including execution. In one case China executed eight men in one of 'the biggest cases of public embezzlement since the 1949 communist revolution.' The eight were financial workers, mostly accountants, who took advantage of the weak management systems in the banks in which they were employed.[19] These executions apparently were supported at the top levels of government to bring order to the primitive financial sector and crack down on corruption.

Efforts to clean up the system extend to the highest levels of government and Communist Party circles. In one case it was announced that government was investigating corruption allegations against Mr. Chen Xitong, deposed Communist Party boss of Beijing and member of the ruling politburo. The Chinese media referred to another high official, Mr Wang Baosen, a Beijing vice-mayor, as morally degenerate. The official Xinhua news agency reported Mr Wang's main criminal acts as embezzling, diverting Yn300 million to associates, and leading a morally degenerate life.[20]

3 Regional Development: Special Economic Zones

In 1979 Deng Xiaoping opened China to closer economic contacts with the world. This opening was the beginning of China's economic integration with other nations, and required parallel actions on the political side in the form of improved intergovernmental relations between China and other nations. Beginning in 1979 China adopted a policy of improving commercial and investment relationships with its trading partners, including neighboring countries and the western industrial nations.

The opening in 1979 and later years focused on development of coastal cities and regions, and the creation of Special Economic Zones (SEZs) located strategically near more developed urban population centers. If China is to achieve superpower status, it must develop all regions of the country in an optimal manner. Until the present, interior regions of China have lagged far behind the coastal areas and urban population centers. This uneven regional development must be corrected. How this will be done represents a key part of the future development strategy needed to assure a stable political future for China.

Regional disparities in development have been a continuing problem for China's authorities. This chapter describes how China has fostered investment and economic development in the coastal provinces. Three coastal cities are discussed in detail. The successes in coastal development have begun to spread into the hinterland and rural China. This chapter also focuses on rural development, including the efforts made to reorganize business and economic activity in rural areas in China's large interior provinces.

THE OPENING AND REGIONAL DEVELOPMENT

Since 1979 China has achieved a transformation in attitude, behavior, and business organization. A new dynamism has taken hold, bringing about a broader outlook, increased coordination of productive pursuits, and wide-ranging efforts to improve managerial and administrative systems and processes.

China's isolated lifestyle in the decades prior to 1978 must be compared to the new energies and innovations that followed. Prior to the opening China's isolated economic development was characterized by spurts of growth followed by long periods of decline and stagnation. China's isolation from the industrialized countries, evidenced by a low ratio of trade to GNP, reflected a 'lack of horizontal coordination within China.'[1] Instead of one China, there were 40 000 during the great proletarian cultural revolution, consisting of isolated provinces, prefectures and industrial plants. In this period large factories had to be self-sufficient, due to lack of adequate transportation, inferior quality of components made domestically, breakdowns in supplier inventory management, and widespread preference for direct barter.

By contrast, the open policy has led many areas of China to introduce business and economic reforms, and to experiment with market-oriented capitalist methods. While confined largely to the coastal region, the open policy is creating incentives that will result in a 'spatial redistribution of development efforts from the interior to the coast.'[2]

CHINA'S COASTAL CITIES AND SEZs

Development along China's coastal region has been rapid. This development has been attributed by many analysts to the driving force of the coastal port cities. The term 'coastal cities' is used loosely in current analysis of China's development. Only 32 of the 324 cities in China can be classified as coastal port cities.[3]

Strategic Importance of Coastal Cities

The disproportionate importance of these 32 cities is reflected in the following data:[4]

1. They account for 16 per cent of China's urban population and 20 per cent of the nonagricultural labor force.
2. They generate 28 per cent of total value of industrial production.
3. They account for 25 per cent of retailing value and 90 per cent of export trade value.
4. Approximately 60 per cent of national industrial production is concentrated in the eastern coastal cities, of which one-third comes from the coastal port cities.
5. They generate over 26 per cent of the national industrial tax base.

Economic growth in the coastal cities has far surpassed that of the interior, reversing a past pattern in which interior development was emphasized due to fears of vulnerability of coastal cities and regions to military aggression. It has been estimated that as a result of this former policy the coastal region suffered a 12 per cent decline in its share of national industrial output over the 40-year period ending 1982. In this period the interior regions gained relatively and absolutely.

Resurgence of growth in the coastal region since the late 1970s can be interpreted as a rational rebalancing of national priorities. More importantly, the coastal cities now can be viewed as playing the role of catalytic spearheads aimed at accelerated growth.

By opening doors to the outside world, China's open cities have become more integrated into the international production process and global financial markets. While this development inevitably will lead to unevenness in China's internal growth, larger gains should accrue in the form of spurring growth rates in adjacent interior provinces and municipalities.

In the discussion below we make specific references to the following two groups:

1. Special Economic Zones (SEZs).
2. Fourteen Open Cities.

The Chinese government has initiated measures to accelerate development. In 1979 four SEZs were established in Shanghai, Zhuhai, Xiamen, and Shantou. These zones enjoy a greater degree of economic autonomy in connection with taking initiatives to promote investment and technology inflows. A major goal of the SEZs is to create a favorable climate for foreign investment. In 1984 the open policy was extended. Fourteen coastal cities were declared open, forming an almost uninterrupted coastal belt linking China with foreign markets.[5] The open cities include some of the most attractive seaports in the world.

Open Cities

An open city is characterized as follows. It enjoys a high degree of autonomy, so that it can pursue externally oriented economic activity. Also, foreign investment enjoys special privileges. To further improve the investment climate, eleven coastal cities have established Economic and Technological Development Zones (ETDZs). This includes providing necessary infrastructure: transport, water, electricity, telecommunications.

In addition, important services have been improved, including labor force training, legal framework, administration, and preferential policies.

Since 1984 open regions along the coast continued to expand. In 1985 the open policy was extended to the Chang Jiang (Yangtze River) Delta, Zhu Jiang Delta, and Golden Triangle (Xiamen, Zhangzhou, and Quanzhou) in Fujian. The open policy has exerted a demonstration effect on regions adjacent to the open cities and interior provinces. These have attempted to emulate the open coastal cities in providing incentives for entrepreneurial activity.

As catalysts of development, open coastal cities provide windows for the importation of capital and technology, and the inflow of management skills needed to train the labor force. Second, they operate as regions where advanced technology and management methods are put in place for subsequent transfer to the interior. Third, coastal cities provide locations for processing and packaging of raw materials and agricultural products for the international market. Fourth, coastal cities provide market opportunities and a meeting place for domestic and foreign buyers and sellers. Fifth, these cities operate as demonstration centers where new forms of business, new management systems, and new trading techniques can be shown to China's socialist society.

As the coastal cities develop new industrial, commercial, financial, and business activities; older and more mature activities may be relocated to interior provinces and municipalities.

SEZs

When in 1979 the four Special Economic Zones (SEZs) were established, one of their most important roles was to generate new sources of foreign exchange.[6] In the following 14-year period the role of the SEZs has evolved, along with the adoption of different national development strategies. In 1979 the leadership coalition in China needed to finance projects incorporating advanced technology. These required financing with foreign capital. Several strategies were adopted to attract this capital. Taiwan and South Korea had successfully used the Export Processing Zone (EPZ), which applied comparative cost advantages in labor and land to attract the capital, technology, and management skills of foreign investors.

In 1979 two types of EPZs were promoted by the State Council to expand exports. The first, the Export Commodity Processing Base (ECPB), was given stronger management regulations and increased government subsidies. Important export commodities were centralized in coastal and interior bases. The second type was the SEZ. Designed to generate foreign exchange under an export promotion strategy, the SEZs were envisaged as motivators of overseas Chinese in Hong Kong and Macao. The SEZs were to permit Chinese residing in offshore areas (Hong Kong) to invest directly in enterprises in China. Early gains included a sharp rise in foreign investment to finance infrastructure and construction of new factories. Between 1979 and 1984 Shenzhen's economy grew 39 times over 1979 levels. Other SEZs modernized rapidly through construction of roads, port facilities, and improved water and electricity facilities.

Very soon after establishment of SEZs it could be seen that economic interchange between traditional sectors in the domestic economy and SEZs was becoming a key benefit. The benefits included (1) SEZs providing China with scarce goods, (2) SEZs purchasing components from Chinese suppliers, (3) transfer of technicians to SEZs for educational exchange, and (4) establishment of inter-regional enterprises by domestic Chinese and SEZ-based partners. By 1984 over 500 interregional enterprises were established in Shenzhen alone.

In Table 3.1 we provide summary, comparative information on the four regional SEZs, as well as data on Hainan, also given SEZ status. Shenzhen accounts for a major portion of the combined trade flows of the SEZs. In 1991 the five SEZs attracted a combined investment inflow of $2.1 billion. These figures pre-date the foreign investment surge that took place in 1992–4.

The success of the SEZs led some Chinese leaders to consider broadening the role the international market should play in spurring China's economic development. A more outward-oriented approach, designated the Coastal Development Strategy, called for transforming the more prosperous coastal regions into major foreign trade centers. This approach would enable the interior provinces to gain from diffusion of technology and managerial innovations. With this concept, coastal areas benefited from foreign trade and investment privileges, access to foreign exchange and tax abatement schemes. In 1984 the Central Committee designated 14 cities as 'Open Coastal Cities,' In the following section we describe the role played by these coastal cities in furthering China's opening to the West.

OPEN COASTAL CITIES

The decision in 1984 to create 14 open coastal cities was closely linked to the success of the SEZs, and the need to extend the outward-oriented development approach to a wider area. As in the case of the SEZs, the coastal cities were given power to approve investment projects, offer

Table 3.1   Comparison Data on Four Special Economic Zones and Hainan

	Population	Major Industries	Exports	Imports	Foreign Investment Dollars	Contracts
Shenzhen	1.0 m	Electronics toys, textiles	$5.1 bn	$4.3 bn	$683 m	795
Zhuhai	0.5 m	Textiles electronics, foods, metals	$678 m	$882 m	$433 m	425
Xiamen	0.6 m	Electronics, textiles, agric. prod., granite	$900 m	$889 m	$485 m	
Shantou	8.3 m	Textiles, agric. prod., paper prod., porcelain	$497 m	$727 m	$239 m	
Hainan	6.5 m	Light industrial, prawns, agric. prod., metals & minerals	$326 m	$490 m	$289 m	
Total (US$ m)			$7501	$7288	$2129	

Source: *The China Business Review,* November–December 1991.

incentives to foreign businesses, retain a large part of foreign exchange earned, and import equipment and technology duty free.

With the creation of 14 coastal cities, the SEZs found a new function, namely as role models and experimental stations for coastal reform strategy. A second change in the status of the SEZs was that they now were forced to compete with the other coastal areas for domestic inputs, and foreign investment. As a result of this competition, the SEZs became far more efficient.

The following discussion considers the development role and achievements of several leading coastal cities.

Shanghai – World City

At the time that China was embarking on its opening, Shanghai led the nation in industrial output, per capita income, and energy consumption.

As China's largest industrial city, Shanghai contributed over 12 per cent of the nation's gross value of industrial output (GVIO). When in 1984 Shanghai was designated as an open port city, it was expected that successful economic development would be diffused throughout the Yangtze Delta. In this light, Shanghai is viewed as a catalyst for urban and regional development in Central and East China.

Shanghai has long been China's principal gateway to the outside world. The city is strategically located at the midpoint of China's east coast. In the late nineteenth century Shanghai emerged as the country's largest economic center, providing key banking, financial, commercial, and manufacturing services. The expansion of modern manufacturing was closely linked to the local shipping industry. At the end of the First Five Year Plan (1957) Shanghai was China's most important industrial base. It retains this position despite vigorous industrial growth in cities such as Beijing, Tianjin, and Guangzhou. In 1988 the value of Shanghai's industrial production was over 39 per cent of the total attained by the 14 open coastal cities.[7]

Since the First Five Year Plan, Shanghai has experienced a broad-based industrial development, including a more highly skilled labor force, and a high level of sophistication in manufacturing design. Textile manufacturing includes production of cotton, wool, jute, and silk, and is the second largest industrial sector. Shanghai ranks second nationally in steel production (after Anshan, the steel-producing center in China). In addition, Shanghai is an important production base for various metal products. Shanghai's first ranking manufacturing sector is machinery, which accounts for one-third of the value of manufacturing output. Other important sectors include power-generating equipment, ships, watches, bicycles, and cameras. New manufacturing production includes synthetic materials, electronic calculators, precision instruments, scientific gauges, and precision lathes. Shanghai produces a high percentage of manufactured consumer goods, including television sets, radio and tape recorders, washing machines, and refrigerators.

Some years ago a writer on Shanghai observed that its vocation had never been government services, art, or philosophy; it had been money-making. Like religious converts, Shanghai's communist leaders have embraced the city's zest for commerce with rare enthusiasm. Mayor Huang Ju is most enthusiastic about his plans to make Shanghai the 'dragon head' of the Yangtze River valley, the gateway to the world outside China.[8]

Shanghai's current importance as an industrial and manufacturing center also is related to the following:

1. Shanghai's industry is the leader in production efficiency for all China.

2. Shanghai trains workers, who migrate and bring their skills to other industrial centers.
3. As a capital city, Shanghai attracts advanced technology and production of new types of industrial goods from foreign countries (via technological exchanges and joint ventures, and direct investment), and transfers this knowledge and related skills to other manufacturing cities in China.

In 1986 Shanghai established the Special Economic Zones of Minhang and Hongqiao, with the objectives of attracting foreign investment, introducing advanced technology, management skills, and developing international cooperation. Minhang is Shanghai's first industrial satellite town. More recently the city established an ETDZ at Caohejing, southwest of Shanghai. This was the first high-tech development center among the coastal ETDZs. A multi-billion dollar project to develop the Pudong area has resulted from a set of new regulations promulgated by Shanghai municipal authorities. According to the plan, 350 sq. km of farmland in Pudong are being converted into a new development area. Foreign investors have been granted special incentives as they invest in projects encouraged by Shanghai. The following types of foreign investment are welcomed in Pudong:

(a) Manufacturing enterprises, especially those that are advanced in technology or export oriented.
(b) Projects involving development of large tracts of land, energy, transport, telecommunications and other infrastructure projects.

Incentives include low taxes, tax exemption, reductions on import duties, exemptions from property taxes, priority lending from financial institutions, and others.[9]

Tianjin – North China Metropolis

In terms of its population Tianjin is the largest port city in north China. In 1987 its aggregate population was reported to be 8.2 million.[10] Located only 130 km southeast of Beijing, Tianjin enjoys a strategic position. With the development of a railway system in northern sections of China, Tianjin became the second largest port city in the nation measured by foreign trade value (pre-World War II).

In its early years Tianjin was developed as a trading port to serve the capital city of Beijing, and it rapidly developed into a major industrial center. Over the period 1952–87 industrial production increased from 49 per cent to 62 per cent of gross product, at the expense of services and agriculture. Tianjin's economy has long been more oriented toward heavy industry than other large coastal cities. In the early years of communist government Tianjin became one of the key heavy industrial centers in north China, producing iron and steel, power generators, chemicals, machinery, and tractors. More recently the city has become specialized in producing petrochemical machinery and oil-drilling equipment, elevators, cranes, light duty trucks, and ship propellers.[11]

Compared with other coastal cities, the value of Tianjin's industrial output is second only to Shanghai. However, the city has made great efforts to preserve historic (nineteenth-century) buildings, and to develop tourist/visitor activities. Urban renovation has been undertaken to preserve traditional architecture, and is an important aspect of urban renewal.

The city has implemented a series of modernization projects, including sewage treatment, new expressway links, the replacement of coal with cooking gas, and beautification through parks, gardens, and green areas.

Tianjin's favorable strategic position and economic prosperity is based on the following. First, it is located near a densely populated region in north China, enjoying good rail links with Inner Mongolia and northeast China. Second, the adjacent region is well endowed with fossil fuels, minerals, and other essential industrial inputs. Third, Tianjin's physical expansion into neighboring areas has not been at the expense of rich agricultural land. Adjacent land utilized for urban expansion is made up mostly of salty swamps and sandy areas with low agricultural productivity. Fourth, the city's leaders were quick to appreciate the need for investment in infrastructure. As a result of the substantial investment in energy, transport, and telecommunications Tianjin enjoys the reputation of being one of the most desirable cities in China in which to live.

Guangzhou – Southern Metropolis

Guangzhou is the sixth largest city in China. Traditionally China's unrivaled southern metropolis, Guangzhou, is the largest port and city in south China.[12] The economic importance of Guangzhou has been enhanced with the open economic policy and ability to attract foreign capital. Situated in the subtropical region of Guangdong Province on the populous Pearl River Delta, Guangzhou enjoys a year-round growing season, making for a wide range of fresh agricultural products. In 1988 the population of Guangzhou was approximately 6 million. Close proximity to Hong Kong and Macao affords this metropolis the advantages of commercial contacts, good transport, international financial services and good communications. A concentration of educational and research institutions has facilitated development of Guangzhou's urban economy.

Not too distant from central Guangzhou (25 km) is Huangpu, a designated Economic and Technical Development Zone (ETDZ). Huangpu is able to import advanced technologies, expand production capacity, and focus on technological improvements. Huangpu has developed a mix of high value-added and import-substitution industries. The Huangpu ETDZ focuses on microelectronics, communications technology, biotechnology, and high-efficiency products (optical fiber). Additional product lines include artificial heart valves, integrated circuits, health foods, and embroidered products.[13]

Development of the Huangpu ETDZ has not been without problems and criticism. Among these are (1) excessive external orientation and lack of economic links with other parts of China proper, (2) overinvestment in infrastructure, requiring long payback, and (3) lack of balance between available local resources (land) and their use in investment projects. By 1989 when the zone had been in operation five years, 318 development projects had been signed and put into operation with foreign and domestic firms worth 1.2 billion yuan (approximately $210 million). In addition, 115 foreign companies had invested $160 million in the zone.

Guangzhou bears the burden of many years of neglect of basic investment needs. The city faces severe housing shortages and inadequate local transportation facilities. The acute housing shortage and low standard of repairs can be traced to the attitude that housing is a public good rather than a commercial good. Residents expect a large element of government subsidy, and rents are at artificially low levels. In the early 1980s household surveys found that housing rental absorbed barely 3 per cent of household income. Low rental rates result in deferral of necessary repairs, shortening the lifespan of housing units. One remedy to the housing problem is the promotion of housing as a commercial good. Rents must be raised to more realistic levels. Finally, incentives must be found to induce urban residents to relocate to outer areas of the city, or even to satellite towns.

The transportation system in Guangzhou suffers from inadequate and poorly maintained roads, and deficiencies in transport capacity (particularly buses). The city lacks a comprehensive transport management system, with a multiplicity of agencies responsible for different component parts of the system. Central government and provincial agencies are not subject to municipal authorities. Guangzhou will continue to suffer inadequate transport services until the conflict of jurisdiction and authority is settled between the various levels of government.

Economic planners have developed several models for future development of the Guangzhou economic region. These aim at a more rational integration of the city and outlying regions. These models take into account exploration and development of petroleum resources in the South China Sea. This activity can be expected to stimulate petrochemical industries and speed up development of numerous service activities. Another development likely to spur the growth of business activity in the Guangzhou region is the political integration of Hong Kong and Macao from 1997 onward. This integration will lead to increased business and financial links within this economic region and promote an increased inflow of investment and technology.

RURAL DEVELOPMENT

The development and expansion of rural nonagricultural enterprises in China is an important and unique experience. In a very short period of time industrial activity has taken hold, flourished, and allowed profitable enterprises to spread across rural areas throughout China. As a result, rural personal incomes have increased, and the labor force structure has become more diversified.

China's rural development is a critical factor in attaining superpower status. Its importance should not be underestimated.

1. Regional disparities in economic development and income levels have persisted as a key problem for many decades. These disparities retard development, and are a source of potential political instability. Rural development reduces and removes these disparities.
2. Close to 80 per cent of the population lives in interior regions, and rural areas in the coastal provinces.
3. A key factor in achieving economic growth is the mobility of labor. When comparing rural and urban labor, labor productivity differences are extreme. In future labor must be free to move from occupational areas of low productivity to areas of higher productivity. Rural development facilitates this mobility.
4. Economic reform has fundamentally altered population flows. Urban population has experienced rapid growth, 80 per cent of it due to migration during the reforms.[14]

Institutional Framework

Rural communities in China include township, village, and production team.[15] With implementation of the production responsibility system (PRS) in agriculture early in the 1980s, the production team lost most of its functional importance. The term 'community government' refers to all three levels of rural community listed above. The following describes the growing importance of the township-village-production team (TVP) sector, and its institutional framework.[16]

China's rural communities operate with a stable population membership. This is related to a low historic incidence of migration. In the past the government has frowned on worker migration, but recently has permitted temporary migration to cities and other rural areas for employment. Immobility of population translates into immobility of human resources. The gradual breakdown of these immobilities has provided the additional worker resources needed to allow development of the TVP sector.

Income-sharing within the community is another important feature of rural life. Jobs are allocated to balance family incomes. Community decisions on location of new firms take into account income-sharing. With the implementation of PRS, equal distribution of agricultural land assisted in maintaining balanced distribution of income. More important, allocation of jobs in TVPs has proven useful in balancing family incomes.

Local governments can promote industrial and commercial development through establishing TVP-type activities. Many local governments depend heavily on TVPs for extra budget revenues to meet their needs. These take the form of profit remittances and management fees. In the more industrially developed rural communities TVPs generate a large share of budgetary tax revenues.

Since the late 1970s rural communities have been much affected by economic and political reforms. A most important reform was introduction of the production responsibility system (PRS), which gave households agricultural land rights, formerly in the hands of community production teams. Another important change was the relaxation of restrictions on large-scale expansion of nonagricultural activities by rural communities. The wage structure shifted toward direct payment for services on a performance basis, year-end dividends, and profit bonuses. These changes provided strong incentives toward efficiency in the TVP sector, and the personal motivation to offer better services and longer working hours. All of these contributed to raising productivity levels in the TVP sector.

Growth Impact

Early growth of the TVP sector has been phenomenal. Over the period 1978–86 nominal gross output value increased at 24 per cent per annum.[17] Employment in rural areas outside agriculture grew in the same period at close to 13 per cent annually. Growth in China's TVP sector has been very uneven from year to year.

With the rapid growth described above, overall dimensions of the TVP sector have changed substantially. Measured by real Gross Value of Industrial Output (GVIO), China's industrial TVP sector was roughly four times as large in 1986 as it was in 1980. Table 3.2 illustrates these dramatic changes. The share of crop cultivation fell to less than one-third in 1986, but the share of industry rose to over 30 percent. In 1987 rural GVIO exceeded value of agricultural output for the first time.

Accompanying the growth in TVP industry were shifts in structure of the rural labor force. The total rural labor force expanded to 379.9 million (an increase in the period 1980–6 of over 19 per cent). The share of labor employed in agriculture and forestry declined from 89.2 per cent to 80.2 per cent. The share in industry increased from 6.1 per cent to 8.3 per cent. The share in construction-transport-commerce increased sharply from 1.6 per cent to 6.1 per cent (Table 3.3).

The TVP sector has become one of the most dynamic parts of industry in China:

1. It is an important producer in most industry sectors and dominant in several.

Table 3.2 Composition of Rural Gross Social Product, 1980 and 1986

	1980	1986
Total rural gross social product (billions of yuan)	279.2	755.4
Share of total (per cent)		
Agriculture (cultivation)	49.3%	33.1%
Forestry, livestock, fishery, and related	19.5	20.0
Industry	19.5	31.5
Construction, transport, and commerce	11.7	15.4

Source: W.A. Byrd and Lin Qingsong, eds., *China's Rural Industry*, Oxford University Press, London, 1990, p. 15.

Table 3.3   Structure of the Rural Labor Force, 1980, 1984, 1986

	1980	1984	1986
Total rural labor force[a]	318.4	359.7	379.9
Share of total (per cent)			
Agriculture (cultivation)	82.8	70.9	80.2
Forestry, livestock, fishery, and related	6.4	13.3	
Industry	6.1	6.7	8.3
Construction, transport, and commerce	1.6	4.4	6.1
Other	3.1	4.7	5.4

Note: a. Millions.
Source: *China's Rural Industry*, p. 16.

Table 3.4   Contributory Share of TVP Sector in National GVIO

1971	3%	1983	12%
1978	9%	1986	21%

Source: *China's Rural Industry,* p. 16.

2. Its share of national GVIO has risen sharply, from 3 per cent in 1971 to 21 per cent in 1986 (Table 3.4). The TVP sector has almost doubled its share of China's industrial output every 5 years.
3. The TVP sector facilitates moving rural labor into more productive employment outside agriculture. As long as restrictions are maintained against permanent migration into large cities, the TVP represents the main channel for shifting the enormous rural labor resources of China into more productive activities.
4. All segments of the TVP sector have risen in importance in Chinese industry. Private enterprises have demonstrated the most spectacular growth.

TVPs are active in all but one industrial subsector: petroleum. The most important subsectors are machinery, construction materials, textiles, chemicals, and food processing.

The TVPs are a key part of China's economy. They play a decisive role in industrialization of rural areas and modernization of the national economy. The TVP sector offers the opportunity to shift rural labor from agriculture to higher productivity employment. Without the TVP sector, the efficiency gains realized from agricultural reforms could not have been possible. The TVP sector is important to Chinese industry as a supplier of inputs, partner with state industries, and competitor promoting greater efficiency. TVPs have been important in allowing experiment and demonstration of the effectiveness of economic reforms.

4 Emerging Superpower

China is an emerging superpower. Greater China (including Hong Kong) will attain superpower status early in the 21st century, based on its strategic geographic position in the Eurasian land mass, possession of a large conventional military force, a large national economy, and nuclear weapon capability.

Over the next several decades China will be uniquely positioned to achieve high economic growth. In this period China will come to dominate regional political and economic affairs, and will challenge Japan for number 2 position in the world league of national economic rankings. The superpower status attained by China will pose many vexing problems for the US and Europe. America's former hegemonic influence will be undermined in international trade and investment, as well as in the realm of international political relations.

TOWARD SUPERPOWER STATUS

What is a superpower, and why is it important that China shortly will become recognized as one? Superpower status confers upon a nation vast responsibilities as well as immeasurable benefits. These take a political, economic, and military form. As a superpower the US shouldered the responsibilities of providing political leadership in the face of global and regional problems; extending economic assistance to countries in need; and providing military support where aggressors threatened the legitimacy of individual nations (e.g., Kuwait in 1991). A superpower may benefit from this status. Would-be aggressors steer clear of formidable superpowers. Probably more important, superpowers are listened to regarding political and economic issues and problems. Superpowers possess an agenda-setting capability in international affairs and within international organizations.

Defining Today's Superpower

During the second half of the twentieth century the concept of superpower status has been unique and without precedent. This is due to the fact that in this period, a superpower by definition possesses nuclear capabilities.

While the UK, a superpower in the nineteenth century, now possesses nuclear capabilities, it is lacking in other attributes.

Today's superpower possesses four attributes, which confer upon it this status.

1. large diversified national economy;
2. major conventional military force;
3. nuclear weapon capability;
4. strategic geographic location;

During the period 1950–90 two countries satisfied the four conditions for superpower status; these were the US and Soviet Union. The US represented the largest national economy as measured by current production and income, and the Soviet Union was considered to have the capacity to produce between one-third and one-half the volume of goods and services as the US. In this 40-year period the US and Soviet Union possessed large conventional military forces, and both enjoyed substantial nuclear weapon capabilities. Finally, both nations enjoy a strategic geographic position. In the case of the Soviet Union, that nation occupied a major part of the Eurasian land mass. This represents the single largest land mass on the globe, and it has long been considered that the nation that controls this possesses an important geopolitical advantage. In the case of the US, the North American continent is protected on US eastern and western borders by the Atlantic and Pacific Oceans. In the past this has made it most difficult for potential aggressors to pose a serious threat to America's national security.

The breakup of the former Soviet Union after 1990 seriously reduced that country's claim to superpower status, although we should not be hasty in writing off the remaining core of the former Soviet Union (FSU). For the foreseeable future it is not likely that the many new republics of the FSU will be able to federate in a format that can quickly restore superpower status.

Who Is Eligible?

Given the eclipse of the Soviet Union, which other countries today might claim superpower status? Three countries may be considered, namely Japan, Germany, and China (Table 4.1). Germany and Japan clearly lack two requirements: a major conventional military force and nuclear weapon capability. In addition, Germany's economic size may be insufficient unless we consider the European Union with Germany at its centerpoint as

Table 4.1   Four Requirements for Superpower Status

	Large National Economy	Major Conventional Military Force	Nuclear Weapon Capability	Strategic Geographic Position
United States	$5610	Yes	Yes	Yes
Soviet Union	498	Yes	Yes	Yes
China	369	Yes	Yes	Yes
Japan	3362	No	No	Doubtful
Germany	1574	No	No	Yes

Note: Data for 1991 GNP in US dollars (bn). Data for Soviet Union refers to the Russian Federation only.

a possible candidate. However, the internal politics of the EU suggest strongly that it may not hold the potential for superpower status in the visible future.

China appears the most likely candidate to achieve superpower status. China possesses a large conventional military force, the largest in the world. Second, China has developed a modest-sized nuclear weapon capability.[1] Most important, China occupies a pivotal position in the Eurasian land mass. Its position may be superior to that of the FSU, since China possesses a lengthy coastline, with many large ports and natural harbors. China's ship construction industry is now one of the world's largest, and China enjoys a growing comparative advantage in this industry sector.

The single question-mark relating to China's attaining superpower status is the overall size of its national economy. As of 1991 China ranked tenth in aggregate GNP, far behind Germany, Japan, and the United States.[2] We turn to the question of China's economic growth in a later section of this chapter. Today the US remains the sole country that can claim undisputed superpower status.

WORLD LEADERS, EMPIRES, AND SUPERPOWERS

In the previous section we set down the four attributes that, when realized, confer superpower status. During the latter half of the twentieth century two countries were able to meet these requirements: the USSR and US. During the initial years of the 1990s the FSU appears to have fallen away from superpower status.

The four criteria for superpower status in the last half of the twentieth century are peculiar to that period. Prior to 1950 superpower status represented a different mix of national attributes. For example, in the years following World War I the US could be considered to have enjoyed this status, even though it lacked nuclear weapons, and possessed a conventional military force subject to questionable superiority. In this period superpower status was based on economic leadership and strategic geographic position. During the mid-twentieth century the US enjoyed clear economic leadership. In 1948–51 the Marshall Plan assisted European postwar reconstruction. In 1950 US energy consumption was close to 45 per cent of the world total, twice the level of consumption in Europe, and almost three times the amount of energy consumption in the USSR and Eastern European bloc countries.[3] In 1983 US consumption of energy still represented almost one-quarter the world total and five times that of Japan.

Over the past five centuries world leadership and superpower status has shifted from country to country (Figure 4.1). This shifting in status is paralleled by fundamental changes in the world balance of power. Underlying the shifts in balance of power are many types of change, such as the Age of Discovery and related colonial rivalries in the sixteenth and seventeenth centuries, the Industrial Revolution which occurred in the eighteenth century, the rise and fall of colonial empires, and gradual development of more open global trade and investment system that allowed technology to be transmitted around the world. According to Brian Reading, a UK-based analyst, the world may be entering a period of changing power relationships, in which we may expect new competition for hegemonic power, instability, and painful economic adjustments.[4] The rise of the Asian economies, including China, may create great difficulties for the established powers, including downward pressures on wages and incomes in industrial economies.

The first European countries to vie for leadership status were Portugal and Spain. Early in the fifteenth century the explorations of Prince Henry the Navigator carried the flag of Portugal to distant lands. Spain followed closely on the heels of Portugal, and endured through the sixteenth century and into the seventeenth century as a contender for world leadership. Defeat of the Armada in 1588, the rise of new challengers (France and Netherlands), and weak internal governance led to Spain's eventual decline (Figure 4.1).

In 1602 the creation of the Dutch East Indies Company placed the Netherlands in contention for leadership. However, the Netherlands was almost constantly at war, exhausting it physically and financially. France

43

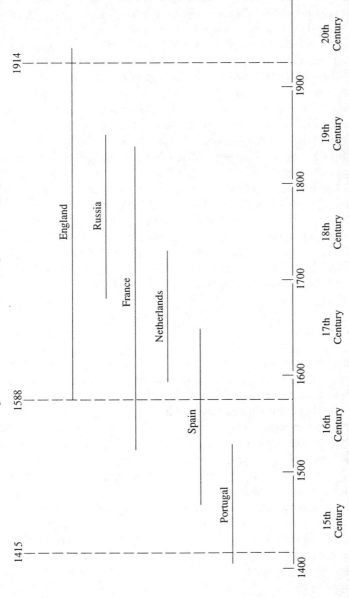

Figure 4.1 Six Centuries of Empires and Superpowers

Notes: Some key dates are indicated, namely 1415 when Prince Henry the Navigator launched Portugal as a naval power and country of exploration, 1588 when British naval power was proven, and 1914 when the British colonial system started to fall apart.

provided a far more enduring challenger for world leadership, and the assemblage of an enormous colonial empire placed France high on the list of countries for nearly three centuries. Soon after France embarked on its imperial mission, the English took to the seas for the same purpose. Defeat of the Spanish opened the way for global ambitions to be realized. The British defeat of the French in 1763, the Louisiana Purchase by the United States, and the defeat of Napolean prevented the French attaining super-power status. This left the way clear for England to rule the seas and con-solidate control over its empire throughout the nineteenth century, largely unopposed.[5] One footnote should be added to this brief account. Russia was in contention for leadership status. Under the reigns of Peter the Great and Catherine the Great, Russia was a 'flank' nation contending for leader-ship status from the closing years of the seventeenth century to the end of the eighteenth century.

A key question that emerges when examining Figure 4.1 is the follow-ing. It appears that superpower (or leadership) status has been passed from country to country. In steady succession, Spain was replaced by the Netherlands and France as leading nations. In turn Great Britain sup-planted France, and the US took the place of Great Britain. The USSR appeared on the scene as a superpower, but could not endure. Will the US position be supplanted? If so, when and by whom?

POST-COLD WAR

The end of the cold war raises the question whether a major global transi-tion in the balance of power can occur in an orderly way. Does the end of East–West conflict mark the beginning of a newer and more vibrant US hegemony? While the US now enjoys clear superiority in military affairs, the world of economic relationships is more complicated. First, there presently exist three economic 'poles,' i.e., North America, Europe, and Japan. Second, economic relationships are changing more rapidly. Are we at the 'end of history,' as Francis Fukuyama suggests?[6] Or are we at the beginning of a new epoch?

In 1978 one writer declared the end of the 'American century' and the commencement of Japanese economic hegemony.[7] This analysis is based on relative industrial decline in the US, especially in comparison to Japanese industrial performance in developing high-tech manufacturing, increasing world export market share, and in maintaining high levels of investment spending. Prestowitz points to the key role played by

Japanese financial muscle, the increased role of yen financing, the increased share of Japanese banks in international lending, and the ability of Japanese investors to acquire massive amounts of overseas productive assets.

There is much to be agreed with in Prestowitz's analysis of the shift in relative economic strength in favor of Japan relative to the US. This shift has affected global political as well as economic relationships. Economic performance and political power are closely related.[8] While the US is accused of Japan-bashing, China doggedly pursues superpower status and continues to regard both Japan and Russia with suspicion.[9]

To the extent that Japan's ascendancy in world affairs is related to its rise as a 'trading state,' will the appearance of other important successful trading states (China, South Korea, Indonesia) spell the imminent end of US hegemony in world economics? One writer denies an end to US world leadership based on relative economic status.[10] According to Nye, the relative decline followed close on the end of World War II when US military superiority was at an artificially high level. Since that time, the US has maintained its leadership position. Further, it leads in 'soft power' such as cultural trends, support of international institutions (United Nations, IMF, World Bank), and the democratic ideal.

Other writers are not as sanguine as Nye. They look to the continued prosperity and high economic growth achieved by the trading nations, especially in the Asia-Pacific region. They also consider the emergence of rival trading blocs in Asia, Europe, and North America as the crowning end of US hegemony.[11] On a regional basis these analysts view Japan and China as contenders for hegemonic patrimony. Tokyo and Beijing are aware that America's retreat in world affairs will remove the buffer that keeps them separated. Domestic politics in Japan already contains a range of viewpoints regarding renewal of the Nuclear Nonproliferation Treaty, which expired in 1995, and the role to be played by Japan in this regard.[12]

The world may be in the midst of a fundamental power transition. One aspect of this transition is the decline in Marxism with the breakup of the former Soviet Union, and a shift toward capitalism which is taking place in most former communist bloc countries. Whatever else, China will become a key factor both regionally and in global relationships. While it may take a few years for Beijing to gain international recognition as a superpower to be dealt with, its massive population, own self-consciousness, military preparedness, and high economic growth make it a nation that cannot be ignored.

CHINA'S ECONOMIC GROWTH

Recent Past

China has achieved a successful economic growth. Over the period
1965–90 per capita income advanced at an annual rate of 5.8 per cent
(Table 4.2). Overall GDP growth was 6.8 per cent in the period 1965–80,
and 9.5 per cent in the decade 1980–90. These achievements are most
noteworthy, especially if we consider the political disruption accompanying the Great Leap Forward and the Cultural Revolution.

The data in Table 4.2 suggest that China has the potential to achieve
above-average growth over sustained periods. The downtrend in population growth rate indicated in the table is cause for increased optimism,
since lower population growth will impose less pressure on resources and
supply bottlenecks.[13]

International comparisons show that China can achieve a GDP growth
double that of Japan, and several times higher than OECD countries. The
only countries in the table that reflect superior or comparable GDP growth
are South Korea, Singapore, and Hong Kong. In all three cases these countries achieved high prosperity based in part on their ability to share in the
fruits of an expanding world trade and investment system. In all three
cases direct investment inflows contributed capital and modern technology

Table 4.2   International Comparisons of China's Economic Growth
(average annual rates)

	GDP Growth		Per Capita Income	Population Growth	
	1965–80	1980–90	1965–90	1965–80	1980–90
China	6.8	9.5	5.8	2.2	1.4
India	3.6	5.3	1.9	2.3	2.1
South Korea	9.9	9.7	7.1	2.0	1.1
Singapore	10.0	6.4	6.5	1.6	2.2
Hong Kong	8.6	7.1	6.2	2.0	1.4
Japan	6.4	4.1	4.1	1.2	0.6
Mexico	6.5	1.0	2.8	3.1	2.0
Germany	3.3	2.1	2.4	0.2	0.1
High Income OECD	3.7	3.1	2.4	0.8	0.6
United States	2.7	3.4	1.7	1.0	0.9

Source: World Bank, *World Development Report*.

to produce for export markets. An open world trading system permitted these countries to function as export platforms for multinational company investors.

In recent years the Special Economic Zones (SEZs) and coastal cities of China have been following the pattern of rapid economic development and industrialization of South Korea, Singapore, and Hong Kong. These regions have enjoyed, and continue to enjoy success in the form of industrial modernization and accelerated growth.

Greater China Zone

Given the recent political and economic changes taking place in and around China, it is meaningful to refer to the 'Greater China Zone.' Politically, the Greater China Zone includes three distinct areas: interior China, coastal China, and Hong Kong. Economically, the Greater China Zone includes the three areas referred to above, plus Taiwan. Data pertaining to the politically defined Greater China Zone can be found in Table 4.3. This table provides a measure of the size of the Greater China Zone as of 1990, and provides projections of GDP for the Greater China Zone for the years 2000, 2010, and 2025.

In 1990 Greater China enjoyed a population of 1140 million and an aggregate GDP of $425 billion.[14] At this time Greater China included a highly modern metropolitan center possessing the most advanced financial institutions and markets (Hong Kong), capable of carrying out a full range of global financial services. In addition, it included a coastal area encompassing the Special Economic Zones and numerous large urban centers in the process of achieving rapid modernization and continued industrialization. Finally, Greater China includes a vast interior region, with a massive land area and natural resource deposits, and an enormous labor force capable of shifting from traditional activities (farming, handicrafts, small-scale manufacturing) to industrial and service employment in the rapidly growing modern sectors. While some observers might regard this third component as a 'drag on China's future,' this is not a valid assessment. The vast interior of China represents a stored-up treasure of productive resources, which are waiting to be exploited.

Looking into the future, it is possible to project China's economic growth into the 21st century. These projections are presented in Table 4.3 for each of the three components of Greater China. Currently China ranks ninth in the world as measured by total output. This is impressive, especially when we consider the extremely low per capita income levels prevailing in China's hinterland ($200–300 per capita). However, China's

Table 4.3   Greater China Zone Economic Growth, 1990–2025

Year	China Coastal	China Interior	Hong Kong	Greater China Total	World Rank
1990					
Population	134	1000	6	1140	
Income[a]	$1240	$200	$10 000		
GDP[b]	$165	$200	$60	$425	9
2000					
GDP[b]	$391	$473	$118	$982	7
2010					
GDP[b]	$844	$1119	$211	$2174	6
2025					
GDP[b]	$2677	3549	$506	$6732	3

Notes: a. Per capita income in US dollars.
        b. GDP in US dollars bn. Population data are in millions.
            Growth rate assumptions as follows: coastal 1990–2000 9 per cent,
            2000–10 8 per cent, 2010–25 8 per cent, interior 1990–2000 9 per cent,
            2000–10 9 per cent, 2010–25 8 per cent, Hong Kong 1990–2000 7 per cent,
            2000–2010 6 per cent, 2010–2025 6 per cent.
Source: World Bank, *World Development Report*.

coastal regions with a population of over 130 million are modernizing
rapidly, and already enjoy per capita income levels several times higher
than in interior China. Finally, Hong Kong already enjoys the status of a
modern metropolitan center, with high per capita income and the ability to
render whatever type financial services may be required by the Greater
China Zone.

China's high growth rate will persist at least into the first two decades
of the 21st century. The factors that will allow this impressive growth are
described in a later section of this chapter. By the year 2000 China's GDP
should be $982 billion, with China ranking seventh in the world. By 2010
China's GDP should reach $2174 billion. At the quarter century mark
China's GDP should be $6732 billion, with China ranking third in world
GDP levels.

If we consider the Economic Greater China Zone which includes
Taiwan, we have the potential for very high sustainable economic growth
well into the 21st century. Taiwan adds a considerable range to the many
favorable factors present in Greater China (Figure 4.2). These include

Figure 4.2 Role Played by Each Component of Greater China Zone in Future
Growth

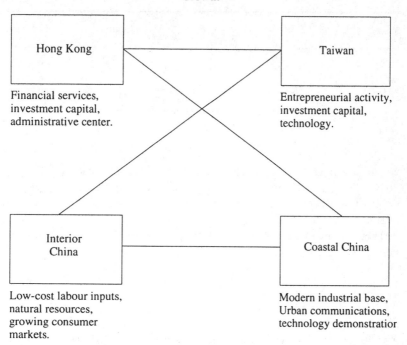

Hong Kong	**Taiwan**
Financial services, investment capital, administrative center.	Entrepreneurial activity, investment capital, technology.
Interior China	**Coastal China**
Low-cost labour inputs, natural resources, growing consumer markets.	Modern industrial base, Urban communications, technology demonstratior

entrepreneurial activity, investment capital, and a modern technology base
which far-sighted Taiwan businessmen have been investing in year-by-
year.

The four components of the Economic Greater China Zone each can
play a unique role in furthering overall economic growth. Interior China
possesses low-cost labor inputs and natural resources. Equally important,
it provides the potential for mass consumption markets as per capita
income levels rise throughout China. Coastal China provides a rapidly
modernizing industrial base, located in the many cities and economic
zones now operating there. Finally, Hong Kong provides financial services, investment capital, an efficient financial market, and an efficient
administrative and communications center.

China should be able to achieve overall economic growth equal, if not
superior to that of recent decades. More important, China should be able
to achieve sustained economic growth rates nearly double these of most
G7 countries. This will quickly propel China into the status of a leading

Table 4.4   Dragon Superpower, China in the 21st Century
(China GNP as a per cent of G7, US, Japan, Germany)

Year	G7	US	Japan	Germany
1990	3.2%	8.3%	13.8%	29.4%
2000	5.4	14.2	22.5	48.1
2010	7.9	21.3	32.3	69.0

Source: Author's estimates, and Table 4.3.

world power and superpower status early in the 21st century. By year 2010 China's GDP should be equivalent to 8 per cent of aggregate GDP of the G7 countries, and 69 per cent of the GDP of Germany (Table 4.4).

There are many reasons for projecting high growth rates for the Greater China Zone. These include:

1.   basic economic potential;
2.   size and scale of Chinese economy.

The following detailed comments focus on China's economic potential and size-scale factors.

Economic Potential and Scale Factors

The following seven factors elaborate on the reasons for expecting well above average economic growth.

1.   Large, capable workforce. In the past the workforce in China has demonstrated flexibility, adaptability, quickness to learn, and the potential to implement changing work practices resulting in high productivity gains.
2.   Vast land area, with enormous untapped natural resource deposits. This offers opportunities for highly profitable investment in infrastructure to unify internal markets. Favorable investment opportunities abound. These include the rail transport, highway, electric power, air transport, and coastal seaport and inland waterways sectors. The

returns (and productivity levels) on these investments should be very high in terms of their social marginal productivity.

3. Ability to attain near self-sufficiency in food production. Modest incentives offered in the later 1970s resulted in significant increases in agricultural productivity.

4. Potential for massive shifts of resources from low to high productivity use. This applies especially to labor inputs. Shifting 1 million workers from low- to high-productivity employment each year can add $1 billion to GDP, an incremental growth of approximately 0.25 per cent per annum. At this rate it would take several centuries for China to accomplish a shifting of all workers from traditional low-productivity to modern high-productivity sectors.

5. Potential for interregional trade based on internal comparative advantage. The 'gains from trade' can be substantial, due to the sharp differences in level of economic development from one region to another.

6. Potential for acquiring large amounts of modern technology from overseas, to bring about large increases in total factor productivity.

7. Potential for expanding international trade and investment, to achieve industrial modernization. In recent years China has achieved substantial business investment inflows, in excess of $10–20 billion per annum.

Growth Comparisons into the 21st Century

By the turn of the century China will be approaching a 1 trillion dollar economy (Table 4.3), and before the year 2025 China's annual output will exceed $6 trillion. At that point China will rank third in GNP, behind the US and Japan. But from that point on China will be moving to overtake Japan to become the second largest country in the world economy. By 2050 China could be the second-ranking country in the world measured by current GNP. At that point China's GNP will exceed that of Japan by a wide margin, will be more than twice as large as Germany, and within a few percentage points of overtaking the US economy.

Given these growth comparisons, China's superpower status should occur long before the year 2025, perhaps by 2010 or earlier. By the year 2015 China will have 60 cities with a population of 1 million or more, China's interior regions will be developing rapidly, and China will be the world's largest producer of many raw materials, manufactured products, and agricultural products.

China will be the largest or second largest trading partner of most Asian nations, and will enjoy diverse financial linkages with these countries based upon direct business investment flows, securities investment, bank lending, and other financial relationships. At this point China will possess one of the largest stock markets in the world, as measured by capitalization value, surpassing many of the European national markets and most of the emerging stock markets.

Finally, China will have become an important provider of services to the rest of the world, including shipping services with the world's largest merchant fleet, and other (financial, tourist) services.

China and Japan

In the previous section we provided a brief analysis and description of China around the year 2015, when China is expected to have attained superpower status. But what of the other large nations? At present Japan is considered to be second only to the US in economic power and potential.

In the period 1950–90 Japan achieved tremendous success in economic growth, industrial development, raising technology levels, and penetration of world export markets. These achievements have been most impressive. But we must examine the fundamental economic potential of Japan, and there are many problems. First, Japan has only limited land area; second, the resource base is extremely narrow – Japan must import most of its raw materials and nearly all of its energy inputs; third, Japanese labor is very-high cost and this tends to work to the detriment of the comparative advantage position of many industrial sectors in Japan.

On the economic side Japan may be approaching the zenith of its position as a national economy. Its trading partners are extremely concerned with their trade relations with Japan, particularly protracted trade deficits in their bilateral relationships. This leaves little margin of flexibility for Japan to maneuver and negotiate in its economic relationships.

We have compared China and Japan in five areas: domestic economy, resource base, labor market, international trade and investment, and geopolitical status (Table 4.5). In all respects the comparison clearly favors China, especially in connection with long-run potential. China possesses a potentially much stronger domestic economy. China enjoys a vast land area and ultimately will become an economic colossus. Japan's fragile economy possesses only a limited land area, in which careful control must be exercised in land and resource use.

China's resource base is large, diversified, and relatively undeveloped. China's production of metals, chemicals, and fossil fuels is growing

Table 4.5 China and Japan Compared

		China	Japan
1.	Domestic economy	Vast land area, population, and resources. Ultimately China will be a colossal national economic entity.	Limited land area, large population relative to land area and resources. High-cost labor supply. Fragile economy based on careful control of system.
2.	Resource base	Large, undeveloped resource base. China likely to become one of leading producers of world manufactures.	Extremely limited resource base. Economy already paying high cost to maintain self-sufficiency in food.
3.	Labor market	Potential to shift labor from low-productivity to high-productivity activities. A source of high growth.	Limited potential from labor market reallocation. Wages high in Japan, making many industrial sectors noncompetitive in international markets.
4.	International trade and investment	China depends on trade and investment to achieve an economic transition. Fast becoming major importer, exporter, and recipient of investment.	Japan probably has reached zenith of position in trade and investment. Trading partners adopting a harder line relative to Japanese exports and investment relations.
5.	Geopolitical	China already takes a very aggressive role in international affairs. Likely to increase its pressures to play greater role as its economy grows relative to G7 countries.	Japan has demonstrated unwillingness to play a key role in many areas of international relations. Some countries appear unwilling to accept Japan's playing a dominant role in regional economic and political affairs.

steadily, based on relatively generous natural resource deposits. By contrast, Japan must import nearly all of its resources and energy. The Japanese economy already is bearing high costs to maintain a trade surplus and self-sufficiency in a number of lines of production.

Japan's economy is constrained with limited potential from labor market resources. Wages are high in Japan, leading to difficulties in maintaining competitiveness in global markets. By contrast, China enjoys the luxury of a massive labor supply, most of which is presently found in low-productivity activities. This gives China the potential to shift tens of millions of workers from low-productivity to high-productivity employment over the next several decades. This will be an important source of incremental growth for China for many years into the future.

China is at the beginning of a long period in which increasing exposure to international trade and investment will yield positive gains to the economy. The transition to an open economy is still quite recent. China has demonstrated the ability to adopt policies needed for successful trade on both the import side and export side. Japan probably is nearing the end of a long period of increasing exposure to international economic relations. Japan's share of world export markets has grown steadily over the period 1950–90, and the realized gains from trade have been considerable. However, Japan's trading partners are adopting a harder line relative to Japanese exports.

Japan has demonstrated an unwillingness to play a key role in many aspects of international relations. By contrast, China has demonstrated a more aggressive posture and a willingness to cooperate with other countries in economic development projects. China has donated resources to infrastructure development projects in many smaller countries, and is likely to expand the role played in regional and global affairs.

IMPLICATIONS FOR US POLICY

The rapid progress achieved by China toward superpower status poses serious questions and issues for the US. These are listed below, and discussed in later chapters of this book.

1. As China moves toward superpower status, will its social and political systems develop in parallel fashion? Will China become more democratic and open its doors to the rest of the world?
2. What relationship will be most appropriate between the US and China, to bring about full and complete adoption by China of policies and attitudes appropriate to an emerging superpower?

3. The US–China economic relationship must generate gains or benefits for both sides. How will these be shared? And what policies must the US follow to insure it receives an adequate return flow of benefits?
4. How can China fit into the delicate world power balance, as its economic system grows and expands? Is there a possibility of increased tension and even conflict between China and Japan, the two largest economies in the Pacific region? If this tension increases, what role can the US play?
5. In what way can the relationships between nation states and international organizations (United Nations, European Union, World Bank, GATT) be accommodated to the expected rapid growth in importance and influence by Greater China?

Western publications have characterized China's modernization and economic expansion as 'breath-taking.'[15] There is no doubt that no other country can demonstrate the scale and size of economic expansion as China. Further, there is little doubt that China can, in the not distant future, satisfy all the required characteristics of superpower status. Nevertheless, problems remain, relative to overcoming poverty, human rights abuses, and foreign trade in military weapons. Those issues are discussed in subsequent chapters.

5 Growth: Past, Present, and Future

ECONOMIC GROWTH RECORD

Record over 1980–93 Period

Over the period 1980–93 the People's Republic of China achieved a 9 per cent average annual increase in real GNP (Table 5.1). This growth was made possible by China adopting a more liberal economic policy vis-à-vis its domestic economy and foreign trade with the rest of the world. High growth followed the shift away from former autarkic policies aimed at self-sufficiency, and toward increased interdependence with the world trading system based on international specialization in production.

With real output increasing by over 9 per cent annually, the size of the Chinese economy has nearly quadrupled. Productivity gains have facilitated substantial increases in incomes and living standards. Many of the distortions and rigidities of the former central planning economy have been reduced. Economic units increasingly make their own decisions based in large part on prices and other market related indicators.

China has developed a healthy nonstate industrial sector, which accounts for over half of output and 65 per cent of GDP. The economy has become more integrated with the rest of the world through rapid growth in foreign trade and investment. The average annual growth in industrial output has exceeded 13 per cent, and foreign trade has grown at an even faster rate (Table 5.1).

China's successful economic growth cannot be understood without reference to the high levels of saving and investment that are characteristic in this country.[1] The share of fixed investment in GNP rose from 20 per cent in 1980 to 32 per cent in 1987–8 and has remained above 30 per cent into the early 1990s. With economic reforms the share of fixed investment increased in 1992–3 to 32–8 per cent.[2] As economic reforms have taken hold, central authority control over investment gradually eroded. For example, state enterprise investment fell from 80 per cent of fixed investment in 1980, to approximately 60 per cent in 1988–93.

Table 5.1 Selected Macroeconomic Indicators, 1980–93 (annual per cent change, unless otherwise specified)

	1980	1981	1982	1983	1984	1985	1986	1987	1988	1989	1990	1991	1992	1993
Real GNP	7.9	4.4	8.8	10.4	14.7	12.8	8.1	10.9	11.3	4.4	4.1	7.7	13.0	13.4
Real gross industrial output	9.3	4.3	7.8	11.2	16.3	21.4	11.7	17.7	20.8	8.5	7.8	14.5	22.0	21.1
Real gross fixed investment	2.9	-12.5	28.0	14.7	22.7	27.3	13.3	14.7	10.4	-15.5	1.2	18.8	28.2	22.0
Retail prices														
Period average	6.0	2.4	1.9	1.5	2.8	8.8	6.0	7.3	18.6	17.8	2.1	2.9	5.3	13.0
End of period	22.2	2.6	0.1	3.7	4.8	10.7	6.2	9.1	26.7	6.4	2.2	4.0	6.7	17.6
Broad money	24.1	19.7	13.1	19.2	42.4	17.1	29.3	13.2	21.0	18.4	28.0	26.4	31.3	24.0
Domestic credit	22.3	13.1	11.2	12.8	31.4	31.3	34.1	22.3	18.9	17.1	23.7	20.2	22.8	22.4
Net domestic assets	–	–	–	–	–	–	33.9	21.5	20.7	18.3	24.1	25.0	32.7	25.4
Merchandise exports (per cent change in US dollar terms)	33.7	20.5	-4.0	-2.0	15.4	5.0	2.6	34.9	18.2	5.3	19.2	17.8	18.6	8.0
Merchandise imports (per cent change in US dollar terms)	24.8	12.6	-16.4	-10.9	27.6	60.0	-8.7	4.3	27.4	5.3	-13.3	22.3	26.2	29.0
Trade balance (in billions of US dollars)	1.9	–	3.0	0.8	-1.3	-14.8	-12.0	-3.8	-7.7	-6.6	8.7	8.1	4.4	-12.2
							(% GNP)							
Current account balance	0.3	0.9	2.1	1.5	0.8	-4.0	-2.6	0.1	-1.0	-1.7	3.9	3.8	1.8	-2.5
Overall budgetary balance	-3.3	-1.3	-1.4	-1.7	-1.5	-0.5	-2.0	-2.2	-2.4	-2.3	-2.1	-2.5	-2.5	-2.1
Revenue	29.4	29.0	27.2	27.4	26.4	26.6	25.1	22.8	20.0	20.4	20.1	18.1	16.3	15.4
Expenditure	32.7	30.3	28.6	29.1	27.9	27.1	27.1	25.0	22.4	22.7	22.1	20.5	18.9	17.5

Source: China Statistical Yearbook, 1992; and Chinese authorities.

Growth with Cycles

The economy of the PRC has been prone to cycles of macroeconomic instability. These cycles cover four areas of high volatility over the period 1982–93. Three full cycles appear in this period, in which real GNP growth, industrial production, and retail prices display close conformity in cyclical rises and declines.

Fixed investment also conforms reasonably well with aggregate activity over the cycles covered in this time period. Growth in monetary aggregates moves pro-cyclically. Over the period 1980–93 domestic credit has increased in importance as a source of financing fixed investment, reflecting the greater role of financial markets in this respect.[3] Finally, the trade balance displays a countercyclical movement.

SOURCES OF HIGH GROWTH

China's high growth rate can be explained through a combination of domestic and external economic forces. Briefly, they can be summarized as follows:

1. High ratio of domestic investment relative to GNP.
2. Development of a free market economy, in which economic resources are free to be used in the most efficient manner.
3. Successful mobilization of international capital.
4. Liberalized trade and import of technology.

High Investment Ratio

Before 1978 fixed investment was allocated through the Ministry of Finance after approval by the planning agencies. In addition, working capital allocated to state enterprises was channeled through the Ministry of Finance. In 1978 a decentralization process was introduced, and over time a greater share of investment became subject to provincial and local authorization. Moreover, nonstate enterprise investment increased in importance. These changes were paralleled by shifts in the financing of investments.

Since 1978 the PRC has sustained a higher ratio of fixed investment to GNP, by stimulating sectoral and regional investment and by providing the means for its effective financing. The changing sources of financing investment are reflected in Table 5.2. The rapid decline in state budget

Table 5.2   Total Fixed Asset Investment: By Sources of Financing
(per cent of total fixed asset investment)

	1980	1985	1990	1991	1992	1993
Total fixed investment	100.0	100.0	100.0	100.0	100.0	100.0
By sources of financing						
State budget	33.0	16.0	8.7	6.8	4.2	–
Domestic loans	–	20.1	19.6	23.5	27.4	–
Foreign investment	–	3.6	6.2	5.7	5.8	–
Self-raised funds	–	60.3	52.4	52.2	51.2	–
Other	–	–	13.1	11.8	11.3	–
Memorandum item						
Total fixed investment/GNP	20.4	29.7	25.1	27.2	32.7	37.7

Source: *China Statistical Yearbook,* various issues.

financing is evident. Domestic loans necessarily filled part of the gap associated with the decline in the state budget role. This reflects a reform in the former monobank system, an increase in bank loans (policy loans), and a limited discretionary role in lending by the specialized banks. Also, new lending institutions were created. State enterprises were allowed to retain depreciation funds, and profit retention was introduced.[4] By 1988 over 90 per cent of state enterprises were following a contract responsibility system with fixed profit remittances and investment targets. Parallel to this taxes were assigned on a more systematic basis to central and local governments.[5] Foreign investment activities have played an increasing role in financing fixed investment. Finally, the government has encouraged development of the capital markets, and bond financing now is becoming a more important source of financing fixed investment.

Development of Free Market Economy

The more liberal policy following 1978 has promoted a more market-oriented economy. Private sector initiatives play an increasingly more important role. Entrepreneurs visualize the potential of a large mass-consumption market. Prices have been 'freed,' and are no longer fixed according to government fiat.

The market economy allows greater unification of markets on a regional basis. Equally important, productive resources (labor and capital) are more mobile. In the following chapter we discuss mobility of factors in detail.

As we describe in a later section of this chapter, labor mobility can be an important component source of higher economic growth.

Mobilization of International Capital

China has provided incentives for inward foreign investment, and has made great efforts to enhance its international credit standing to attract funds from the international capital markets.[6] In a later chapter we discuss China's efforts to attract large amounts of foreign capital. Also, we discuss China's growing importance as a global mobilizer of capital.

China's ability to attract foreign capital increases the amount of fixed investment that can be sustained, and also probably increased the efficiency of this investment. As noted in Table 5.2, in the early 1990s foreign investment was financing close to 6 per cent of fixed investment.

Liberalized Trade and Import of Technology

The neoclassical theory of trade posits that a nation's production-consumption level should be higher on a welfare basis as a result of engaging in international trade. All other things equal, this allows a larger year-by-year growth in income.

On a statistical basis, China's foreign trade gives all outward manifestations of serving as an engine of economic growth. Between 1978 and 1994 total trade (exports plus imports) increased tenfold. As China's external orientation improved after the economic opening, the value-added performance of its exports increased. That is, higher value exports made up an increasingly larger share of the total. Manufactured exports increased from 49 per cent of total exports in 1980 to 82 per cent in 1993.[7] Exports of electrical equipment, including telecommunications equipment, was a dominant part of this export expansion.

Since the opening China's imports have become more technology-oriented. The share of industrial products in imports rose during the decade and a half following 1978. Machinery and transportation equipment imports grew sharply, embodying higher levels of technology than could be produced domestically.

China's trade has become more closely directed toward countries enabling it to better capture gains from trade and to benefit from import of higher technology machinery and equipment. China's trade with Eastern European countries was relatively stagnant. By contrast, trade with the US grew rapidly. China is now one of the world's top ten exporters and its share of world trade increases continuously.

DECOMPOSITION OF ECONOMIC GROWTH

In this section we estimate the magnitude of several of the major sources of China's economic growth. In brief, they include:

1. mobility of labor;
2. efficiencies from implementing free markets;
3. foreign trade and technology import;
4. foreign and domestic investment.

Mobility of Labor

Much progress has been made in expanding the role of the market in allocating labor. Development of the township and village enterprises (discussed in Chapter 3) has given rural labor markets a dynamics similar to that found in large urban centers. By 1993 this sector employed over 110 million workers. Employment also has grown rapidly in the large urban centers, in the special economic zones, and in the coastal cities. Workers in these sectors can earn at least 3–5 times as much as peasants who continue to work as agricultural producers.

Opportunities for higher income and living standards have operated like a magnet, attracting workers from rural areas. As a result, tens of millions of workers are 'in motion,' either as migrant workers moving from one location to another based on opportunity, or already relocated and in some instances still unemployed. Estimates of this mobile and growing population component range from 70 to 100 million workers.

Several different interpretations can be applied to this mobile population:

(a) Shock absorber theory. This mobile population can flow from one sector of the fast-changing economy to another, cushioning shocks generated in the transformation of the Chinese economy.[8]
(b) Source of potential instability. Surplus labor among the peasant population is estimated to be between 150 million and 200 million. Many incidents of rural unrest are reported.[9] Migrant workers could become a source of social and labor frictions and instabilities.
(c) Means of maintaining high growth. Workers move from lower productivity peasant farming to higher productivity modern sector industrial and commercial employment.[10]

We take this third interpretation as a basis for estimating the impact of labor shift on growth in value of output.

To estimate the effect of such a shift of workers on economic growth rate, we must use the following estimates.

1. Number of workers shifting from low to high productivity employment.[11]
2. Differential in value of output of worker in former and subsequent employment.
3. Relation between increased value of output of workers that shift employment to total output value.

Using an estimated 5 million workers shifting from low to higher productivity employment each year, and a differential in value of output of $1500, we obtain an increased output value for these mobile workers of $7.5 billion ($1500 × 5 million).[12] Taking the PRC's GDP at approximately $500 billion, we have an incremental growth of 1.5 per cent.

Efficiencies from Implementing Free Markets

While labor mobility has led to improved efficiency in the application of labor inputs, a similar efficiency gain is possible when capital moves from one region of lower productivity to another of higher productivity. It is difficult to measure the extent of capital mobility in China for several reasons. First, movement of capital from one region or industrial sector to another may escape notice and remain largely undetected. Second, even when observed, the movement of capital from one use to another leaves open the question of measuring its change in efficiency or productivity. Third, a considerable amount of capital flows through the country in the form of migrant worker remittances. It was reported that in 1993 migrant workers from Anhui Province sent home remittances of $862 million, which exceeded the provincial governments annual revenue by $230 million.[13] Finally, labor compensation takes the unambiguous form of wages or salaries which are identified and measured relatively easily. By contrast, the return to capital takes the form of profits or interest. Profits have been anathema in communist China, but became 'acceptable' after the opening. However, in state enterprises it became difficult to distinguish profits from taxes when the central government moved through several stages of liberating SOE financing with the objective of having these enterprises learn to operate effectively in a competitive market system.

Given these measurement problems, the approach taken here is to impute efficiency gains to capital. This can be done on the basis of the relative role or contribution non-labor inputs such as capital make to the value added process. In this case a conservative imputation is called for. This imputation is based on an 80:20 distribution of wage and non-wage factor income. That is, the wages share is taken as 4 times as large as the non-wages share. Attributing the non-wages share to capital, and working on the simplifying and conservative assumption that proportionately as much capital is moving from low productivity to high productivity use as labor, we must infer that the impact of capital mobility on incremental growth is one-quarter as large as in the case of labor mobility, or 0.38 per cent (1.50 × 0.25).

Foreign Trade and Technology Import

Foreign trade can improve the effectiveness of investment in capital goods by facilitating the import of higher technology machinery and equipment. Investment in capital goods leads to higher output value, based on the productivity level that can be achieved with the newly acquired capital goods.

China has followed a clear policy of promoting high growth in foreign trade, which allows industries in the PRC to import capital goods which embody higher technology. These yield clear benefits in terms of higher efficiency and growth of output.

The impact this can have upon overall economic growth rate can be estimated given the knowledge of how important capital goods imports are relative to total fixed investment, and the margin of productivity advantage of imported capital goods as compared with domestically produced capital goods. From Table 5.3 we can observe that incremental GDP is 0.50 per cent. This results from the higher efficiency of imported capital goods, or their lower capital:output ratio. The capital:output ratio is discussed in detail in the following section.

Foreign and Domestic Investment

During the early 1990s the saving:investment ratio climbed to 36 per cent of GDP. Approximately one-sixth of this is associated with foreign investor activity.

It is possible to complete our decomposition of growth analysis by utilizing the investment ratio. This requires application of the incremental capital:output ratio. The equation below states that the growth rate is a

Table 5.3   Technology Import and Growth Rate

1. Ratio of imported capital goods to GDP[a]	4.4%
2. Ratio of fixed investment of GDP	36%
3. Ratio of imported capital goods to fixed investment[b]	12.2%
4. Productivity differential of fixed investment[c] from imported capital goods	0.50%

Notes:

a. Obtained by multiplying imports/GDP by imports of capital goods/total imports (11 × 0.40).

b. Divide line 1 by line 2.

c. With a $500 billion GDP, the 12.2 per cent of fixed investment is $21.9 billion out of a total fixed investment of $180 billion. A 50 per cent more productive capital good would have a capital:output ratio of 2.7 compared with a national average of 4.0. This yields $2.5 billion of incremental GDP. Relative to the $500 billion GDP, this is 0.50 per cent.

positive function of the saving ratio and an inverse function of the capital:output ratio.

$$g = \frac{s}{k}$$

In the equation *s* represents the savings = investment rate relative to GDP; *k* represents the incremental capital:output ratio; and *g* represents the potential growth rate.

This growth model defines potential growth as based on the increased capacity to produce. The capital:output ratio represents the current value of investment required to increase output equivalent to one current unit. A capital:output ratio of 4 means four currency units of investment are required to produce one current unit value of additional output.

In the case of China the aggregate S = I ratio is taken at 36 per cent, its value in the early 1990s. The growth rate is taken as the increased output that can be attributed to an increase in the capital stock. Other factors bringing about increased growth are to be regarded separately. In this case we use a growth rate calculated as follows:

China's aggregate growth rate	−	Effect on growth of factors other than an increase in capital stock	=	*g*

Substituting

$$9.20 - (1.50 + 0.38 + 0.50) = g$$
$$9.20 - 2.38 = g = 6.82$$

Substituting

$$6.82 = \frac{36}{k}$$

$$k = 5.28$$

The contribution of all economic growth factors in China's aggregate growth is summarized in Table 5.4.

PROSPECTS FOR FUTURE GROWTH SUSTAINABILITY

In this section we consider the sustainability of the growth rate contributions summarized in Table 5.4. This analysis is required as an input for the final section of this chapter, the forecast of PRC growth to 2010.

Labor Mobility

In the recent past mobility of labor in China is estimated to have contributed 1.5 per cent to annual GDP growth. This is the second largest component. It is based on an annual shift of 5 million workers from lower to higher productivity employment. Further, it is based on an initial differential of $1500 in income/productivity per worker. How far into the future are these two relative orders of magnitude applicable?

China probably has a sufficient number of low-income farmworkers to be shifted into higher productivity employment to continue this aspect of the growth process for many decades. Also, this reserve army of underemployed will grow in future, along with population growth. However, the

Table 5.4   Decomposition of China's Growth Rate

1. Mobility of labor	1.50
2. Efficiency from free markets	0.38
3. Foreign trade and technology import	0.50
4. Domestic and foreign investment	6.82
Total	9.20

sustainability of the productivity differential may be a different matter. First, farm incomes may rise at a sharp rate in the future, narrowing the productivity differential between the peasant labor force and industrial urban workers. This narrowing could be brought on by the shifting balance between production of foodstuffs and their growing demand. China's economic boom and natural forces are shrinking the country's farmland, raising questions about the future ability to feed a growing population.[14] In China's breadbasket provinces farmers are abandoning the land to chase prosperity in towns and big cities. Provincial governments are paving over agricultural land for freeways and factories, shopping centers and golf courses. A Princeton University scholar, Perry Link, observed that a 10 per cent reduction in China's rice harvest in 1990 (190 million tons) could not be covered by the 12 million tons of surplus rice on the international market.

China has been suffering a net annual loss of 659 000 acres of farmland since 1991 because of the overheated real estate boom. Agricultural Minister Liu Jiang noted that disruptions to farming patterns touched off shortages and panic buying in 1994, sending farm prices skyrocketing 43 per cent in major cities.[15]

China has 20 per cent of the world's population, but only 7 per cent of the world's arable land. Total farmland has declined by nearly 20 per cent since the 1950s. Government officials maintain China is so big, it is impossible for other countries to provide sufficient food. Therefore, China must remain self-sufficient in food, and not allow the continued destruction of precious farmland.[16]

These trends threaten the PRC's self-sufficiency status in food, and could bring an upward shift in prices of farm staples. This in turn could increase real and nominal incomes of farm workers at the expense of urban residents. Rising farm incomes would reduce the positive effect on GNP growth from rural workers shifting to industrial and urban employment.

Free Markets

Free markets allow capital to move freely to where it can be most effectively used. In addition, free markets support competitive behavior and more rational resource allocation.

As discussed previously, China appears to be moving slowly and steadily toward a free market economy. Price distortions between plan and competitive market prices have narrowed. Also, the growth of wholesale and retail trade adds to the pro-competitive tendencies.

China's continuing introduction of capital market and banking reforms enhances the efficiency allocation of capital. As discussed in a later chapter, capital market financing is growing at a higher rate than the real economy. The contribution of free markets and improving resource allocation to economic growth appears to be sustainable well into the next century.

Trade and Technology

Since 1978 China's foreign trade has grown at rates far exceeding real economic growth. This high growth is expected to continue, perhaps with a modest deceleration after the year 2000, based on the following assumptions:

1. China will enjoy comparative advantage in labor-intensive goods for several decades, based on its large and only partially developed reserve labor supply.
2. China will gain stronger comparative advantage in higher technology goods in the early years of the next century. This will be based upon the ability of the PRC to continue to attract more advanced production processes through inward business investment and through import of high-quality machinery and equipment.[17]

Domestic and Foreign Investment

Currently fixed investment is a dominant contributor to China's economic growth, accounting for over 70 per cent of the high growth rate (9.2 per cent, of which investment contributed 6.8 per cent). For investment to play a sustainable role, the ratio of fixed investment to GDP must remain relatively high and the efficiency of fixed investment also must perform favorably.

Investment levels in China are subject to high cyclical volatility. Therefore, it is possible that China may continue to enjoy a high average investment ratio and growth rate. But this is likely to be accompanied by high instability in the level of investment and GDP growth.

A more favorable outlook may apply to the efficiency level of fixed investment. We have measured this efficiency level in terms of the aggregate capital:output ratio. Earlier, we noted that this currently is estimated at 5.29. That is, 5.29 units of investment are required to provide fixed investment capacity to produce one additional unit of output each year. This tends to be at the high end of the range of possible capital:output ratios. It can be hoped that in future China will enjoy a lower aggregate capital:output ratio, and therefore more efficient investment performance relative to economic growth. Several factors suggest this may be possible.

1. The increased use of capital market financing will in future screen out lower efficiency investment. Similarly, banks will be shifting more and more away from policy lending toward loans that offer promise of higher productive efficiency.
2. Foreign investor firms are increasing the size and scale of their commitments in China, in many cases enjoying production cost economies from this.
3. China may be entering a new stage in its infrastructure investment, wherein construction of electric powerplants and telecommunications facilities will be moving to the decreasing cost stretch of the growth and learning curves.
4. Production of infrastructure equipment is gaining efficiency via use of lower cost inputs, better technology (radio-transmitted messages), and more intensive competition among suppliers of equipment and components.

FORECAST OF GROWTH TO 2010

In the previous chapter we developed a forecast of China's economic growth, based on the three part analysis of coastal China, interior China, and Hong Kong. In this section we make use of this forecast to compare the projected growth of China and the G7 countries.

In the decade 1991–2001 China can be expected to more than double its production and income (Table 5.5). In the following years to 2010 there should be at least another doubling of income. These projections are based on growth rates in the 7–9 per cent range for China and Hong Kong. Over the same period the G7 countries are expected to enjoy annual economic growth rates of 3.0–3.5 per cent. As a result, by 2010 China will be 'catching up' and even surpassing several of the G7 nations in total production and income. In that year China's GDP will exceed that of Canada and the United Kingdom by a wide margin. At the same time China's GDP already will be almost 70 per cent as large as Germany's, and 32 per cent as large as that of Japan.

Table 5.5   Projected Growth of China and G7 Countries to 2010

Year	Greater China	US	UK	Germany	France	Japan	Canada	Italy	G7	China as % G7
1991	463	5610	876	1574	1199	3362	510	1150	14281	3.2%
2001	1070	7539	1177	2222	1693	4747	720	1623	19721	5.4
2010	2174	9837	1536	3039	2315	6492	985	2220	26424	7.9

Note: GDP in billions of US dollars. China growth rates are detailed in Table 4.3, US and UK 3 per cent per annum, remaining G7 countries 3.5 per cent.

Source: World Bank, *World Development Report*, and author's estimates.

Comparisons based on aggregate income do not tell the whole story. By the year 2010 China will have leaped ahead of all but two of the G7 countries (US and Japan) in many other respects. China will be a leading producer of many industrial products, ranking first, second, or third in production of steel products, cement, and many chemicals products. Further, China's annual fixed investment will be larger than all countries with the exception of the US and Japan.

These accomplishments will give the PRC a respected and carefully observed status around the world, especially among its neighbor countries in Asia. China will increasingly use its growing industrial strength to assemble and project a strong military establishment and naval presence, especially in the South-east Asia region where trade and investment ties can be expected to grow rapidly.

6 Development of Internal Markets

China has achieved much in developing internal markets. This progress can be evaluated in various ways, in connection with narrowing provincial income inequalities, price behavior, interregional trade flows, mobility of productive resources, and evolution of the distribution system.

In its strategy to modernize the industrial sector, China has borrowed the best from other countries. This ranges from the close working relations of government and industry as in Japan, to the export-promoting strategies of the four Asian Tigers. On the eve of China's opening in 1978, the country faced fundamental problems related to a shortage of energy and outmoded manufacturing equipment. Since the opening China's industrial expansion has been impressive. It has developed an industrial strategy that copes with these problems. A consistently high growth in output has been supported by the inflow of foreign capital, technology and equipment. Foreign investors have participated in developing China's industries and internal markets, making it possible for Chinese producers to become more competitive in world markets. As a result, China's foreign trade sector has become a second engine of economic growth.

MICROECONOMIC MARKET DEVELOPMENT

At the Eighth National People's Congress held March 1993, China committed itself to the creation of a market economy, with greater emphasis on microeconomic determination of the production and distribution processes. At that time the Congress ratified the earlier 14th Party Congress October 1992 decision for development of a socialist market economy. Development of China's internal market has been fostered by the following broad market-oriented trends:

1. The government progressively decontrolled prices. Three categories of prices have operated (planned, guidance, and market prices), with gradual movement of goods from more regulated to less regulated categories. Dual-track pricing introduced in 1985 permitted free market sale of production that exceeds plan target levels. Table 6.1

Table 6.1   Reduction in Scope of Price Controls

	Domestic Retail Goods			Agricultural Produce Sold		
	Fixed Prices	Guided Prices	Free Prices	Fixed Prices	Guided Prices	Free Prices
1978	97.0	0.0	3.0	92.6	1.8	5.6
1985	47.0	19.0	34.0	37.0	23.0	40.0
1990	30.0	25.0	45.0	31.0	27.0	42.0
1991	20.9	10.3	68.8	22.2	20.0	57.8

Note: All figures refer to per cent of total.
Source: World Bank, *China: Internal Market Development and Regulation*,
Washington, DC, 1994, p. 193.

indicates the progress made in reducing the scope of price controls over the period 1978–91. The proportion of domestic retail goods and farm produce subject to planned prices has fallen drastically.

2. Allocation of goods was moved out of the mandatory plan. In 1980 90 per cent of industrial goods and 837 production materials were allocated under the economic plan. By 1993 less than 10 per cent of industrial goods were allocated under the plan and the number of production materials under the plan administered by the Ministry of Materials and Equipment had fallen to only 13.

3. Distribution channels in the PRC expanded gradually. Until 1979 the system of unified purchase and sale of manufactures, and unified purchase of farm products accounted for nearly all sales. By the 1990s sales could be made to private purchasing agencies or to consumers. Related to this, new distribution agencies have sprung up.

4. Sophisticated commodities markets have been established for agricultural products and industrial raw materials. By 1993 there were 21 centrally sponsored commodities exchanges in China, many equipped with computer technology and modern trading facilities.

5. The government has planned and in part initiated a major program of legislative change, this is aimed at establishing an improved framework for a comprehensive market economy.

It is possible to evaluate the micro-market development in China, based on the extent to which progress has been made in the following areas:

(a) reducing interprovincial income inequalities;
(b) promoting a greater entrepreneurial role in industry, in part through increased private ownership;
(c) price behavior and reform;
(d) interregional trade flows;
(e) mobility of productive resources;
(f) evolution of distribution system.

Provincial Income Differences

According to a recent World Bank report, China has achieved moderate success in reducing interprovincial income inequalities. Analysis of shifts in regional levels of per capita income over time indicates a decline in per capita income variation. For example, over the period 1983–91 the coefficient of variation in regional income declined from 0.77 to 0.59.[1] Over the same period there was a parallel decline in regional coefficients of variation in per capita industrial output (from 1.24 to 1.03), and an erratic decline in regional variations in per capita investment (from 0.84 to 0.75).[2]

Equally impressive have been shifts in sectoral industrial output. The ownership of industrial output has been changing steadily. Gross output value accounted for by the state sector has declined from 76 per cent in 1980 to 53 per cent in 1990, and has continued to decline since 1990. The number of firms and the contribution to output of collective, individual, private, and other enterprises (joint ventures), which comprise the non-state sector have grown steadily. Similarly, retail sales value by ownership has exhibited a similar change in composition (Table 6.2). Therefore, while retail sales increased from Yn214 hundred million in 1980 to Yn941 hundred million in 1991, the share of state-owned units fell from 51 per cent to 40 per cent, and the shares of individually owned units increased from less than one per cent to close to 20 per cent.

Despite these shifts in ownership shares of industrial output and retail sales, the structure of industrial output in China has remained remarkably static. Further, each major industrial group is represented in virtually all provinces. Considering eight principal groups of industries (coal mining, tobacco, textiles, chemicals, building materials, machinery, electronics and telecommunications), these are represented in all provinces.

Price Behavior

One important indicator of the extent to which markets are functioning is the behavior of prices. We have already observed (Table 6.1) China's

Table 6.2 Composition of Total Retail Sales Value by Ownership, 1960–91 (Yn100 million and per cent)

| | Total Value of Sales (Yn100 m) | Retail Sales by Ownership | | | | Sales of Agricultural to Non-agricultural Residents % |
		State-owned Units %	Collective units %	Jointly Owned Units %	Individual Units %	
1960	67.45	86.7	9.9	0.0	2.1	1.2
1975	127.11	55.7	42.2	0.0	0.1	2.0
1980	214.00	51.4	44.6	0.0	0.7	3.2
1985	430.50	40.4	37.2	0.3	15.4	6.8
1990	830.01	39.6	31.7	0.5	18.9	9.3
1991	941.56	40.2	30.0	0.5	19.6	9.7

Source: World Bank, *China: Internal Market Development and Regulation*, Washington, DC, 1994, p. 224.

progress in deregulating prices. Unfortunately, the inflationary period of 1988–9 brought a halt to price reforms, but by 1991 price deregulation had resumed and surpassed the achievements of 1985. In the 1990s rapid progress was achieved in deregulating prices where there existed heavy government subsidies (coal, transport, grains, edible oils).

How successful was the decontrol of prices? If markets function efficiently, prices of the same or similar goods in regulated versus free market sectors should conform more closely. Parallel markets developed in China where scarce goods sold in unregulated exchange at prices above state-regulated levels. With dual-track pricing and progressive decontrol, the gap between free market and controlled prices should have fallen. A useful measure of the efficiency of markets is the extent of convergence between state regulated and market prices. In 1975 free market prices were 80 per cent above state-regulated prices, in 1980 48 per cent above, in 1985 28 per cent above, and by 1991 only 5 per cent above state regulated prices.[3]

Another measure of the efficiency of the internal market in connection with price behavior, is the extent of regional price convergence. If we examine regional prices, the immediate observation is that variations have been large. The World Bank has published a comprehensive analysis of regional price differentials for producer and consumer goods covering all provinces in China. This covers the period from 1986 to 1991, in which seven broad categories of consumer goods are analyzed. For all products, regional variations in prices increased after 1986. In short, regional price variations were significant in 1991 and have not noticeably diminished since 1986. The price decontrols of 1992 and 1993 were not incorporated in the World Bank analysis.

Interregional Trade Flows

Many provinces in China have set up barriers to internal trade. These include physical restraints such as roadside barriers and checkpoints, levying fees and fines on truckers transporting goods from one province to another, and preferences in the procurement of goods and services.[4] In some cases these trade restrictions are related to the authority given provincial and local officials to collect revenues under a fiscal contracting system or export earnings retention scheme. In other cases provincial officials seek to divert scarce raw materials from processing units in other provinces. In periods of overvalued exchange rate, provinces would attempt to increase their holdings of exportables to maximize retention of foreign exchange.

In 1990 the State Council issued a circular banning interprovincial trade restrictions. Since 1990 this has been echoed in prohibitions against unfair competition.

It is possible to gauge the impact of trade restraint, and how government policy in this direction may have affected internal trade flows. Taking all provinces together, over the period 1985–92 retail sales grew annually at 9 per cent, whereas interprovincial trade grew at a lesser rate, 4.8 per cent per annum. By contrast international exports and imports grew at rates of 17 and 10 per cent, respectively (Table 6.3). This suggests that there is a tendency for individual provinces to behave as independent economic countries, increasing their links with the external world or other provinces based on local economic needs.

Individual provinces exhibit interesting differences in terms of domestic and foreign trade behavior. Considering export ratios, domestic inter-provincial exports as a per cent of retail sales declined over the period 1985–92. However, in the case of several provinces these ratios increased (Liaoning, Jiangsu, Zheziang, Fujian, Jiangxi, Guangdong). These are all relatively rapidly growing coastal provinces. The provinces of Fujian, Jiangxi, and Guangdong raised their domestic import ratios, suggesting that more rapidly growing coastal areas may also be able to develop stronger trade links in domestic exports with other interior areas.[5] Over the same period three major cities, Beijing, Tianjin, and Shanghai, exhibited declining ratios of domestic trade with other provinces.

The World Bank study has compared domestic and foreign trade for five provinces. Domestic trade ratios are highly variable across provinces. Shanghai has been the most open in trade links with other provinces. Until 1990 the ratio of external trade exceeded domestic retail sales. Since 1990 Shanghai's domestic trade ratios have dropped to levels comparable to

Table 6.3   Growth of Domestic and Foreign Trade, 1985–92

Domestic trade	
Growth in retail sales	9%
Growth in interprovincial trade	4.8%
Foreign trade	
Growth in exports	17%
Growth in imports	10%

Source: World Bank, *China: Internal Market Development and Regulation*, Washington, DC, 1994, pp. xv and 40–1.

other provinces. The same study finds that unlike domestic trade ratios, external trade ratios have been rising strongly in Guangdong, Sichuan, Shanghai, and Liaoning. This suggests that external markets are more attractive and that trade has tended to develop more easily with the external world than with other provinces.

How does China compare with other countries, in terms of internal trade flows? Detailed comparisons are available for the former Soviet Union and the European Union (EU). The results from these comparisons are summarized in Table 6.4. They show that when taking interregional trade as a per cent of GDP, internal trade in selected provinces in China (22.1 per cent of GDP) was lower than trade in the EU (28.3 per cent), and among the nations of the FSU excluding Russia. This further suggests that there is considerable opportunity for expanding internal markets in China through increased internal trade.[6]

How should we interpret the previously described decline in regional mobility of goods in China? Four possible explanations should be considered. First, there has been a decline in centralized allocation, which has been considered most inefficient due to the long-haul nature of this model. Second, the relative decline in interprovincial trade may be due in part to the rapid growth of township and village enterprises, and consequent growth of intraprovincial production and consumption. Third, some of the decline can be attributed to the dual pricing system and the embargoes on trade placed by some provincial authorities on exports of specific goods. Finally, there is an absence of guidelines and rules (statutory or adminis-

Table 6.4   China and Other Regional Trading Areas:
Interregional Trade Comparisons

	$\dfrac{\text{M}}{\text{GDP}}$	$\dfrac{\text{X}}{\text{GDP}}$	$\dfrac{\text{Total Trade}}{\text{GDP}}$
China[a]	12.7	9.4	22.1
EU	14.2	14.2	28.3
Former Soviet Union:			
Excluding Russia	15.4	11.8	27.2
All FSU	8.7	8.7	17.3

Notes: a. All data expressed as percentages. M denotes imports, X denotes exports.
Source: World Bank, *China: Internal Market Development and Regulation*, Washington, DC, 1994, p. 42.

trative) on interregional trade at the national level. For example, in the US there exist constitutional prohibitions on constraints against interstate commerce. A similar legal provision, appropriate to the PRC governmental system, may be required. Also important is the effect that the fiscal contracting system has on interprovinial commerce.

Mobility of Capital

International economists tell us that factor mobility is an appropriate substitute for mobility of goods. International trade and international factor movements have similar effects in promoting the competitive efficiency of markets.

Capital is generally considered the most mobile among the factors of production. Capital mobility takes place through enterprise investment, through the banking system, and through the capital market. In this section we focus on enterprise investment. In later chapters we discuss capital mobility provided through the banking system and the capital market.

Enterprises select locations outside their current area of operations if there are favorable locational factors, such as labor and materials costs, subsidies and incentives, and other cross-provincial investment regulations that affect costs.

In the early transition years (1979–83), under the profit retention system, enterprises were discouraged from transferring funds to use in other locations. This was due to arrangements established between central and local governments for the sharing of enterprise profits and taxes that discouraged capital mobility. At that time the fiscal system was characterized by centralized revenue collection and centralized fiscal transfers. Revenue-sharing distinguished between centrally fixed, locally fixed, and shared revenues. Local revenues included enterprise retained profits where the state enterprises were owned by local governments. Local governments were reluctant to see their enterprises transfer resources outside their jurisdictions.

Beginning in 1983 the PRC began to introduce modifications to the revenue-sharing system. Taxes and profits were separated at the enterprise level. Retention of profits accrued to local industrial administrative units. Incentives were favorable toward retaining investments within local jurisdictions. By 1988 over 90 per cent of state enterprises were following the contract responsibility system, which fixed profit remittances, retention rates and investment targets, usually for a period of three years. Also, a system of fiscal contracting was introduced between central and local governments specifying the sharing of tax revenues. Regulations concerning the taxation of interprovincial investment under this system require that enterprises established through investment from another region pay turnover taxes in the host area but continue to remit income taxes to the home province. For joint (venture) enterprises with investment funds from the host and outside areas, turnover taxes are paid the host area, and income tax can be paid in one of two methods. The first is to divide revenue and then pay taxes to the respective home jurisdiction. The second is to first pay taxes and then divide profits. In this case the joint venture pays taxes in the host area, and the two parties divide after-tax profits according to the contract. Usually, the second method is applied.

Under the open door policy initiated in 1979, the central government opened some areas to foreign investors, offering various tax incentives. Some of these open areas provide similar incentives to domestic investment. These concessions profoundly affected foreign capital inflows, but also influenced investment flows between the coastal and inland regions to a modest extent. In the past enterprises with foreign investment in the SEZs enjoyed a 15 per cent income tax rate. Lower tax rates apply to investments based on amount of investment and level of advance technology. Additional incentives include tax holidays, and exemption of import duties. At many SEZs tax concessions available to foreign investors have also been made available to domestic investors from other provinces. Since 1984 the 14 coastal cities Economic and Technological Development Zones have enjoyed the same preferential tax policy as the SEZs.

To equalize the tax treatment with the centrally approved special zones on the coast, all thirty provinces and many counties and townships launched their own 'special zones.' By 1993 there were 1800 zones at the county level, or higher level. Most offer preferential tax policies similar to those applied in the SEZs, and some offer even more aggressive tax relief. Most of these tax exemptions are not approved by the central taxation authority, and in some cases may be considered illegal.

What are the implications of these developments since 1979 for regional capital mobility in China? First, regional capital mobility is limited, and to the extent that it occurs, it may not be efficiency-enhancing. Interregional capital flows are likely to be based on competing regional tax differences, rather than on real differences in capital need or productivity.

Government policy adjustment should address disincentives to regional mobility based on local government and local industry administrator interests in revenue retention. There is a very strong case for more equal treatment of investors in all regions, and from all regions. The current regulations on cross-provincial investments are lacking in credibility. This is based on the lack of enforcement and lack of sanctions in cases of violation. If future flows of interregional investment are to be encouraged, the government must develop uniform regulation and enforcement applicable to all investors.

Evidence regarding interprovincial investment is available for six provinces, Guangdong, Shaanxi, Sichuan, Beijing, Shanghai, and Liaoning, covering the period 1985–92. Total investment in these provinces accounted for 30 per cent of national investment.

It should be noted that interprovincial investment is a very small share of total investment, in all provinces except Shanghai representing only 3 per cent. Exceptionally, in Shanghai interprovincial transfers account for almost a third of total investment. In three of the six provinces the ratio has declined. In Sichuan the ratio has been constant and in Liaoning there was a small increase. Shanghai is the single province with a large increase, in part reflecting inflows to the Pudong investment zone.

In the early 1990s interprovincial investment flows have been less significant than external investment. As a proportion of total investment, foreign investment has been as high as 10–13 per cent in Shanghai, Liaoning, and Beijing, and higher in Guangdong (32 per cent). Over time there has been an increase in this ratio. However, in the interior provinces (Sichuan and Shaanxi) there has been a decline in foreign investment.[7]

Mobility of Labor

In the period before 1979 China's policy toward mobilization and deployment of labor was based on two guiding principles: minimizing unemployment and assuring lifetime job security. Most urban workers were assigned to permanent positions in state enterprises. At the same time rural–urban migration was prohibited. This was enforced by the household registration system, and urban grain rationing, which severely discouraged worker movement.

This system imposed unfavorable economic consequences and financial burdens. At the state enterprise, the burden of providing housing services, hospital and medical facilities, and social security grew to an unbearable level. Segmentation of the rural from the urban labor force made it difficult to meet growing needs for industrial production. Further, it led to an increased differential in urban versus rural wages, leading to the overpricing of urban labor. Enterprises had little incentive to use more labor-intensive techniques of production, resulting in a constraint on urban jobs.

Job security and wage rigidity became associated with low incentives and reduced labor productivity, and underemployment among urban workers.

One analysis of China's labor market gives the peasantry a key potential role in influencing the employment situation, social stability, and even political equilibrium. This thesis holds that China's 800 million peasants are China's active volcano. In the past China's dynasties were wrecked by uprooted, migrant farmers. Chairman Mao's solution was to 'chain the peasants to the soil.' The current genie in the bottle is every farmer's 'lust for development and search for money; the desire to hold his fate in his own hands.' Once farmers have left the fields, their actions become uncontrolled. What solution? Return to Mao's method of locking up the peasants with work brigades. Estimates of the superfluous rural labor force of about 100 million suggest that this approach may require considerable effort and ingenuity.[8]

The onset of reforms came with a growing recognition of the negative effects of the previously described labor market policies. Since 1979 officials have sought to increase the flexibility of the labor market. These reforms came in successive stages. In the late 1970s the breakup of the commune system in the rural areas increased the visibility of the formerly disguised surplus rural labor force. Within a few years millions of peasants became redundant. A second development permitted migration of rural labor to urban areas. Initially, temporary migration was permitted, but a year later in 1984 permanent migration was allowed in the case of peasants who were self-reliant in terms of money, food, and living accommodation. A few years later some provinces (Gansu and Sichuan) developed unskilled labor export programs to ease shortages in labor deficit regions. Millions of rural workers are drawn from the countryside every year by dreams of high wages. With overtime pay, building workers earn about twice the average Chinese salary.[9] At present university graduates are permitted to take jobs in township and village enterprises without losing their urban residence permits and their access to urban subsidies. Talent exchanges have been set up for highly specialized personnel.

Large cities have acquired illegal workers from rural areas, as a reserve pool of labor. This differs from the above described migrant labor, since it is only eligible for temporary residence. In 1990 there were an estimated 60–80 million persons in this category. These floaters provide a large and docile labor force, vulnerable to exploitation due to lack of formal status.

At the enterprise level, much greater latitude has been granted in hiring, including use of temporary migrant workers in lieu of permanent labor. The hiring of such labor falls under the guidance of the Ministry of Labor. Under the relatively new labor contract system entrants are required to sign a contract, which specifies duration of the agreement, responsibilities and benefits of both parties, and terms for renewal or cancellation. First introduced in 1983, this system greatly increased the flexibility for enterprises to reject unsuitable workers.

A bonus system provides mechanisms for linking wages to performance, and in 1985 a 'floating wage' system was introduced that permits linking of a portion of wages and bonuses to performance. The share of bonus payments out of total compensation has increased in state enterprises. It was estimated in 1992 that over 100 000 state-owned enterprises with 41 million workers (over half of such workers) gave various forms of efficiency related wages.

Under the enterprise contract responsibility system, managers were given authority to set production targets and flexibility in pricing. The managerial role in risk-taking also was made more explicit. In a number of enterprises managers now bid for a position, and enter into a personal management contract. This states their expected achievements. To stem the high level of underemployment in state enterprises, in 1985–7 an Optimal Labor Reorganization program was launched. This allows for comprehensive organization of the work unit, along with retraining aimed at increasing overall worker productivity. Parallel to this, there have been efforts to retrain workers, to mitigate the social dislocation from increased job turnover. In 1995 the Ministry of Labor initiated a nationwide re-employment program to stave off unemployment, estimated to hit the 18 million level by the turn of the century. The government estimated an average of 3 million people losing their jobs in the run-up to 2000, due to floundering state enterprises, bankruptcies, and other types of job losses. Incentives are provided for enterprises that hire the unemployed.[10]

From 1991 the government has allowed increased action on the part of enterprises to remove surplus labor. This is a departure from the former 'three irons' policy – iron salary, iron chair (permanent jobs for officials), and iron rice bowl (lifetime jobs). In 1992 greater flexibility came with a set of Regulations on Transforming the Management Mechanisms of State-owned Enterprises. These give enterprises the right to make their own decisions about hiring, to terminate contracts, dismiss workers, demote managers, and reduce or increase pay. Enterprises may terminate labor contracts before their expiration.

During the first half of 1992 it was announced that 1.4 million urban workers had lost their jobs (compared with 0.7 million in all of 1989). Some of the largest worker cutbacks include China National Coal Corporation (100 000 workers), with plans for further reductions of 400 000 in 1993–5. Wuhan Steel, one of the larger steel plants shed

80 000 of its 120 000 workers. The goal is to raise output per capita from 40 tons of steel to international norms.[11]

There exist natural limits to the shedding of jobs by enterprises and the ability of the state to provide new jobs. Based on a survey of 200 large and medium state enterprises in nine cities, some 17 million workers were rendered redundant from the reform process, but the state is able to provide jobs for only 7.32 million.

DISTRIBUTION SYSTEM

In this section we consider the role of the state in distribution, efficiency of the current distribution system, and the role of the transportation system. Emphasis is on distribution of producer goods, where the state traditionally has played an important role.

Allocation–Distribution

Since 1979 the state's role in material allocation has declined, with a very small number of goods now subject to allocation through government procurement. In 1993 only 19 commodities remained subject to state allocation, and even in the case of these products the share of supply by government contract declined steadily after 1985.[12] In the case of five products, the role of the government in controlling supply is still relatively high, 25 per cent or more of the total allocation (soda ash, nitric acid, caustic soda, coal, and steel products).

The increased role of the market in the allocation of goods is clear. But while the role of the state in allocation has declined, it continues to play a large role in distribution. In short, the state has not completely withdrawn from its dominant role in distribution.[13] For example, state enterprises have aggressively organized retail-oriented joint ventures, in many cases with foreign partners possessing great skills in this activity.

Prior to the economic reforms of 1979 onward, State Council planned allocations determined the distribution of production materials. Individual ministries or government departments oversaw production of these goods. In 1979 with the launching of economic reform, China initiated a decentralization of the distribution function, and production goods service companies were established. Some producer goods were removed from the central plan allocations, and large fairs were organized where buyers and sellers could meet to trade in producer goods.

In 1982 the distribution function was given increasing recognition, and the State Council provided Yn6 million via bank loans to augment the working capital of materials supply and marketing units.

Materials market reform accelerated in the mid-1980s with dual-track pricing. A given commodity could be sold partially under the plan and partially outside the plan, simultaneously subject to fixed prices and free prices. Specialized materials bureaux were set up for individual products, as the function of distribution was assigned increasingly to the Material Supply Bureau. Specialized markets and comprehensive trading centers were created for steel products, automobiles, and other products. By the end of 1992 the Ministry of Materials and Equipment (MME) reported the operation of 3000 retail markets, and 500 comprehensive trading centers whose combined turnover totaled 45 billion renminbi (RMB) in 1991. Also, over 300 wholesale markets had been created specializing in the sale of steel products with a turnover in 1992 exceeding 21 million tons.[14]

The above illustrates that deregulation and price decontrol did not automatically lead to the creation of markets for these goods. Second, the state-owned distribution system adapted to changing circumstances, undertaking new experiments to mold more efficient distribution channels. Third, this evolutionary process has taken a decade and a half to reach its present state, which is far removed from the distribution network of a developed market economy.

Current Distribution System

The distribution system in China today reflects several important features.

1. The state's dominance of distribution functions in producer goods has continued.
2. The system represents a hybrid with core elements geared toward central planning, but with several modifications.
3. New elements have been introduced gradually, with wide regional variations.
4. The major city of each region has a parent organization which is a Materials and Supply Equipment bureau. This bureau is delegated by local government to organize producer goods distribution.
5. Many materials bureaux also have a comprehensive trading center as one of their companies. Delivery systems are traditional.
6. New features in this system include a broader geographic reach of distribution enterprises, ability of distribution companies to buy from

producers in any province, and sell to state-private-collective users anywhere in China.

7. New privately or collectively owned distribution organizations are allowed to compete with state-owned distributors in most product categories.

The efficiency of the present materials distribution system must be considered in connection with the unique aspects of the Chinese system and comparisons between China and other countries at a similar stage of evolution toward developing a market economy. With regard to features specific to China, many bureaux are branching out into a variety of non-distribution type activities. These include investments in real estate which can be speculative, and diverse industrial and commercial activities. Expansion into real estate should be questioned. For example, the Suzhou Materials Bureau operates a real estate company, engaged in building offices and hotel facilities. This bureau explains the diversification in terms of the increased risks faced as a result of price decontrol, intense competition, and tendency of construction firms to buy materials directly from suppliers. This real estate activity should be questioned on the basis of possible cross-subsidization that masks inefficient activities, leading to investments not justified by competitive market prices.

One possible explanation for the diversification of materials bureaux is the restrictions placed on deepening their trading activities. In a more market-oriented economy such bureaux could evolve toward general trading companies (GTCs). These GTCs offer the potential advantages of integrating external and domestic distribution functions, similar to the *sogososha* of Japan. Restrictions against directly undertaking foreign trade, and limits on volume of trading, seriously impair the ability of these bureaux and the Ministry of Materials and Equipment to adjust demand and supply according to the operational level of the market.

Transportation and Telecommunications

Efficiency of a distribution system depends on the available infrastructure for the movement of goods, and also on communications services. In the early 1990s it could be said that the level of such services in China was roughly comparable with other large developing countries, such as Brazil, India, and the former Soviet Union, but below the level of advanced industrial countries such as Germany or the US. For example, China employs approximately 15 per cent of its workforce in transport and trade, close to the shares of India and the former Soviet Union (Table 6.5). By contrast,

China Superpower

Table 6.5 Employment in Transport and Trade, China
Compared with Other Countries

	Employment in Transport % of Total	Employment in Trade % of Total
China	6.33	9.70
India	11.91	1.64
Brazil	3.76	11.59
Germany	5.57	14.75
USSR	8.05	7.77
United States	5.61	20.65

Note: Data for China, Germany, USSR, and United States apply to 1989, for India 1988, for Brazil 1987.
Source: World Bank, *China: Internal Market Development and Regulation,* Washington, DC, 1994, p. 88.

Germany and the US employ 21–5 per cent of their workforce in these sectors.

Since 1983 the transport system in China has exhibited slow growth, in contrast to the high overall rate of economic expansion. For railways, new routes grew by only 0.43 per cent per year (1983–92), and waterway routes 0.09 per cent. On a per capita basis the growth rates in these two sectors were negative, and in highways only marginally positive.

In 1989 an estimated 200 million tons of required freight transportation remained unsatisfied, representing almost 10 per cent of freight capacity. The railway system suffers from severe underinvestment in facilities. Over the last few decades China has been investing amounts equivalent to 1–3 per cent of GNP, compared with other countries investments of 2–4 per cent of GNP.[15] China's rail investment must be increased to at least 2 per cent of GNP (approximately $9 billion in 1993) to bring supply into balance with demand by the end of this century. If tariff rates were adjusted to properly reflect operational costs, a favorable profit rate could finance a larger part of the required investment.

Truck transportation also suffers serious limitations on capacity. Plans are in place for development of an extensive intercity highway network. Fragmented ownership of the truck fleet results in low efficiency in use. With its enormous economic surge, China is straining the foundations of its nineteenth-century transport system. Though road-building is taking place at a frenzied pace, China has fewer paved roads than Depression era

America. Traffic congestion on some roads can be so severe, it will take more than two days to cover a 240-mile trip.[16]

Rapid changes are taking place in the trucking sector, including licensing of for-hire vehicles, collective as well as private ownership, liberalization of the fuel allocation system, and deregulation of truck haulage rates. Nevertheless, many constraints remain. Business licenses are required in the case of for-hire trucking services, and there are many differences in provincial regulations.

The state needs to encourage growth of trucking companies that specialize in intercity and interprovincial hauling. Further, China must consider the introduction of intermodal systems. These systems require that freight be shipped in containers, which can be moved between truck, railroad, and barge as necessary. The long-term goal must be a system that facilitates delivery of goods to buyers at lowest possible cost.

To break the stranglehold the overburdened transport system has on the economy, China is planning a radical shift in pricing policies to encourage efficiency. By selectively lifting price controls, Beijing hopes to open the way for more foreign investment. Enterprises operating general transport facilities (ports, airports, highways) would be given complete autonomy to set prices. Deregulation of railways would be gradual. Further, there would be reforms to improve management, establish an improved fund raising system, and develop a clearer separation of the roles of local and state government.[17]

INDUSTRIAL DEVELOPMENT

Industrial Policy

Industrial policy serves as a means toward achieving the broad social-political objectives of a centrally planned economy. China's industrial policy was given explicit expression in the seven Five Year Plans that operated over the long period ending in 1990.

In the 1950s, industrial policy was patterned loosely after the Soviet Union, emphasizing heavy industry and development of large state enterprises in key product lines. The subsequent political rupture with the Soviets led to a broadening of production targets, giving agricultural production greater priority. The Great Leap Forward (GLF) was conceived by Mao ZeDong in 1957 and adopted by the National People's Congress a year later. This drive to increase small-scale production was prompted by a desire to catch up with the more advanced industrial countries. Emphasis was given to agriculture, national self-sufficiency, and labor-intensive production methods. After an initial surge of production (1958), it became clear (1960–1) that the GLF was not successful, and a more moderate economic policy followed.

Over the next several decades, wide-ranging programs of investment in industrial plant and equipment led to higher industrial capacity. In 1977–8 the Four Modernizations were introduced. These modernizations of agriculture, industry, science, and technology aimed at turning China into an advanced industrialized nation by the year 2000. The subsequent opening of China to foreign trade and investment played an important role in making modernization a real possibility. In the 1980s, China's international trade and investment grew rapidly.

The Seventh Five Year Plan (1986–90) aimed at furthering the modernization process. This plan called for greater responsiveness to consumer demand, increased efficiency, and assimilation of modern technology. By the early 1990s the industrial sector in China had grown to rank eighth in the world. More importantly, it had achieved a much higher level of efficiency, employing under 20 per cent of the labor force but accounting for nearly half of national output. State enterprises still account for almost half of industrial output, but private sector industrial production has been increasing both absolutely and relatively to total output.

Borrowing the Best

In its desire for industrial superiority, China is seeking to borrow the 'best from all worlds.' This includes the best from American financial capitalism, exploitation of export market opportunities to the US and other important consumer markets, the Japanese government–industry nexus, the export success of the Asian Tigers, investment from Taiwan and Hong Kong, and Singapore's government-linked entrepreneurial effort (Table 6.6).[18]

The Chinese have assessed the usefulness and adaptability of the Japanese economic miracle to China's economy.[19] Those Chinese analysts writing about this issue focus on three questions: (1) How did postwar Japan achieve the high rate of industrial development? (2) How did Japan achieve modernization of its national economy and eliminate the disparity in economic well-being with Europe and America? (3) What experiences in the case of Japan can be applied to China?

Analysts in China consider six aspects of Japanese success:

1. Japanese economic development was given priority.

Table 6.6   Borrowing the Best

Country	Technology	Government Industrialization Policy	Capital	Export Market	Financial Capitalism
US	X			XX	X
Japan	X	XX	X		
Asian Tigers			=	X	
Singapore		+			

Notes: + Singapore style of government-linked enterprise.
        = Taiwanese investment is sought, but is a highly sensitive issue.
        X Desired strategy or target.

2. During the four decades of the 1950s to the 1980s Japan chose indus-
    trial development priorities in a flexible and consistent manner. This
    implies that there has been a proper sequencing of industrial sector
    development, which includes an appropriate balance in developing
    industrial, financial institution, and export trade activities.
3. Consumption was allowed to increase, but held to a level that made
    possible a savings surplus and capital accumulation, necessary to
    develop capital-intensive industries.
4. Japan concentrated on importing and achieving marginal improve-
    ments of existing technology, to be able to catch up with the level
    prevalent in the advanced industrial nations. This proved to be a more
    advantageous approach than one emphasizing wholly independent
    research. This permitted Japan to catch up with other industrialized
    nations that formerly led in technology, and to even surpass them in
    some respects.
5. Japanese managers gave high priority to achieving a high rate of pro-
    duction (and labor productivity) growth, leading to its achieving
    'number 1' rank in this respect.
6. The Japanese educational system is recognized as one that develops
    human resources and intelligence to a high level of efficiency. This
    makes Japanese people highly adaptable to changed circumstances
    and working conditions.

    When describing Japan's economic success, Chinese writers gave the
role of government a central position. Private enterprise receives only secondary attention. The Ministry of International Trade and Industry (**MITI**)

is given high credit for cooperating with and coordinating the activities of private enterprise. This facilitated development of superior technology, better planning, and efficient specialization.

The image described by Chinese writers is one of Japan's economic model pointing the way to China's industrial future. In this regard, one might expect the Chinese political leaders to hold closely to the 'limited opening' pattern, which has prevailed since 1978. Efforts by western countries to 'pry open' China through diplomacy, sanctions, and negotiation may come to experience frustration and even failure.

Chinese leaders have consistently emphasized the central role of industry in the development of their country. Moreover, they have had to be flexible about how they achieve industrial development. For example, in the first decade of communism (until 1957) emphasis was given to heavy industry and investments in large state enterprises. Subsequently, industry's relative role changed, with more emphasis given to assisting agriculture. This flexible approach was also applied to regional development. Initially, government leaders wanted to develop inland locations, but later focused more heavily on developing traditional industrial (coastal cities) centers more intensely. Recently, there has been a more even balance between regional development as well as between types of industry.

Industrial progress has been rapid, but subject to unevenness. According to Howe, very high growth in small-scale output in the period 1949–52 was followed by much lower growth in 1952–60, and extremely low growth in 1960–5 (Table 6.7). Industrial output growth picked up to satisfactory levels in the periods 1965–70 and 1970–5.[20]

In evaluating China's industrial performance, Howe refers to the erratic growth rates, but notes that several sectors performed particularly well in achieving high growth and absorbing modern techniques. These are electricity, machine tools, and petroleum. In 1978, he notes that several sectors posed serious problems. For example, iron and steel finishing capacity was

Table 6.7   Annual Growth in Industrial Output (per cent, per annum)

1949–52	33.89
1952–60	18.29
1960–65	1.58
1965–70	9.50
1970–75	8.79

Source: Christopher Howe, *China's Economy: A Basic Guide*, Basic Books, New York, 1978, p. 98.

too small in relation to crude steel output, and more modern technology was required.[21] In coal, China possesses large reserves, but there are problems of quality and location. In 1978, remote and underdeveloped regions of Western China accounted for close to 60 per cent of reserves but only 10 per cent of output. Finally, the textiles industry lacked modern techniques. Stagnation of this sector in the 1970s resulted from the inability of agriculture to supply raw cotton.

Development since 1978

Beginning in 1978, the government of China launched reforms to increase industrial efficiency and speed up modernization. These reforms cover a number of areas, including:

(a) ownership, organization, and management of enterprises;
(b) role of market forces;
(c) treatment and role of foreign owned enterprises.

The government has enacted legislation which promotes development of various forms of enterprise ownership and organization. Small-scale rural and urban enterprises have been beneficiaries of these reforms, especially in southern China and in the special economic zones. Medium and large-scale enterprises, which have been the core of China's industrial base, have been slower to reform. Nevertheless, the larger state enterprises have been subjected increasingly to market pressures and incentives.

The share of total industrial output produced by state-owned enterprises has been declining steadily since the economic opening of the late 1970s. In 1980 their share of output was 76 per cent, and seven years later it was below 60 per cent. This decline is expected to continue, so that by the year 2000, their share will be around 30 per cent of the total. In the past, the large state enterprises have played an important role. The government relies on those enterprises for its revenues; they provide essential or even strategic goods and services in the energy, raw materials, heavy industry, transportation, and ammunition sectors; and they provide a training ground for a large part of the workforce in skill areas such as administration, office practices, technical skills, and mechanics.

Operating at low efficiency and generating large operating losses, state enterprises have been subject to public criticism and debate. They continue to maintain workers on their payrolls, who sit idle at home. One estimate is there are 15 million such idle workers.[22] Millions more still punch a clock, but are grossly underemployed. Such enterprises cannot pay wages that keep pace with inflation. Consequently, there are increasing numbers of arbitrated labor disputes. In 1993 there were 12 358 such disputes, over half in state enterprises. Reforms have been introduced to impose greater financial discipline. One such reform allows selected state enterprises to be converted into joint stock limited companies and to issue shares to public and private investors. Some of the latter have had their shares listed on the Shanghai and Shenzhen stock markets.

Reforms since the late 1980s permit state enterprises to issue shares, replacing exclusive government control with mixed ownership (including different government entities and ministries, employees, and other enterprises).[23]

In addition to the large state enterprises, several different types of enterprises are growing in importance in China as market forces increase and as foreign capital and technology are permitted to play a greater role in industrial development (Table 6.8).

1. Collective enterprises. These are located mostly in well-populated areas, and organized on a community level. In cities, collectives are organized by neighborhood associations. These enterprises generally have a narrower range of business, are less capital- and technology-intensive, have a closer consumer orientation, and fall outside the strict control of the state plan.
2. Family and industrial enterprises. Small family business, owned by private persons, generally engaged in crafts, retailing, and personal services.

Table 6.8 Share of Industrial Output by Type of Enterprise

Type	1987	1990	1991	2000
State enterprises	59.7	54.6	52.9	30
Collectives	34.6	35.6	35.7	
Industrial	3.6	5.4	5.7	70
Other[a]	2.0	4.4	5.7	
	100.0	100.0	100.0	100

Note: a. Includes foreign investment enterprises.
Source: Shanghai Petrochemical Company Limited, *Prospectus* dated July 23, 1993, p. B3, and author's estimates.

3. Semi-foreign joint ventures. Joint ventures between Chinese and foreign partners that take two forms – equity joint ventures and cooperative joint ventures. The operation of these forms of ventures is subject to extensive laws governing registration, capital, accounting, taxation, foreign exchange and labor.

Foreign Participation in Industrial Development

To attract foreign capital and technology needed for China's modernization, the government enacted laws authorizing establishment of Sino-foreign joint ventures and wholly owned enterprises. Since 1978 the number of Sino-foreign joint venture enterprises has increased rapidly. By 1992 about 84 000 foreign investment enterprises with an aggregate amount of contracted investment of approximately US $110 billion had been established. In 1991 foreign investment enterprises contributed approximately 5.7 per cent of the PRC's total industrial output (Table 6.8).[24]

Pomfret describes two problems in measuring the flow of direct foreign investment into China: the definition of foreign investment and the large gap between amount pledged (or contracted) and actual investment.[25] He notes that by June 1985, only $2.4 billion of an approved $8.5 billion of inward investment had been realized.[26] Further, Chinese statistics recognize six different kinds of direct foreign investment:

1. Wholly foreign owned ventures.
2. Equity joint ventures.
3. Cooperative ventures.
4. Joint development, returns are specified shares of physical output.
5. Compensation trade.
6. Imported inputs for processing and assembly.

Generally, other countries do not consider items 5 and 6 as foreign investment. In addition, in some cases, item 3 may not involve any significant foreign control, and therefore could be excluded from foreign investment figures.

Considerable American investment is attracted by the enormous gap in infrastructure in China. In a visit in 1994 a US engineering executive counted 19 subway systems and 82 airports moving into design or construction phases in the next few years.[27] Taiwanese investment into China faces a political stalemate. Much Taiwanese investment has been indirect, through safe channels (Singapore, Hong Kong), to avoid such difficulties. One large Taiwanese company, Evergreen Group, has waited for the lifting of a cross-strait shipping ban. Normalization of trade ties, including direct flights between Taiwan and the mainland, could take several years.[28]

Foreign infrastructure investment has played a big role in facilitating China's industrial expansion. Despite rapid expansion in number of loss-making domestic airlines (28 new airlines had been approved by early 1994), the industry flourishes.[29] Foreign airlines seek partnerships with Chinese carriers, and foreign service companies invest in aircraft maintenance and airport technology projects. China's desire to become a member of the World Trade Organization could lead to a greater opening of the aviation sector to foreign investment. Overseas banks expect China to spend US$89 billion on 1200 new passenger aircraft between 1994 and 2010. Air transport has grown in China 21 per cent annually since 1980. Alliances and management contracts with European and American carriers can nurture the many PRC airline enterprises, as well as compete with them.[30]

Rapid development of the Chinese telecommunications market has been a boon for equipment suppliers worldwide. Ericsson, the Swedish group, has been one of the biggest beneficiaries. In 1993 China was Ericsson's sixth biggest market, accounting for $500 million in sales. In August 1994 Ericsson landed a $400 million contract to extend the phone network in Guangdong province.[31]

In the decade 1994–2004 China will spend more than $120 billion to realize its planned electric power expansion. Much of this will be financed by foreign companies, which supply equipment and technology, carry out construction, and participate in build-operate-transfer (BOT) agreements. One difficulty is the insistence by Beijing officials that profit rates on power projects be limited to 15–20 per cent on capital.[32] Foreign investors face construction, level of output, and political risks. Foreign exchange rules introduced early in 1994 compounded these risks. The replacement of foreign exchange swap centers with a centralized electronically linked foreign exchange market imposed the following changes on foreign investors:

1. prevent electric prices from being denominated in foreign exchange;
2. guarantees can only be provided in yuan;
3. people no longer have easy access to the swap markets to convert money following the restructuring of the foreign exchange markets.

Investors must look to firm off-take obligations by a creditworthy company, and a firm fuel supply if they wish to enjoy limited risk. Such arrangements are not easily made in the PRC.

China's strategy to attract foreign investment to spur industrial development is a complex issue. It is discussed in much greater detail in a subsequent chapter.

Industrial Market Structure

With a large geographic land area, it is necessary to consider the question of market integration-fragmentation. Most important is the extent to which China's industrial structure has become 'cellular' by province or region.

Examining industrial structure and output, two observations must be made. First, in China as a whole there have been large shifts in the ownership structure of industrial output. The proportion of gross output value (GOV) accounted for by state enterprises declined from 76 per cent in 1980 to 65 per cent in 1985, and to 53 per cent in 1990. This decline continues into the decade of the 1990s. Collateral with this, the number of firms and the output contribution of collective, individual, private and other (including joint venture) that comprise the non-state sector have grown steadily (Table 6.9). Most especially, the number of individual firms almost doubled over the period 1985–91, and their average GOV more than tripled.

Nevertheless, the structure of industrial output over the period since 1980 has remained fairly stable. This can be seen most clearly in Table 6.10, using a 15 branch industry classification. For example, the share of light industries (including food processing, textiles, apparel, leather goods, paper and publishing, and cultural and craft goods) was 33.3 per cent in 1980 and 32.8 per cent in 1990. This stability is not due to offsetting changes in the composition of state enterprise and non-state enterprise output, or offsetting shifts in urban and rural output. The relative composition of each of these groups has also been virtually unchanged.[33] This stability is an interesting phenomenon, considering the major policy shifts, move from plan toward market allocation and pricing system, changes in industrial ownership, and opening toward increased foreign trade.

Each major industrial group is located in virtually all provinces. Considering eight principal groups of industries (coal mining, tobacco, textiles, chemicals, building materials, machinery, and electronics and telecommunications), these are represented in all provinces. Moreover, the variation across provinces in terms of numbers of firms and total employment in each sector is low.[34] Firm size also is similar across provinces.

Table 6.9 Number and Gross Output Value of Industrial Enterprises by Ownership, 1985–91

	Total			State Enterprises			Collectives			Individual		
	No. of firms 10 000	GOV[a] Yn100 m	Avg GOV Yn10 000	No. of firms 10 000	GOV[a] Yn100 m	Avg GOV Yn10 000	No. of firms 10 000	GOV[a] Yn100 m	Avg GOV Yn10 000	No. of firms 10 000	GOV[a] Yn100 m	Avg GOV Yn10 000
1985	518.5	9716.5	18.7	9.4	6302.1	672.6	174.2	3117.2	17.9	334.8	179.8	0.5
1987	747.4	13 388.7	17.9	9.8	7996.7	819.3	181.9	4634.8	25.5	555.3	487.0	0.9
1988	810.6	15 425.0	19.0	9.9	8761.0	884.1	185.3	5575.4	30.1	614.8	669.0	1.1
1989	798.1	16 741.9	21.0	10.2	9385.6	917.5	174.7	5975.3	34.2	612.4	804.3	1.3
1990	795.8	18 041.1	22.7	10.4	9851.2	943.6	166.9	6426.9	38.5	617.6	973.0	1.6
1991	808.0	20 660.7	25.6	10.5	10 937.8	1044.7	157.7	7376.0	46.8	638.7	1176.9	1.8

Notes: a. Gross Output Value (GOV) deflated into 1985 constant prices.
The numbers of the three ownerships do not add up to the sum because of 'other ownership.'
Source: China Statistical Yearbook (1992)

Table 6.10 Trends in the Branch Composition of China's Industrial Output,[a] 1970–90 (per cent)

	1970[b]	1980	1981	1990
Metallurgy	10.5	8.6	8.8	7.3
Electricity	3.5	3.8	3.8	3.0
Coal	2.6	2.3	3.0	2.1
Petroleum	4.8	5.1	5.5	3.8
Chemicals	18.5	12.5	11.4	12.7
Machinery	30.0	25.5	20.9	28.9
Building materials	2.9	3.6	3.8	4.3
Forest products	1.7	1.7	2.0	1.3
Food processing	9.2	11.4	13.3	10.5
Textiles	15.0	14.7	16.5	14.0
Apparel	10.0	2.7	2.8	2.8
Leather goods	0.0	1.0	1.1	1.2
Paper and publishing	1.3	1.3	1.3	1.3
Cultural and craft goods	0.0	2.2	2.4	3.0
Other	0.0	3.4	3.3	3.8
Total	100.0	100.0[b]	100.0	100.0

Notes: a. Excluding village-level firms.
        b. Adjusted to take account of adding-up inconsistency.
Source: World Bank, *China: Internal Market Development and Regulation*, 1994, p. 13.

The similar industrial structure across provinces, and the fairly stable industrial structure over time, carries important implications. This suggests that China has not benefited from opportunities for regional specialization that a large internal market might permit. Further, this indicates China has taken relatively little advantage of opportunities for regional specialization based on comparative advantage, while the potential in this direction may be substantial.[35] Additional evidence that internal trade flows have been declining in relative terms reinforces the need to explore means toward market integration, as a key part of the evolution toward the establishment of a more efficient market economy.

Government Regulation of Markets

China is developing a more market-oriented economic system. In this system resource allocation, production, and investment decisions increasingly are being guided by market forces and opportunities for profit. Development of a competitive market system has many aspects, including the existence of a large number of buyers and sellers, free entry and exit of producers and distributors, an absence of barriers to interregional trade, and independent price-setting by producers based on expectations of profit.

The aim of the government in this context should be to steer the economy toward a situation of greater competition. From a regulatory standpoint, this requires that government create instruments and conditions insuring competitive behavior. A range of regulatory instruments have been put in place to safeguard the competitive market. These include laws concerning freedom of entry, licensing procedures, laws on competitive behavior, and regulations on monopolies and unfair trade practices. The following briefly analyzes the role of government in regulating the economy with a view toward promoting competition in markets.

Promoting a Competitive Environment

Well-designed competition laws can be important in maintaining and developing more competitive markets. This works through the impact of such laws on market structure and participant behavior. The economic environment in which laws and pro-competition rules are applied also is critically important. In China, as in other former centrally planned economies in transition, there are extensive problems of monopoly due to the typical large size of state enterprises. A central issue in the transition toward a freer market system is the breakup of large enterprises, or introduction of safeguards against improper exercise of monopoly power.

The industrial structure in China is far from concentrated. In part this is because specialization has taken place at the provincial or local level. Former emphasis on local self-sufficiency has led to duplication of industries from one province to another. This duplication tended to be reinforced by decentralization of investment decisions to the provincial level in the early 1980s. A good illustration of this is the automotive sector, with 2531 enterprises producing motor vehicles or parts, with an average employment of 620 employees. Shanghai Volkswagen, probably the most important car producer in China in the late 1980s, produced about 17 000 Santana cares in 1990. In that year there were over 110 producers, each accounting for less than 10 000 units of production.[36]

Another example of non-concentrated or diversified production is the machine tool sector. With every province manufacturing machine tools, the top five machine tool enterprises in China account for 20 per cent of national production, compared with 42 per cent in Japan and 69 per cent in the US.

More detailed information on industrial concentration is available in Table 6.11, which contains estimates of regional concentration of output by sector. The data indicate:

1. For most sectors the share of the lead province is below one-third of national output.
2. The top four provinces account for less than two-thirds of total output.
3. Only in two cases (railway coaches and power-generating equipment) is there significant sector concentration.

Table 6.11   Industrial Concentration Ratios for Selected Industries, 1986, 1987

Product	Share of Commodity Output Value		Leading Producer
	Top Province	Top Four Provinces	
Railway coaches	57	100	Hebei
Railway freight wagons	38	82	Heilongjiang
Motor vehicles	24	62	Liaoning
Transformers	22	49	Hebei
Electric wire	22	53	Tianjin
Washing machines	16	55	Shanghai
Sulfuric acid	9	34	Liaoning
Ammonia	9	33	Hebei
Insecticide	25	57	Tianjin
Silicon	12	29	Habie
Cotton cloth	15	41	Jiangsu
Bicycles	16	50	Tianjin
Sewing machines	33	66	Shanghai
Power-generating equipment	45	70	Anhui
Machine tools	17	50	Zhejiang
Large/medium tractors	38	84	Shanghai

Source: World Bank, *China: Internal Market Development and Regulation*, 1994, p. 136.

Change in Market Structure through Mergers

Under central planning in China, cases of enterprise mergers were government-initiated. After ten years of transition toward a freer market economy, it became clear that guidelines were needed regarding how mergers might occur, acceptable methods for valuation of assets, and acceptable impact on employment and fiscal revenue. In 1989 the State Commission for the Restructuring of the Economic System, the State Planning Commission, the Ministry of Finance, and the State Assets Administration together issued guidelines on mergers covering these matters and others.[37] The guidelines were addressed to provincial authorities. By year-end 1989 17 separate regional authorities had established their own policies for the merger of enterprises. An increasing number of mergers led to the organization of 'enterprise property rights markets' to promote mergers. Development of these markets was reportedly supported by the State Administration of Industry and Commerce (SAIC).

The policy of voluntary mergers was formalized in 1992 in the Regulations on Transforming Management Mechanisms of State-Owned Industrial Enterprises. These Regulations recognized the right of enterprises to merge operations with other units. The government department with authority may withhold approval of a merger if competition will be reduced.

Mergers have been used as a government method to rehabilitate loss-making enterprises. This issue of loss-making state enterprises is discussed in some detail in a subsequent chapter. Voluntary or market-driven mergers have been few in number, as have mergers between enterprises based in different provinces. A number of obstacles constrain merger activity:

1. Burdensome payments, such as fees for land transfer, auditing fees, and legal fees.
2. Insufficient audit capacity with which to value assets of firms to be merged.
3. Government officials continue to hold discretionary power over which enterprises should merge.
4. Long time period required to gain approvals from many government departments and levels of administrative authority.

Enterprise Groups

Enterprise groups represent an alternative to outright merger, as a means of organizing associations of companies for mutual benefit. Beginning in

1980, 'horizontally associated' groups operated through loose structures. From 1986 these horizontal associations were upgraded into more formal groups. Over 50 of these very large groups have direct dialogue with the central government relative to enjoying special status in the state economic plan. Almost one-third of these have core activities in machine building electronics, seven in energy, six in defense, four each in steel, chemicals-pharmaceuticals, and building materials, three in banking, and several others in transport and foreign trade. Several prominent enterprise groups include Second Auto Works, Great Wall Computers, and Nanjing Zhongshan Electronic Works.

Enterprise groups enjoy preferential treatment in that they are permitted to establish their own financial companies, business promotion travel rights, and to conduct foreign trade. Beginning in 1988, when shareholding companies could be established, these groups could establish affiliated enterprises with ownership participation.[38] Based on the complex of business activities permitted and the opportunities for share-ownership participation, many typologies of enterprise groups currently are operating. The SAIC defines several types, including 'regular enterprise groups' composed of a center (mother) enterprise and three or more subsidiary (daughter) units tightly linked to the center. Also, there are 'half tightly linked' subsidiaries where the center unit is not a majority shareholder. Finally, there are 'loosely linked subsidiaries,' which operate under long-term contracts with the center but without management links. Over 80 per cent of enterprise groups in China are of the loosely linked type. An alternate typology is published by the State Statistical Bureau (Table 6.12). Of the 6780 enterprise groups existing in 1988, less than 8 per cent operated as 'dominant firm with a leader.' Three-quarters operated as vertical integration or conglomerate groups, suggesting small anti-competitive effects.[39]

With four-fifths of enterprise groups of the loosely linked variety, it may be expected their significance in concentrating capital assets is limited. However, cartel like activities within the group membership are possible.

Market Conduct and Competition Policy

Close communication between enterprises in the same industrial sector can lead to cartel like behavior in setting prices and production. In 1993 such behavior was reported in the case of the washing machine market in Beijing and the air conditioner market in Nanjing. In that year three important laws affecting competition policy in China were put in place. These were the Product Liability Law, Consumer Protection Law, and an Anti-Unfair Competition Law.

Table 6.12   Enterprise Group Typologies

Typology	Number of Groups	Per cent Groups
Dominant firm with a leader	536	7.9
Specialization group	285	4.2
Vertical integration group	1674	24.4
Horizontal integration group	1008	14.9
Conglomerate	2754	40.6
Subtotal	6257	92.0
Other	523	8.0
Total	6780	100.0

Source: World Bank, *China: Internal Market Development and Regulation*, Washington, DC, 1994, p. 142.

The new law on unfair practices has four objectives. These are to insure healthy development of the economy, to encourage and protect fair competition, to prevent unfair competition, and to protect the lawful rights of businesses and consumers. The law focuses on deceptive trademarks and advertising, violation of trade secrets, and injurious practices. There is specific reference against interregionally restrictive trade practices. This new legislation includes in its scope both domestic and foreign enterprises, and private and public companies.

Entry of New Firms

Ease of entry by new suppliers is an effective source of competition in a market economy. Previous sections of this chapter examine the regional mobility of goods and factors of production. The registration of new firms is another dimension of ease of entry. The State Administration of Industry and Commerce (SAIC) was set up in 1980 as a ministerial level government department directly under the State Council. The SAIC and its bureaux have responsibility for the supervision and regulation of the economy, including the enforcement of laws affecting economic markets. Since 1980, with the increased market orientation of the economy, the role and functions of the SAIC have increased rapidly, and cover a wide range of market regulated activities.

The SAIC currently carries out three major functions:

1.   Licensing and registration of enterprises.

2. Organization and administration of markets, including consumer goods and producer goods.
3. Market supervision and investigation, relative to conformity to economic laws and regulations.

A central priority of SAIC is to protect consumer interests in an environment of fair competition.

In China enterprise registration aims at compliance with existing legal requirements. This includes starting operations, alteration in scope of operations, change in registered capital. Detailed documentation is required by SAIC, and in some instances a very large number of permits and other forms must be completed or obtained. Penalties are levied for failure to obtain necessary documents or payment of required fees. These requirements impose a burden on the scarce talent and resources of new entrants. There clearly is a need for procedural simplification. Easing the procedures for entry certainly would promote an increase in market competition.

CONCLUSION

China has made significant progress toward establishing the regulatory framework for a market economy. There does not appear to be a problem of firm size or share of market. Rather, there is the need to focus on enhancing market conduct that will promote competition. The 1993 legislation is appropriate in focusing on improved market conduct.

China has made significant progress toward establishing the regulatory framework for a market economy. There does not appear to be a problem of firm size or share of market. Rather, there is the need to focus on enhancing market conduct that will promote competition. The 1993 legislation is appropriate in focusing on improved market conduct.

The entry of new firms is complex and subject to administrative discretion. These issues must be addressed. Efforts must be continued to simplify procedures for entry and to remove corruption in the administration and supervision of enterprises.

The role of government in economic activity is to create an environment favorable to competition and the development of transparent markets. Today China faces the task of transforming the role of government. Government policy necessarily is different in a market economy as compared with one of central planning. There continue to be problems of a proliferation of regulations, and lack of spatial integration in China's markets. China must analyze the internal barriers against trade and movements of factors of production, and take effective action where such barriers reduce competition.

7 Banking, Money, and Credit

For China to continue to achieve high economic growth rates into the 21st century, it will be necessary to improve the efficiency of banks and financial institutions, so that scarce capital can be allocated to high productivity uses. Moreover, China must continue to attract foreign loan and business capital. This chapter gives some insights concerning the prospects in these areas over the near future.

CURRENT BANKING SYSTEM

Since the introduction of reforms in 1978, the financial system has experienced many changes. These include the emergence of the People's Bank of China (PBOC) as Central Bank, a growing distinction between bank policy lending and commercial lending activities, and the increased importance of nonbank financial institutions and foreign banking institutions.

The PBOC and four specialized banks operate a decentralized branch network, with over 120 000 branches. The four specialized banks include the Bank of China (BOC), the Industrial and Commercial Bank of China (ICBC), the People's Construction Bank of China (PCBC), and the Agricultural Bank of China (ABC). Since 1985 the PBOC and the specialized banks have diversified their activities, providing policy loans, agricultural loans, and loans financing external trade. The assets of selected state banks at year-end 1994 are presented in Table 7.1.

Table 7.1   Assets of Selected Chinese Banks, 1994

	HK$ bn
Industrial and Commercial Bank of China (ICBC)	2610
People's Construction Bank of China	1414
Bank of China	822
Bank of Communications	211

Source: *South China Morning Post*.

107

The Chinese banking system (Figure 7.1) also includes universal banks, a number of development banks, rural and urban credit cooperatives, and over 300 offices and branches of foreign banks engaged primarily in foreign currency banking.

China has a variety of nonbank financial institutions. Prominent among these are the trust and investment companies. In most cases these are affiliated with a specialized bank. Trust and investment companies receive trust deposits, trade securities, and issue guarantees. A growing number of securities companies operate in China, including foreign-owned brokerage and investment companies. These companies are engaged in trading securities of all types. In addition, China's financial institutions include leasing and insurance companies.

Banks

To achieve the objectives of economic reform, in 1978 the PBOC was separated from the Ministry of Finance. Later, in 1984, the commercial banking function of the PBOC was transferred to the Industrial and Commercial Bank of China (ICBA) and other specialized banks. Under this reformed system, the PBOC operates more like a Central Bank, with functions similar to those of its counterparts in Europe and North America.

In 1995 China began to issue shorter term government bonds to improve the ability of the Central Bank to conduct open market operations.[1] The PBOC also functions as the official representative of China in international monetary organizations such as the International Monetary Fund. The State Administration of Exchange Control (SAEC) is an arm of the People's Bank of China. The SAEC is part of the PBOC regulatory apparatus, responsible for control of all foreign exchange transactions in China including foreign borrowing. An important question for the future development of the PBOC as an independent Central Bank is the extent to which the Ministry of Finance will become dependent on the Central Bank to facilitate financing via sale of bonds.

In the 15-year period since China's opening, the specialized banks have provided the major part of bank financial services. These specialized banks are state-owned and carry out a wide range of activities. These include granting loans to enterprises in accord with state policy, borrowing and lending funds at interest rates set by the PBOC, facilitating settlements of financial transactions, administering the transfer of funds throughout the economy, supervising cash management of enterprises that carry on business with the bank, and conducting international financing under the guidance and approval of the State Council and PBOC.

Figure 7.1 China's Banking System, 1995

The People's Bank of China
(Central Bank)

Policy banks
State Development Bank
– finances key state infrastructures projects

Export and Import Bank of China
– provides trade-related credits

Agricultural Development Bank
– supports government purchase and distribution of food and cotton
– funds key agricultural projects

Specialized banks (pending commercialization)

Industrial and Commercial Bank of China

People's Construction Bank of China

Agricultural Bank of China

Bank of China

Corporate commercial banks (11 banks)

Combined operations and assets insignificant compared with those of the specialized banks

Prominent examples:
– Bank of Communications
– Everbright Bank
– CITIC Industrial Bank

Urban cooperative banks (proposed)

The People's Livelihood Bank
(China's first private commercial bank)

Source: South China Post, weekly edition, April 15, 1995.

In addition to the specialized banks, other commercial banks are active in China. These include the Bank of Communications, CITIC Industrial Bank, Hua Xia Bank, China Everbright Bank, Guangdong Development Bank, and several other regional banks. The first four banks listed above operate across the nation with extensive branch systems.

Banks manage their liquidity positions through the interbank market. To participate in this market, a bank must receive approval from the Central Bank. The market allows banks that are short of liquid funds to borrow these from banks holding excess liquidity. This market has developed rapidly since 1985, when tight credit policies by the PBOC caused some banks to run short of funds.

Nonbank Financial Institutions

Several categories of nonbank financial institutions operate in China. Of particular importance are the trust and investment companies, Leasing companies, securities firms, and cooperatives. These institutions have challenged the near-monopoly position of the banks, and compete with them for deposits and loans. The nonbank financial institutions are subject to less regulation, are more innovative, and more efficient and profitable.

Most trust and investment companies were established by state banks and local governments to circumvent the credit controls of the People's Bank. The banks have the incentive to divert funds to the affiliated trust and investment companies for greater flexibility of use and profit.

The China International Trust and Investment Corporation (CITIC) was established in 1979, and is the largest conglomerate of this type. It is engaged in finance, trade, manufacturing, services, and other related activities. CITIC is unique among its kind, since it actively participates in the international financial markets, and has initiated numerous foreign investments and joint ventures. One of its activities is the import of advanced technology and management. CITIC has made investments in countries such as the US and Australia in natural resources and manufacturing. CITIC has much more power and flexibility in its activities than other Chinese business-financial enterprises. Its leadership has excellent connections in the central government, and its areas of operation are of strategic importance in China's evolution from central planning to a more capitalist-type system. CITIC owns CITIC Industrial Bank which offers a wide range of financial services, including deposit-loan in domestic and foreign currencies, securities brokerage and underwriting, foreign exchange, credit cards, and financial consulting. CITIC has made important progress in bringing foreign management and capital into the PRC and in demonstrating how to succeed by adopting a competitive, market-oriented business style.

Another nonbank institution is China Venturetech Investment Corporation, established in 1985. China Venturetech is supervised by the PBOC and raises capital for new technology investment in smaller companies. This institution has offices in Hong Kong, the US, France, Japan, and Australia.

China's Urban Credit Cooperatives and Rural Credit Cooperatives are collectively owned. The 3000 credit cooperatives operate 56 000 branches across China, and function as the grass roots units of the Agricultural Bank. China reopened its postal savings deposit service in 1986, and this has exhibited rapid growth. Given the high savings rate in the PRC, this institution plays an important role in mobilizing funds for allocation through the financial system.[2]

MONEY AND CREDIT

The Credit Plan

Over the period 1979–95 the system of economic controls in the PRC has shifted from one dominated by the central plan to one influenced more and more by market mechanisms. This blend of direct and indirect controls operates around an overall credit plan, which is formulated periodically taking into account growth and inflation targets.[3]

Since 1988 the scope of credit planning has been expanded, and includes credit provided by nonbank financial institutions and direct financing of enterprises. Credit to the government is excluded from credit planning. Each year a comprehensive credit plan is submitted to the State Council, and this body must approve the plan in a more narrowly defined scope. This more narrowly defined credit plan includes credit provided by the specialized and universal banks. The PBOC monitors this approved credit plan, as well as the movement of broad monetary aggregates.

An important aspect of implementing the credit plan is the enforcement of credit quotas or ceilings that apply to the specialized and universal banks. This includes ceilings for specific loan categories such as working capital credits and investment loans. Each bank operates under a credit ceiling that fixes its percentage share of total credit.

The Central Bank influences aggregate credit through its lending, changes in administered interest rates, and reserve requirements. Central Bank lending influences bank liquidity and redistributes funds to where the strongest credit demands are observed. Also, Central Bank lending supports the pace of economic advance, closing the discrepancy between credit targets and deposits built up through savings. The form of Central Bank lending varies, and includes short-term credits, longer-term loans (2 years), very short-term lending (for periods of less than 1 month), and commercial paper rediscounts. Specialized banks can borrow directly from the Central Bank, and from financial institutions.

Reserve requirements apply to time and demand deposits in the specialized and universal banks, cooperatives, and trust and investment companies. In China reserve requirements accrue interest income. In 1994 the reserve requirements on domestic currency bank deposits was 13 per cent. Financial institutions in the PRC hold a large percentage of their deposits as excess reserves at the PBOC. This is due to the local branches experiencing liquidity imbalances that cannot be offset on an aggregate basis, a localized interbank market, problems in the payments and settlements system that require holding excess cash for operations, and lack of a strong profit motivation among many state-owned banking institutions.

At the midpoint of the decade of the 1990s it could be stated that interest rates still play a fairly limited role in monetary policy. This can be attributed to the factors mentioned above, which explain the holding of large excess reserves by financial institutions, and more generally due to the soft budget constraint in the case of state enterprises. The limited effect of interest rates on the supply of capital is related to the many new, unofficial ways of raising money.[4] Nevertheless, year-by-year interest rates are playing a more important role in affecting bank operations and management. Most important, interest rates impact the level of household savings and the overall availability of loanable funds.

China's money market is made up of local and fragmented interbank markets for short term funds. These local money market components are utilized by financial institutions, banks, trust and investment companies, securities companies, and the local branches of the Central Bank. These markets are used for funding loans and for liquidity management. Over the years the maturities of government bonds have been shortened, adding to the range of liquid instruments available for money market participants. Also, enterprises now sell a greater variety of financial instruments, including enterprise bonds, financial bonds, commercial paper, and certificates of deposit. Secondary trading of bonds has increased sharply since it was initiated in 1988. The development of a national electronic trading system in 1991 connecting a number of cities also has improved the usefulness of the money market mechanism.

Debt Cycles

The underdeveloped money and credit system in China leads to intensified cycles of debt expansion and contraction. For example, rising inflation in 1993 led to an austerity drive, introduced by Central Bank director Zhu Rongji. Credit expansion was curbed, and many borrowers were required to reduce their loan obligations. Due to a shortage of capital which came about as a result of this austerity move, many companies secretly raised international commercial loans that the Beijing authorities were unaware of. These foreign loans were converted into yuan and used to overcome the credit shortage. According to a report by the State Administration of Exchange Control (SAEC), this represented a violation of state control of foreign debt. As reported at mid-1995 China's external debt was $100 billion as of December 1994, and rapidly approaching the level of $115 billion.[5] The SAEC expressed concern that these illegal borrowing activities built Chinese debt to a potentially dangerous level, undermined monetary policy, and endangered the stability of the yuan. Resurgent inflation in 1994 pushed China's leaders into more extreme measures, including a price freeze on some services such as transport and electricity.[6]

At the same time it was reported the Chinese currency had begun to weaken, falling on the Shanghai foreign exchange market. A strict debt control mechanism now demands that foreign commercial loans may not be converted into yuan for any purpose without SAEC approval. This tightening affected Shanghai investment banks and securities houses unfavorably, and several foreign institutions were reported to be downsizing operations.

Instead of borrowing abroad, the Central Bank decided in 1995 to use some of its large foreign exchange reserves, estimated at that time at US$55 billion. China's conservative money managers fear it will lose its financial independence if it borrows too much. Further, China must be concerned about attracting direct investment. As one European investment banker observed in 1995, strict credit control exercised by the SAEC, plus capital inflows of an estimated $20 billion (one-third of the $60 billion committed by foreign enterprises) will put China in an extremely good external financial position compared with other countries.

Currency Management

Over the period 1979–94 the Chinese economy has experienced a sharp increase in the money to GNP ratio, and most of this growth has been cash-based. Cash remains the only payments instrument for households, producers in the agricultural sector, and it remains the preferred medium of exchange in the industrial enterprise sector. In some regions of the country there is a premium in use of cash, and in some provinces the share of cash in total payments is as high as 80 per cent. Given the high economic growth and inflation spurts, demand for currency has surged.

The PBOC's currency management practices are largely unchanged from the pre-reform period. Cash continues to function as a central planning tool in regulating currency supply. The PBOC prepares the annual cash plan, based on economic forecasts. The State Council approves the plan, with several ministries providing information inputs.

New banking and credit legislation has as part of its intent, to improve the payments system in China. Recent commercial banking legislation seeks to provide a legal framework for reform, which in turn will stimulate competition and innovation. The negotiable instruments law enacted in 1995 is expected to stimulate confidence in the use of new payments instruments (checks). Development of an improved payments clearing and settlement system will provide infrastructure for use of non-cash payments.[7]

FOREIGN BANKS AND FINANCIAL INSTITUTIONS

Foreign banks and financial institutions are attracted to locate offices in China, based on the enormous savings flows and credit demand. Some large American banks have redirected resources to countries like China, where above average returns are expected on investment.[8] China's first international investment bank, China International Capital Corp. is a joint venture including Morgan Stanley (35 per cent ownership), the Government of Singapore Investment Corp. (7.5 per cent), and Chinese investors.[9] With initial capital of $100 million, the bank intends to raise funds in the international capital markets, advise local enterprises, and undertake direct investments. This institution could play an important role in China's effort to raise the $500 billion estimated as necessary to finance infrastructure investment.

Formats Used

China gives a special definition to foreign banks. Three categories are included, namely branches established in China by exterior banks, banks with foreign capital with a China head office (joint venture), and overseas Chinese banks based in Singapore, Hong Kong, or Taiwan.[10]

Foreign banks use several different formats in China. Representative offices provide contacts, service the promotion needs of the parent bank, but are prohibited from engaging in profit-generating activities. The representative office can be the first step along the way to establishing a branch or joint venture. Bank branches offer a more substantial means of entering China's banking markets. They offer a full range of banking services. Joint venture banks permit foreign banks faster and more complete access to the domestic market, but control must be shared.

Several events promoted the expansion of foreign banks in China. To regain its status as China's financial center, beginning in 1989 the Shanghai government implemented several measures. In that year the Pudong New Development Zone was created. This would require investment in infrastructure and industry of $30 billion. To finance this investment Shanghai city took steps to open up the securities markets and permit foreign banking. For the first time foreign banks were allowed to operate branches outside the Special Economic Zones.

By the mid-1990s Shanghai was developing rapidly as a financial center in China. Foreign banks established offices in Shanghai, making this city an important international banking center. China's first national interbank market was established. Also, the Shanghai Securities Exchange trades both class A and class B shares.[11] Finally, Shanghai is becoming a commodities trading center, with grain and metals futures trading expanding steadily.[12]

Early in 1995 government authorities announced a more liberal policy toward foreign banks. This would facilitate foreign banks branching in 10 major cities, that will be declared open financial centers under State Council decree. The Vice-Director in charge of foreign financial institutions said the government gradually would increase the number of new foreign financial institutions permitted, including bank branches, insurance companies, and investment banks. The ten new cities include Beijing, Shenyang, Xian, Hangzhou, Wuhan, and Chengdu. Coastal cities such as Shanghai, Tianjin, and Guangzhou already are open. By end of 1994 some 101 foreign-funded banks, branches, and finance companies had begun operations in China.[13]

Xiamen International Bank was the first joint venture bank to be established. Organized in 1985 with authorized capital of HK$800 million, the bank enjoys a broad base of international support. The original investors were ICBC-Fujian Provincial Bank, Fujian Investment and Enterprise Corp., the Construction and Development Corp. of Xiamen, and Kong Min Xin Holdings of Hong Kong. In 1991 new shareholders came into the venture: Asian Development Bank; LTCB of Japan; and Sino Finance Group.

Hong Kong is Adapting

Previously we described the efforts of Shanghai authorities to develop the financial infrastructure required to render financial services for the high-growth national economy. Our discussion would be incomplete if we failed to consider how Hong Kong is adapting in the final years leading up to reunification with the mainland. Already, the Bank of China has assumed a role parallel to that of Hong Kong Shanghai Bank, and Standard Chartered Bank, as a note-issuing institution.

Hong Kong is growing new institutions, capable of dealing effectively in the highly competitive and open local financial system, or in the myriad channels and contacts required under the crude and often bureaucratic financial system of the People's Republic. One such institution, Peregrine Investments, has become a powerful force in the colony's investment banking and in much of the rest of Asia including China.

Peregrine has built its business with a new establishment of Chinese entrepreneurs, and bet its money on this new establishment.[14] Founded in 1988 with $38 million of capital, by 1993 its pretax profits reached $110 million, and the firm reported capital in 1994 of $550 million. When Peregrine was launched in 1988, Mr Li Ka-shing (of Cheung Kong) was one of its key backers. Other influential backers included Gordon Wu (of Hopewell Holdings) and Larry Yung (CITIC Pacific). These and other supporters have channeled considerable business in the direction of Peregrine. In 1993 the firm led a third of all rights issues in Hong Kong and sponsored 60 per cent of new stock market listings. Since 1993 Peregrine has sought to duplicate its equity market successes on the bond side.

Peregrine has turned its Hong Kong connections to advantage on the mainland. Ties to CITIC Pacific, a 'red chip' company, are quite valuable. CITIC itself is an investor, holding company, and sponsor of emerging enterprises on the mainland.

Peregrine's other China ties include a joint venture with a provincial government, foreign exchange services with authorities in Guangzhou, and a trading partnership with the municipality in Beijing. Most important, Peregrine has been the busiest broker bringing Chinese enterprises to the stock market in Hong Kong. Peregrine was able to get around rules that bar foreign securities firms from seats on the Shanghai stock exchange.

REFORM AND TRANSITION

General Objectives

Government authorities have developed plans to reform the banking and financial system. Basic objectives of this reform are (a) to strengthen the Central Bank, giving it responsibility for formulating and implementing monetary policy, (b) promote development of efficient financial markets with effective regulations, (c) reform the banking system, so that state-owned banking units can operate on a purely commercial basis, and (d) shift government policy lending from existing banks to newly created policy banks.

A proposed new Central Banking law would give the PBOC greater autonomy, with PBOC credit control objectives accomplished through open market operations.

Policy-based lending is to be assumed by three new financial institutions. These include the State Development Bank (SDB) which will provide low interest rate financing for infrastructure, the China Import and Export Bank to finance trade in capital goods, and the Agricultural Development Bank of China which will focus on financing state trading of agricultural products and agricultural development.

The government is encouraging development of a more efficient money market, centered on a broad market for short-term treasury securities. The reforms aim at reducing market segmentation, and promoting a national interbank market. Liberalized interest rates will allow greater flexibility in the money market. Finally, the interbank market is to be strengthened through more effective supervision.

China also announced it will permit clusters of urban credit cooperatives to be transformed into commercial banks. Those will service the growing number of small businesses across the nation.[15]

Obstacles to Reform

In 1995 it could be observed that China's bank reforms were in danger of coming to a standstill under the heavy weight of massive debts owed by state industry to the banking sector. The debt-ridden state enterprise sector absorbs two-thirds of loans generated by China's four specialized banks. During the first half of 1995 bad and doubtful debts climbed sharply, with half of China's state enterprises operating at a loss and relying on bank provided funds to maintain production and pay creditors.[16]

The Chinese government has required these banks to continue to extend loans for critical activities of state firms. To cover loan service payments, public money is injected into the banks, which in turn maintain credit extensions to state enterprises. Under these conditions, it is virtually impossible to introduce further reforms in the banking system. Reform of state enterprises is crucial to change in the banking sector. The speed of state enterprise reform will dictate the pace of banking commercialization.

In an October 1995 press interview Mr Dai Xianglong, appointed governor of the PBOC (effective June 1995), attempted to counter adverse publicity concerning the creditworthiness of China's 'big four' commercial banks. These banks are heavily burdened with loans to loss-making state companies. He noted that China's official foreign exchange reserves of $70 billion reflect the ability of the financial system and Chinese banks to honor their international credit obligations. He noted that bad loans represent approximately 2 per cent of commercial bank loan portfolios. In addition 7 per cent of loans were 'problematical', with interest payments current but some principal repayments overdue. A further 11 per cent of loans were of concern because enterprises were a year or more behind in repayments. China does not use international classifications for bad loans.

The bulk of problem loans are attributable to heavily indebted state enterprises. Mr Dai noted the government was providing a reserve fund to cover the buildup of state enterprise bad debts in the banking system by allocating 0.8 per cent of loans, to grow to 0.9 per cent in 1996 and 1.0 per cent in 1997. He stated the banks would also be obliged to contribute additional reserves net of profits to cover bad debts.[17]

Given that state enterprises produce close to 40 per cent of gross national product, the government simply cannot withdraw credit extensions. This would force plant closings and leave millions of workers unemployed.[18]

One report suggests it will take a full decade for a true Central Bank and commercial banking system to emerge in China.[19] The law enacted early in 1995 confirms the legal status of the People's Bank of China as the nation's Central Bank. But the ability of the PBOC to influence the banking system will be limited by the slow progress of the specialized banks in their transition toward becoming market-oriented commercial banks.

INTERNATIONAL STATUS OF CHINA'S BANKS

China's efforts to achieve banking reform places a number of these institutions in a difficult pivotal position. Instead of treating the banks as if they were an integral part of the government, China is starting to treat them as financial institutions that must stand or fall on their own commercial performance.[20] As long as they were operated as extensions of the government, the main banks have enjoyed uniformly high international credit ratings. In the past credit agencies analyzing Chinese banks were rating a form of Chinese government debt. With the banking reforms these institutions now operate more on a commercial basis and at arm's-length vis-à-vis the government. Therefore, they are evaluated as independent entities.

Bank Debt Downgraded

Early in 1995 Moody's Investors Service downgraded the long-term bond ratings of four of China's biggest banks from A3 to Baa1 (Bank of China, Bank of Communications, People's Construction Bank of China, and Industrial and Commercial Bank of China). China's sovereign rating was reaffirmed A3. Also, the long-term bank deposit rating was cut from A3 to Baa2. This means that the BOC floating rate certificates of deposit (FRCD) cannot qualify for the liquidity adjustment facility (LAF) operated by the Hong Kong Monetary Authority (HKMA).[21] Access to LAF makes debt securities more attractive because holders of securities that qualify can engage in repurchase agreements (repos) with the HKMA, giving greater flexibility in liquidity management. The revised rating is too low for access to LAF. Therefore, the BOC is excluded from a facility for which the debt of other large banks in Hong Kong (Hong Kong Bank, Standard Chartered, Bangkok Bank) has qualified. An official in China's Finance Ministry commented that the commercialization of China's banks was a time-consuming process, and BOC now would pay more for loan funds.

Bad News is Good

The bank debt downgrading appears to be bad news for the banks, but may be good news for China. The ratings of the four institutions are being downgraded not because suddenly they are doing something wrong, but because Beijing is doing something right. Banks are being required to operate in a more market-oriented way and to use objective criteria in evaluating credit requests. Moreover, policy lending and commercial lending are being clearly distinguished, so that different banks can focus on one or the other of these lending areas.

In future these banks will be more under pressure to consider cost of funds impacts from their credit policies, and their operational

Table 7.2 Major International Borrowings since 1990

Launch	Issuer	Amount (Yn/$US/DM m)	Yield	Maturity	Bookrunner
Jun. 91	Bank of China	20 000 Yn	7.502	5	Yamaichi
Oct. 91	China Int'l Trust & Investment Corp	15 000 Yn	–	5	Nomura Securities
Mar. 92	China Int'l Trust & Investment Corp	20 000 Yn	6050	5	Daiwa Europe
May 92	Bank of Communications	70 US	–	5	Daiwa Securities
Jul. 92	Guangdong Int'l Trust & Finance (GITIC)	15 000 Yn	6276	5	Daiwa Securities
Jul. 92	Bank of China	15 000 Yn	–	5	Nikko Securities
Oct. 92	Bank of China	150 US	–	5	OCBC
Nov. 92	People's Construction Bank of China	150 US	–	5	Merrill Lynch International
Nov. 92	Industrial and Commercial Bank of China	50 US	–	6	–
Dec. 92	China Int'l Trust & Investment Corp	30 000 Yn	5.691	7	Daiwa Securities
Feb. 93	Industrial and Commercial Bank of China	15 US	–	5	–
Mar. 93	China Int'l Trust & Investment Corp	150 US	–	5	Singapore Nomura Merchant Banking
Mar. 93	Bank of China	15 000 Yn	4.650	5	Nomura Securities
Mar. 93	Bank of China	15 000 Yn	5.000	7	Nomura Securities
Mar. 93	Bank of Communications	100 US	–	5	OCBC
Apr. 93	Guangdong Int'l Trust & Finance (GITIC)	150 US	–	5	UBS
Jun. 93	People's Construction Bank of China	50 US	–	5	JP Morgan Securities
Jun. 93	People's Construction Bank of China	70 US	–	7	JP Morgan Securities

Table 7.2   Continued

Launch	Issuer	Amount (Yn/ $US/DM m)	Yield	Maturity	Bookrunner
Jun. 93	Bank of China	200 US	–	5	Credit Suisse First Boston
Jul. 93	China Int'l Trust & Investment Corp	30 000 Yn	4.129	3	Nikko Europe
Jul. 93	China Int'l Trust & Investment Corp	250 US	7.035	10	Goldman Sachs
Dec. 93	Industrial and Commercial Bank of China	15 000 Yn	3.429	5	Daiwa Securities
Mar. 94	Bank of China	400 US	6.935	5	Morgan Stanley
Mar. 94	Bank of China	100 US	8.452	20	Morgan Stanley
Apr. 94	Industrial and Commercial Bank of China	50 US	–	6	–
May 94	Industrial and Commercial Bank of China	30 US	–	–	–
May 94	Bank of China	15 000 Yn	4.704	7	Nikko Securities
Jun. 94	Bank of China	300 DM	6.780	5	Commerzbank AG
Jul. 94	People's Construction Bank of China	15 000 Yn	–	7	IBJ Asia, Goldman Sachs (Asia)
Oct. 94	China Int'l Trust & Investment Corp	200 US	9.274	12	JP Morgan & Co.
Nov. 94	Bank of Communications	12 000 Yn	4.806	5	Nikko Securities
Nov. 94	Industrial and Commercial Bank of China	25 US	–	5	–
Nov. 94	Industrial and Commercial Bank of China	16.42 US	–	7	–
Jan. 95	Industrial and Commercial Bank of China	85 US	–	8	–
Jan. 95	Industrial and Commercial Bank of China	15 US	–	8	–

Source: South China Morning Post, April 22, 1995, p. 2.

performance. Shortly after the downgradings officials from these banks indicated they would scale back offshore bond issues because the ratings affected the cost of cross border debt. These banks have been prominent international borrowers over the period 1991–5 (Table 7.2).

Other banks were affected by the downgrades. Guangdong International Trust and Investment Corp. (GITIC) received a similar downgrade, and the giant Chinese investment conglomerate China International Trust and Investment Corp. (CITIC) was put on review for a possible downgrade.[22] One economist noted that China's growing debt and increasing number of commercial disputes over borrowings since 1993 made possible a negative review of CITIC.[23] China ranks as the world's fifth biggest borrower.

Possible Impact on Economic Growth

The four banks whose debt was downgraded together make up half of the country's financial industry, with combined assets of US$641 billion (HK$4950 billion).[24] They have played the role of financial powerhouse, supporting development programs in agriculture and industry.

The downgraded institutions will have to pay more to attract the same level of borrowed funds, due to perceived higher risk. The additional cost will depend on future market conditions for new loans. As an illustration, the Bank of China US dollar floating rate notes were trading in April 1995 at LIBOR plus 60 basis points, a 33 per cent increase over January 1995.

In its downgrading Moody's observed the four specialized banks face huge policy loan writedowns from loans to loss-making state enterprises, and questioned Beijing's timetable for implementing banking reforms.

8 China's Emerging Capital Market

The capital market enables a country to mobilize liquid savings for investment in suitable projects. When operating efficiently, capital markets allocate capital to sectors where investment will enjoy the highest productivity. China is in the earliest stage of developing its capital market. Nevertheless, this market is evolving rapidly, and exhibiting continuous structural adjustment and improvement.

EVOLUTION OF CAPITAL MARKET

The development of China's capital market will rank as one of the most important events of the 1990s. The first national stock exchange was opened in December 1990 in Shanghai. This was followed by establishment of the Shenzhen Stock Exchange in April 1991. By year-end 1993 the value of equity on these two exchanges was $40 billion, and by 1994 close to $60 billion.[1]

Some of the best known Chinese enterprises (Tsingtao Brewery and Shanghai Petrochemical) have been listed on the Stock Exchange of Hong Kong; others are scheduled to be listed. In October 1993 a Chinese enterprise was listed on the New York Stock Exchange for the first time. Government and enterprise bonds have been listed on the Shanghai Stock Exchange and futures contracts for government bonds have been actively traded on the Exchange.

A Challenging Experiment

The successful development of the capital market in China is of special interest for several reasons. First, it illustrates the challenges faced by developing country governments as they attempt to spur financial modernization. Second, China is a country whose economic system is in transition from central planning to a socialist market economy. Transition economies face special difficulties in developing capitalist institutions and learning behavior patterns characteristic of modern financial systems.

China faces a perennial shortage of capital, but its financial markets will play only a secondary role unless issues such as ownership of industry, bankruptcy, and distribution of wealth are dealt with in an appropriate way.[2]

The Chinese authorities introduced capital markets as an experiment, hoping to learn from this experience. Therefore, securities markets were allowed to operate in only a few regions. Market growth quickly outstripped the efforts of government authorities to control such activity. At times an overheated economy contributed to inflation, a decline in bank deposits, and a diversion of funds from investment by industrial enterprises to real estate and securities speculation.[3] This decline in liquidity led the authorities to force banks to recall speculative loans and to reinforce the separation of the banking and securities sectors.

In 1993 and following years significant improvements took place in regulation of the securities markets. The new State Council Securities Policy Committee and its executive arm, the China Securities Regulatory Commission which was established in 1992, assumed its place as the chief regulator and supervisor of securities markets in 1993. For the first time the regulation of bond and equity issues and trading were centralized. A new companies law was passed in 1993, discussed later in this chapter. As of 1995 national securities legislation had not been enacted.

Major Challenges

A country like China faces serious challenges in developing its capital market. First, it must keep the pace of capital market liberalization under control, so that the domestic economy does not become destabilized. China has been buffeted by wide swings in macroeconomic activity. At times, high inflation has required that the authorities slow the capital market reform process, and initiate financial austerity to cope with rising prices.

A second challenge is to respond to the pressures the liberalized components of the financial sector place on the less liberalized components. For example, the government's response to competition for domestic savings is instructive. As high-yielding equities and enterprise bonds outperformed bank deposits, drawing an increasing flow of funds, the government avoided clamping down on these liberalized markets and accelerated the freeing of the controlled sector. Over time the government has shortened the maturity of treasury bonds and increased their interest payments. Further, the policy of issuing bonds by forced allocations was ended in 1991.

A third challenge is to use the development of securities markets as a means of absorbing international financing techniques and practices and as a source of discipline for enterprise governance. The Chinese authorities are using equity markets to encourage enterprises to improve their operational efficiency. For example, the need to prepare a prospectus introduced broadly accepted international accounting practices, and emphasized profitability performance. The Chinese authorities have adopted a skillful approach toward disclosure. Rather than settle on one standard and wait for most enterprises to attain it, they opted for a multilateral disclosure policy. Those enterprises that could meet the highest disclosure standards of the New York Stock Exchange and Stock Exchange of Hong Kong were selected for listing on these exchanges. Those enterprises less known and less able to meet rigorous disclosure standards were selected for domestic listings on the market where international investors participate by means of B shares. Finally, the remaining enterprises can undertake stock listing in the market in which only domestic investors participate, the market for A shares.[4]

A fourth issue is whether to separate banking and securities markets, and how best to bring about this separation. On one side it is very restrictive and even inefficient to maintain an iron-clad separation between bank lending and capital market allocation of funds. If banks are restricted from securities activities to protect them from large losses, the capital market may become less liquid and result in higher cost as securities companies must hold greater capital and reserves relative to possible settlement and default risks. Lack of liquidity in the capital market could increase the likelihood of a settlements failure, adversely affecting investment institutions and stock brokerages.

A fifth issue is to select the firms that are to be listed for trading on the stock exchange. In most countries this function operates through a competitive market filtering system. In China the authorities decided to have securities regulators and government agencies select the firms. For this reason, in part selection is based on noneconomic factors. One such factor has been regional equality. Experience over the period 1991–4 suggests that the authorities chose the most profitable and largest firms.

A sixth issue is how much of a role to give to securities markets as a source of finance. Compared with bank financing, securities markets in China have played a marginal role. For example, the value of new bank loans in the year 1993 was ten times the value of bond and equity issues. Banks are likely to remain the primary source of external finance for enterprises for many years into the future.

Utilizing International Capital Markets

In making use of the international capital markets, China has followed the pattern observed in recent years in other emerging market countries. Given wide spreads and short maturities on commercial bank loans, the government authorities followed the strategy of more extensively using the international capital markets. As noted later in this chapter, China has been one of the leading emerging market borrowers in the 1990s. Chinese borrowers have tapped a wider range of market sectors, and increased the currencies of denomination of debt issues to broaden the base of possible investors. The government of China has enjoyed an investment grade international credit rating. In addition to tapping the international bond markets, Chinese borrowers have become important issuers of equity securities. Finally, foreign direct investment into China has increased steadily, with commitments reaching the level of $100 billion in 1993.

CHINA'S EMERGING BOND MARKET

Humble Beginnings

The systematic development of a bond market in China began in the early 1980s. In 1981 the government issued almost Yn4.9 billion in 10-year Treasury bonds (Table 8.1). These were distributed through compulsory subscriptions to state enterprises, collectives, local governments, and individuals. In 1985 financial institutions were given bond issuing privileges to supplement the funds provided by the Ministry of Finance. These carried higher interest than Treasury bonds, and were of shorter maturity. Subsequently, different types of bonds were issued for various purposes, including construction, capital financing, and enterprise funding.[5]

With the financial reforms of the early 1980s, enterprises found it more difficult to obtain bank financing for investment and for working capital. Approval for issue of enterprise bonds came in 1982, but loose regulation and a draining of funds from the banks caused the People's Bank of China (PBOC) to establish regulations in this area. From 1986 issue of enterprise bonds required approval by the PBOC, with an overall quota limitation and ceiling on interest rates. In that year enterprise bonds accounted for over half of new issues (Table 8.1).

Increased competition for funds, and successive episodes of inflation led to resistance to forced allocation of Treasury bonds. Some non-government issuers increased interest rates paid on bonds, making

Table 8.1 Issues of Securities in China, 1981–91 (billions of Chinese Yuan)

	1981	1982	1983	1984	1985	1986	1987	1988	1989	1990	1991	Total
State bonds	4.866	4.383	4.158	4.253	6.061	6.251	11.787	18.888	18.725	23.416	28.000	130.788
Treasury bonds	4.866	4.383	4.158	4.253	6.061	6.251	6.287	9.216	5.612	9.328	19.900	80.315
Ministry of Finance Notes	–	–	–	–	–	–	–	6.607	–	7.109	6.500	20.216
Construction bonds	–	–	–	–	–	–	–	3.065	–	–	–	3.065
Key construction bonds	–	–	–	–	–	–	5.500	–	–	–	–	5.500
Special bonds	–	–	–	–	–	–	–	–	4.370	3.239	1.600	9.209
'Inflation-proof' bonds	–	–	–	–	–	–	–	–	8.743	3.740	–	12.483
Financial institution bonds	–	–	–	–	0.500	3.000	9.000	15.500	8.319	7.055	16.420	59.794
State investment bonds	–	–	–	–	–	–	–	–	–	–	9.500	9.500
Financial bonds	–	–	–	–	0.500	3.000	6.000	6.500	6.066	6.440	6.691	35.197
Capital construction bonds	–	–	–	–	–	–	–	8.000	1.459	–	0.002	9.461
Key enterprise bonds	–	–	–	–	–	–	3.000	1.000	0.794	0.615	0.227	5.636
Enterprise bonds	–	–	–	–	–	10.000	3.000	7.541	7.526	12.637	24.996	65.700
Local enterprise bonds[a]	–	–	–	–	–	10.000	3.000	3.000	1.483	4.933	11.525	33.941
Short-term borrowing certificates	–	–	–	–	–	–	–	1.172	2.972	5.015	10.444	19.603
Interenterprise bonds	–	–	–	–	–	–	–	3.369	3.071	2.689	3.027	12.156
Certificates of deposit	–	–	–	–	–	–	–	5.926	14.180	50.353	42.685	113.144
Stocks[a]	–	–	–	–	–	–	1.000	2.500	0.662	0.428	2.952	7.542
Total	4.866	4.383	4.158	4.253	6.561	19.251	24.787	50.355	49.412	93.889	115.053	376.968

Note: a. Data for earliest entry include all previous issues.
IMF, International Capital Markets, September 1994, p. 93.

Treasury bonds relatively less attractive. As a result, the Ministry of Finance gradually reduced the maturity of Treasury bonds, and also increased interest rates paid on these securities. In this period of the mid-1980s the amount of bonds issued rose substantially each year (Table 8.1). In the period 1986–91 Treasury bond issues quadrupled in amount, but declined in relative importance.

Secondary Trading Market

The secondary market for debt securities developed slowly. At the outset securities were officially nontransferable. Nevertheless, a thriving illegal market developed in Treasury bonds which had been issued to individuals on a mandatory subscription basis. Speculators could purchase them at deep discounts, and redeem them for profit at maturity. Officially sanctioned securities trading was initiated in August 1986. This was an over-the-counter market for corporate bonds, with prices determined daily by the authorities. An official market in government debt securities was established in seven cities in 1988, and this experiment was extended to 60 cities later that year. In 1988 turnover of Treasury bonds was Yn2.4 billion, and this increased to Yn10.5 billion in 1990 and Yn33.9 billion in 1991. Steps toward development of a unified national market for bond trading came in 1990 with the introduction of the Securities Trading Automated Quotation System (STAQS). STAQS came on line in December 1990 with a satellite link for 17 securities companies located in six cities.[6] STAQS provides screen pricing, centralized clearing, and utilizes the market maker trading structure. Also in 1990 Treasury bonds were listed on the Shanghai Securities Exchange. By October 1993 turnover in the five-year bond on STAQS was Yn133 billion, and on the Shanghai Stock Exchange Yn19.9 million.

In 1993 the National Electronic Trading System (NETS) was officially opened, to provide a nationwide electronic trading system for bonds and stocks. Trading is based on an order-driven book entry system, linked to 100 ground stations. Initial trading on NETS was in institutional shares.

Emerging Problem

The government bond market suffered a temporary setback in 1993 with the availability of more attractive returns in other markets, particularly equities. The Ministry of Finance raised interest rates offered holders of treasury bonds, and also resorted to forced subscriptions. Regional and local governments were assigned bond subscription quotas, and were advised that new equity issues would not be approved until they met their quota. Also employees of state enterprises and government departments were required to purchase bonds, as well as employees in private enterprises. This difficult period witnessed several innovations in the issue of government securities, including issue of short-term financing bills and foreign currency denominated bonds. In June 1993 the Ministry of Finance announced the adoption of a primary dealer system, to which 19 institutions had been appointed. These dealers were required to make a market in treasury bonds.

The development of futures exchanges accelerated after they were first officially recognized in 1992. At least 30 recognized commodities futures exchanges have been established. Financial futures have been introduced. Early in 1993 the SSE listed its first government bond futures contract. Bond futures also are traded on the Beijing Commodity Exchange, with high turnover. In 1994 bond futures were listed on the Shenzhen exchange.

China's rapid transition from a planned to a market economy spurred interest in futures trading. Within a period of three years (to 1994), 40 fledgling futures exchanges sprang up across the country, with 400 registered brokerages and countless other small operations.[7] In April 1994 the government announced a restructuring of this booming industry. Trading in certain commodities (steel and coal futures) was halted. In 1994 the government set up 15 unified exchanges to replace the 40 chaotic trading houses in operation at that time.[8]

Despite its growth strains, China's embryonic bond market might develop into one of the world's most important markets within the next decade, rivaling that of Japan. Factors likely to contribute to this growth are the massive infrastructure needs, possible foreign investor interest and participation, and application of better systems and technology.[9]

CHINA'S EMERGING EQUITY MARKET

Early Development and Growth

Capital market growth in the People's Republic has been substantial due to the need to finance government and enterprise activities in a period of socio-political transition. By 1988 between 6000 and 10 000 companies in China issued Yn7.5 billion (US$1 billion) of securities.[10] Common stock gives the holder a share of ownership in the enterprise. For this reason common stock tends to be in conflict with socialist thinking that gives emphasis to collective ownership of the means of production. Early in the

1980s share issuance was grudgingly allowed, on a limited and experimental basis. Necessity brought about wider acceptance of a shareholding system. The worldwide spread of privatization compelled communist leaders to take a look at the possibilities for transfer of ownership of state enterprises and to open the economy to foreign investors.[11] By the late 1980s government and academic economists were analyzing alternative plans for the development of a stock market system. By 1994 China's proposed Securities Law was in its seventh revision.[12]

Central government control over development of the equity market was first exercised in 1984 with the experimental approval of share issues in five cities. In that year the municipal government of Shanghai permitted state enterprises to issue shares.[13] Official secondary markets for equity shares began to take form in 1986. At that time the Shanghai branch of the Industrial and Commercial Bank of China (ICBC) opened a securities trading counter, offering to buy and sell enterprise shares daily at prices set by the municipal government. By 1988 there were 33 trading counters in Shanghai, transacting seven enterprise shares and eight bonds.

The Shenzhen Securities Market began operating in 1987 with an initial public offering (IPO) of equity of the Shenzhen Development Bank (SDB). An over-the-counter market for SDB shares emerged and by 1989 four additional enterprises had issued shares.

In December 1990 the first recognized stock exchange opened in Shanghai. Initially, seven equities, five state bonds, eight enterprise bonds, and nine financial bonds were traded. The total equity issued by these seven enterprises amounted to Yn235.9 million. A second official stock exchange came into being in Shenzhen in 1991, with five enterprises listed. By year-end 1991 the Shanghai exchange had 9 stocks and 28 bonds listed with a total capitalization of Yn2.9 billion. At this time the Shenzhen exchange had six stocks listed with a capitalized value of Yn7.4 billion. These two exchanges grew rapidly, and by end 1993 there were 183 issues of both A and B shares listed on the two exchanges with a combined value of Yn347.4 billion ($39.9 billion). Turnover of all shares (A and B) in 1993 was Yn331.9 billion ($38.5 billion), most of which was in A shares. Introduction of the STAQS trading system led to increased trading volume of securities.

Selection of Issuing Enterprises

In industrial countries with well-developed capital markets, shares are listed for trading on stock exchanges based on the wide interest of investors in the particular issue or company, and according to the market expectations of profitability of the enterprise. As the stock exchanges have developed in China, selection of issuing enterprises is determined on an administrative basis. Chinese firms that want to list must first be transformed into joint stock companies that have their land and other assets valued by the State Assets Bureau and State Land Administration. Further, they must have their financial statements audited and prepared according to generally accepted international standards. After these processes, they must apply to the local government for approval to issue shares. If successful, they apply to the China Securities Regulatory Commission (CSRC), to insure that the exchange's listing requirements have been satisfied.

The central government has an overall quota of A share listings for the country, which allows control of the pace of market development. The quotas for 1992–4 are presented in Table 8.2. There is no B share quota, but in the approval procedure there must be a proven need for foreign exchange.

A Shares and B Shares

New A share issues are underwritten by a domestic securities firm, usually with a foreign firm adviser. A modified book-building system permits the underwriter to gauge market demand for the issue, and arrive at a suitable offering price. Public share offerings have generally been oversubscribed, and applications are selected by lottery. By contrast, B shares are marketed by private placement, often in Hong Kong.

A and B shares have different liquidity characteristics. B shares are more thinly traded. Therefore, prices of A and B shares for the same company frequently have different prices. We must remember that A and

Table 8.2   A Share Quotas for Stock Exchange Listing

Year	Yn (bn)
1992	10.9
1993	5.0
1994	5.5

Source: International Monetary Fund, *International Capital Markets,* September 1994, p. 102.

B shares differ in their investor base and currency risk, but not in dividend or shareholder rights. For example, in March 1994, B shares in Shanghai traded at a 72 per cent discount to the same companies A shares, but in Shenzhen the discount was 39 per cent. A number of developing countries discriminate between foreign and domestic investors in their capital markets.[14] A possible explanation for the higher price of A shares relative to B shares is the lack of investment alternative for Chinese investors.

Segmentation of Chinese equity markets into A, B, and H shares is a distinguishing feature. One aspect of this is that these market sectors differ in their information and disclosure requirements. Issuers of B shares must provide better information to the market than issuers of A shares. H share issuers need to disclose even more information. Issuers of B shares must prepare financial statements according to international accounting standards, not required of issuers of A shares. Issuers of H shares have added responsibility of meeting Stock Exchange of Hong Kong listing requirements, which are stricter than the two Chinese exchanges.

Experience suggests that investors prefer markets with better disclosure. Foreign investors have gravitated toward H shares more than B shares. When only B shares were available, international investors showed much interest in these shares. When in 1993 enterprises that had issued B shares began reporting 1992 results, some chose not to prepare financial reports according to international standards. Moreover, some had misused funds by speculating in real estate or securities markets. By midyear 1993 liquidity in B shares had fallen. Shortly after, issue of H shares in Hong Kong caught the attention of international investors. The H shares were well received, and market liquidity remained high.[15]

Selection of H share issuers is made by the central authorities at the highest level. In part this approach was difficult to avoid, with the general absence of adequate disclosure, effective market regulation, and market-determined prices for capital shares. Also important is the central authorities' desire to maintain control and carry out an orderly liberalization of markets.

Shanghai's Drive for Status

In 1994 Daimler-Benz, Germany's biggest carmaker, announced it would pass by Hong Kong, and opt for a listing in Shanghai. While in 1994 Shanghai was not quite the competitor to Hong Kong implied by the Daimler-Benz stock listing, there is a growing number of investors and financiers who are betting on Shanghai's emergence as China's future Wall Street. The city has come a long way, and increasing numbers of foreign banks and financial institutions consider it necessary to locate in Shanghai.

The general manager of Nikko Securities capital market division stated: 'Shanghai will one day be the premier center for the whole of greater China.' Shanghai enjoys a number of advantages, including its heavy industrial muscle and educated labor force. The city is spending hundreds of millions of dollars yearly to create the infrastructure, service capacity, and residential structures needed for this status.

While the critical mass for Asian business continues to center in Hong Kong, it is accumulating rapidly in Shanghai. This is especially important in the stock market. Shanghai ranks ahead of Hong Kong in its long-term potential and stronger industrial base.[16] Massive fees are to be earned in the future in Shanghai, as state enterprises and joint ventures come forward with share issues. The Shanghai exchange has begun to implement links with 20 domestic trading centers via satellite.

SUPERVISION AND REGULATION

Corporate Governance

Industrial corporation borrowers are key participants in a national capital market. An important motive in the development of China's capital market is to develop a system of corporate governance that is independent of bureaucratic control. This requires that enterprises be made independent from direct government control.

To accomplish this, authorities have encouraged enterprises to transform themselves into companies with majority state ownership, but with independent management (Table 8.3). By 1994 more than 13 000 enterprises had taken on this status. This selected corporatization is playing an important role in the modernization of the industrial sector. Second, enterprises must be allowed to secure their own financing. This includes negotiating bank loans, and subject to regulatory approval, issue debt and equity securities to the public.

When enterprises are released from direct bureaucratic control, a new kind of managerial discipline must come into effect. This can come from several directions, including reformed banks making prudent credit decisions, and a securities market that values equities and bonds according to the financial prospects of issuers.

Banks impose fiscal discipline by enforcing loan repayment terms, and by analyzing the financial condition of firms. Banks themselves will enforce

Table 8.3　Evolving Status of Corporations

	Pure State Enterprise (pre-1979)	Parallel State Enterprise and Growing Private Enterprise (1979–89)	Selected Corporatization of State Enterprises (1990–2000)
Plan	Central planning	Gradual transition away from planning	Marketized enterprise decisions around small core of central planning
Ownership	State ownership 100%	Private sector and collective sector growing rapidly	Selected selloffs of state enterprise ownership, private sector exceeds SOEs in size
Decision-making	Full conformity of SOEs to plan directives	Small amount of independent, marketized decisions	Ongoing corporatization, growing role for enterprise initiatives and decision-making

credit discipline if they are penalized by bad lending decisions. It could be said in 1995 that banks and financial institutions in China that lend to state enterprises are themselves state-owned. This places cost of funds and interest rates beyond their control. For this reason, to date banks have only limited incentives to enforce loan agreements. And while bankruptcy legislation came into being in 1988, by year-end 1993 only 20 petitions for bankruptcy had been brought to court. Bank managers in China prefer to carry a non-performing loan on their accounts, than force bankruptcy.

Equity markets provide credit discipline via the desire of shareholders to monitor company performance in terms of maximizing shareholder value. Also, the marketability of shares exercises a second market-oriented form of discipline. Shareholders can sell their shares if they are not satisfied with performance. If this depresses share market price, the firm may find it difficult to attract new investors. A substantial price decline may prompt a takeover attempt by a rival management group.

In China equity markets are in their early stage of development, and the disciplining role is at best uneven in its effectiveness. Investors require timely information to monitor performance. Also, institutional investors have not come on the scene, leaving shares in the hands of widely dispersed individual investors. It is unlikely that any one individual holds sufficient shares in any company to warrant close monitoring and aggressive response to weak management. Foreign investors are barred from purchasing any shares other than B share and H shares, which generally amount to no more than large minority holdings.

Centralized Regulation

In 1993 China centralized the regulation of securities markets. Until that time the PBOC had held the initiative in regulating securities markets. This worked through its Beijing securities office. These responsibilities became decentralized in the period up to 1993, as securities centers grew up all across the nation. Local governments and PBOC branches held direct supervisory roles. The PBOC licensed securities firms and markets, and approved new listings. Local authorities regulated these markets. The markets themselves formulated their own rules and regulations, with no clear and consistent regulatory structure.

In October 1992 the State Council initiated a two-tier structure. Under this structure, the State Council Securities Policy Committee (SCSPC) and the China Securities Regulatory Commission became operational in 1993. The SCSPC includes representatives of 14 government ministries, including the Minister of Finance, and is responsible for drafting securities laws and regulations, and formulating rules for securities market development. The exchanges set their own listing requirements and operate as self-regulatory agencies.

The China Securities Regulatory Commission issues general regulations for securities issuance, and practices to be followed in the primary and secondary markets. The PBOC retained its role of licensing securities firms, but the Securities Commission sets conditions of eligibility and capital requirements for these firms. Also, it supervises the daily operations of securities firms. The Ministry of Finance licenses accounting firms and their professionals. The Securities Commission sets eligibility requirements for accounting professionals, and also monitors the securities activities of lawyers.

New Company Law

The Standing Committee of China's National People's Congress approved a new Company Law in 1993, to take effect on July 1, 1994. The law is an important part of the nation's transformation to a market economy. Development of the corporate business sector requires legislation leading to several goals:

1. A legal framework to transform state owned enterprises into more independent market-oriented entities.
2. A body of law and the necessary administrative structures to regulate the issue, sale, and trading of shares, and facilitate development of the securities exchanges.
3. A body of law that will help attract foreign investment.
4. A legal framework that encourages growth of the private sector.

The new legislation provides for establishment of two forms of companies, a limited liability company and a joint stock company.[17] The limited liability company is similar to that allowed under existing joint venture legislation, and provides an alternative to reorganization as a joint stock company with widely held shares. Limited liability companies can have 2 to 50 shareholders, and minimum registered capital (Yn5 million, or Yn30 million for companies with foreign investment).

The new legislation provides for establishment of joint stock companies, which may issue stock through stock exchanges. Joint stock companies should have widespread ownership, in contrast to limited liability companies which can have up to 50 shareholders. Limited liability companies have no shareholder nationality restrictions, but the majority of promoters must be residents of China. To organize a joint stock company the organizers must have approval of authorities designated by the State Council or provincial-local government. The Company Law places few restrictions on transfer of shares in the case of a joint stock company. To support the stability of newly organized companies, the law states promoters of a joint stock company may not transfer their shares in the company for a period of three years after it is established. Directors or general managers may not transfer their shares while in office. The new legislation focuses on rules for listing joint stock companies on securities exchanges, bond issuance, financial accounting, mergers and liquidation, foreign branches, and legal responsibilities.

The new Company Law raises important questions concerning foreign investors. There is the question whether the new law or existing laws concerning foreign joint ventures and wholly foreign owned enterprises takes precedence for existing and proposed limited liability companies with foreign investment. Related to this is the question concerning when national treatment may come. The new Company Law does fill gaps in China's legislation. It requires that a limited liability company establish a supervisory board. Also, provisions in the new law against corruption and self-dealing apply to foreign investment firms.

It is not clear how the new law will affect the tax treatment of limited liability companies with respect to tax holidays and preferential tax rates. Also the law is silent on tax holidays for foreign investment enterprises. Presently, special tax rates are granted to enterprises with foreign investment.

DEVELOPMENTS IN EXTERNAL FINANCING

In this section we consider the growing role of securities markets outside China as a source of financing. China's access to international bond and equity markets increased considerably from 1992 onward. China has tended to follow the global trend of giving greater emphasis to the securities markets for financial resources than commercial banks. Below we analyze international bond financing, China's ability to attain an investment grade rating on international bond issues, and the issue of B, H, and other international equities.

International Bonds

China first issued foreign bonds in the period 1982–89. In the period 1987–8 several Chinese trust and investment corporations and banks raised $2.3 billion, denominated in Deutschmark, yen, and US dollars. In many cases interest rates were near LIBOR, and maturities were relatively generous (seven years or longer). No bonds were sold in 1990 in the aftermath of Tiananmen. In 1991 China resumed bond issues, and in the following two years over $4 billion was placed on international markets (Table 8.4).

In July 1993 for the first time China floated Yankee bonds on the US market. This was in the form of a CITIC 10 year bond paying a 6.9 per

Table 8.4 International Bond Issues by Chinese-based Borrowers (US$ millions)

1991	115
1992	1289
1993	2929

Source: International Monetary Fund, *International Capital Markets,* September 1994, p. 126.

cent coupon.[18] This $250 million issue was used to fund major CITIC projects including the development of Daxie Island, Jiaxing Power Station, an aluminum factory, and Yizheng Chemical Fiber.[19]

Until 1993 China's activities in the international bond markets was carried out exclusively by the so-called ten windows, consisting of the international trust and investment corporations, and several selected financial institutions. The ten windows monopoly on foreign borrowing has been led by the China International Trust and Investment Corp. (CITIC), and the Bank of China (BOC). In the period 1992–3 these two institutions together accounted for over 40 per cent of bond issuance. The ten windows function as intermediary borrowers. They borrow abroad with the benefit of an implicit government guarantee and lend these funds to domestic borrowers. This activity has been regulated by the State Administration of Exchange Control (SAEC), China's supervisor of debt management.

The ten windows have diversified their investor base, including the Luxembourg, Tokyo, Singapore, London, Hong Kong, and New York capital markets for listing bonds. Reportedly, nonstate enterprises have placed unauthorized issues of bonds privately with regional (Asian) investors. In such cases they must pay much higher interest rates for this privilege.

The government entered the international market directly in 1993–4 with several benchmark issues. The Chinese authorities are placing more emphasis on bond financing relative to bank credits, with the advantages of lower cost and longer maturity.

Equity Financing

In 1992 China's stock markets were transformed with the issue of B shares in Shanghai and Shenzhen. These shares are reserved for foreign investors. In Shanghai they are denominated in US dollars, and in Shenzhen in Hong Kong dollars. In all other respects they are no different from A shares sold to mainland investors. By year-end 1992 18 issues of B shares had been listed on the two national exchanges.[20] In 1993 international investors began to reevaluate B shares, with questions concerning adequacy of disclosure. In 1993 liquidity declined in the B share market, especially as Chinese authorities were preparing a list of nine enterprises to be distributed on foreign stock markets.

Given the difficulties in gaining access to the equity markets, and declining liquidity of B shares, some Chinese enterprises reverted to unauthorized listings, also called backdoor listings on the Hong Kong stock exchange. These are takeovers by Chinese enterprises of quoted Hong Kong companies, with the ultimate objective of financing through new rights issues and simultaneously achieving reduced tax rates via a joint venture with the controlled overseas entity. These backdoor listings included large and powerful mainland enterprises, such as China Resources, China Overseas Land & Investment, and CITIC. These 'red chips' injected HK$21 billion into Hong Kong over the period 1991–3 via 29 listings with current market capitalization of HK$100 billion.

At first, the authorities took a neutral view toward these listings. Later, as the transactions became more muddled, and questions emerged regarding the utilization of funds raised through these techniques, the Hong Kong authorities prohibited unlisted companies from taking control of listed enterprises (May 1993). Subsequently, threshold market capitalization limits were raised for new issuers. This tightening up coincided with the listing of mainland Chinese enterprises on the Hong Kong stock exchange. In June 1993 a Memorandum of Regulatory Cooperation between the Hong Kong and Chinese authorities paved the way for these listings. This memorandum requires full and accurate disclosure of information relevant to investors, supervision of trading and settlements, and provides for action to be taken against insider trading.

A key aspect of the Hong Kong listings by Chinese enterprises is the compliance with international accounting standards, and ability to seek arbitration in Hong Kong. Further, this process required modification in the listing enterprises' rules of incorporation, to deal with inadequacies in China's company laws. Subsequent to the announcement and listing of H shares of nine Chinese firms worth $1.5 billion, the authorities announced a second group of 22 enterprises for international listings, with four to have primary listings on the New York Stock Exchange, and the remaining 18 on the Hong Kong stock exchange.

In September 1993 the first Chinese company was floated on the Australian stock market. Guangdong Corporation (GDC) issued approximately 9.6 million shares. GDC is backed by the government of Guangdong Province, a region close to Hong Kong. GDC possesses a complex ownership structure, with 64 per cent of equity held by Guangdong Investment, and 28 per cent by the public investors.[21]

A number of constraints limit the number of firms that can be listed on exchanges outside China. These include (1) the legal framework, and (2) the adoption of appropriate accounting and disclosure standards by the listing enterprises.

Hong Kong's role as a conduit for investment into China stems from its role as a source of bank credits for the region, and as a headquarters for footloose firms seeking offshore business opportunities. Foreign direct investment from Hong Kong into China has represented 60–5 per cent of the total going to China. Over the three year period 1992–4 total investment into China aggregated $70 billion, making Hong Kong's share in excess of $43 billion.

9 Strategic Trade

Over the past decade and a half China's participation and role in world trade has changed dramatically. Until the early 1970s China was essentially a closed economy, with limited exposure to the outside world. Industry was non-competitive and uninterested in penetrating overseas markets.

In 1972 President Nixon made his historic visit to China, to develop better relations between the governments of the People's Republic and the US. Following this initiative, China became a full member of the United Nations and developed a renewed interest in world affairs and of improved global economic relationships. After 1978 under the guidance of Deng Xiaoping, China opened its economy to foreign trade, investment, and technology transfer. Following this, China's economy has experienced rapid adjustment and modernization. China has adopted a flexible foreign trade policy, and PRC trade has grown rapidly in amount and as a per centage of national income. Trade is no longer an exclusive monopoly of a few select government trading organizations. A larger number of business and government entities now are authorized to engage in trade and take an active role in this direction.

The resurgence in foreign trade was accompanied by a shift in the relative importance of China's trading partners. Over the period since 1985 exports to industrial countries declined in importance, while exports to developing countries increased in importance. Exports to Asian neighbors increased from 39 per cent of the total to 57 per cent, while the share of exports to the Middle East, Western Hemisphere and Europe declined. On the import side a similar pattern manifested itself. Imports from industrial countries declined from 70 per cent to 49 per cent of the total. Imports from Asian countries grew from 16 per cent to 41 per cent of China's total.

China's trade strategy has become more aggressive as well as more complex. Somewhat different needs were met in China's trade expansion with the US and Japan, as compared with its Asian neighbors. Trade within the Greater China complex (mainland, Hong Kong, Taiwan) attained almost explosive growth rates.

Overall, China's trade policy has accomplished a number of strategic objectives. Much needed foreign exchange was generated via growing trade surpluses with the US. At the same time growing trade volumes stimulated industrial expansion and technology inflows, and also attracted inward investment.

Projections of mainland China's trade expansion suggest that by the year 2010 the PRC will be challenging other leading exporters for number 2 position in world export markets. By that time the Greater China region will far exceed Japan in global export market penetration, and also could move ahead of the US in world export activity.

CHANGING TRADE PATTERNS FOR GROWTH AND DEVELOPMENT

In examining China's foreign trade, it is essential to understand the complex forces underlying trade volume and commodity composition. China does not operate a free trade system similar to that of the US. Much of China's trade is managed, directly and indirectly, to achieve a number of specific objectives. China's foreign trade can be considered to serve two essential but different purposes: (1) to provide necessary foreign technology and goods, and (2) to promote better relationships with trading partners.[1] Changes in the volume of trade between China and each of its trading partners serves as a barometer of relations between the two trading countries.

Early Years of Communist Leadership

China's leaders have followed the approach that trade can be an important engine for economic growth. The more exported, the more that can be imported. Imports of high-tech machinery and scarce materials furthers the development of China's economy, by leading to higher production for exports. Despite this current view, China's trade operated at sub-par over the period 1960–78. This is due to ideological disputes among Chinese leaders regarding the risks of dependence on foreign capitalists, and shifts in political-economic relations with the West. For example, the Korean and Vietnam wars led to reduced levels of trade between China and the West. As a result, under Mao's rule foreign trade could not play a major role in China's economic development.

During the 1950s China and the Soviet Union were close allies. At that time the Soviet Union was China's most important trading partner, providing strategic goods as well as key weaponry.

In this decade over 47 per cent of China's foreign trade consisted of bilateral exchanges of goods with the Soviet Union. Also, China's trade relied heavily on other communist countries, most particularly the East European satellites (Poland, Czechoslovakia, Hungary, Romania, and Bulgaria). Ideological disputes and disagreements between Mao and Khruschev led to a break in relations in 1960 and cutoff of Soviet trade credits and technical assistance.[2] Bilateral trade between China and the Soviet Union declined steadily in the years following 1960. From that point until the late 1970s China tended to follow a policy of greater economic self-reliance. In the period 1950–59 China's trade with the Soviet Union and Communist Bloc represented 65 per cent of total trade. In the period 1960–71 it declined to 24 per cent of total trade.

From Self-Sufficiency to Opening

The economy's reversion to greater self-sufficiency can be seen in Table 9.1, which provides data on foreign trade relative to national income.[3] In the first half of the decade of the 1960s foreign trade (the sum of merchandise exports and merchandise imports) ranged between 8 and 9 per cent of national income, declined relative to income until 1971 when it was 5.8 per cent of national income. During the 1970s there was no clear trend in the ratio of foreign trade to national income, although the ratio appears to have jumped to a higher level. This jump is in part due to China joining the United Nations and establishing more normalized relations with western industrial nations. From 1980 to 1991 there was a steady, unmistakable rise in the ratio, from 15.5 per cent in 1981 to over 44 per cent in 1991. This steady rise reflects the opening of China under Deng, and the series of policy measures adopted from 1979 onward to make this opening successful.

Following 1971, when China joined the United Nations, more normalized economic relations with the US and Japan led to increased trade activity.[4] Between 1971 and 1978 the volume of China's foreign trade increased from $4.8 billion to $20.6 billion, a 23 per cent annual growth rate.[5] In this period the ratio of trade to national income doubled (Table 9.1). During the 1970s the commodity composition of China's trade underwent moderate change. The share of industrial exports increased, while the share of primary and processed farm products declined. Imports of capital goods increased at the expense of consumer goods imports.

Table 9.1 China's Total Foreign Trade as a per cent of National Income, 1962–1991; and as a per cent of GDP, 1988–93

1962	8.8%	1982	18.2%	
1963	8.6	1983	18.2	
1964	8.4	1984	21.1	
1965	8.6	1985	29.5	
1966	8.0	1986	32.9	
1967	7.6	1987	33.2	
1968	7.7	1988*	32.6	27.2
1969	6.6	1989	31.5	25.9
1970	5.9	1990	37.7	30.8
1971	5.8	1991	44.2	35.0
1972	6.9	1992		36.0
1973	9.5	1993		35.6
1974	12.4			
1975	11.6			
1976	10.9			
1977	10.3			
1978	11.8			
1979	13.6			
1980	15.5			
1981	18.6			

Notes: Total foreign trade means exports plus imports.
* Beginning 1988 new data series used, total trade as per cent of GDP.
Source: International Monetary Fund, *International Financial Statistics*.

CHINA'S FOREIGN TRADE POLICY

Main Characteristics of Trade Policy

For many years China's economy and foreign trade have been subject to central planning. Projects included in a given Five Year Plan require imports of capital goods and materials. Some consumer goods imports have to be included in the economic plan. Projected imports call for the use of foreign exchange resources, and these must be supplied by planned exports of goods produced at home for this purpose.

Three characteristics stand out in any analysis of China's foreign trade policy:

1. Imports are government-controlled to assure that capital goods and consumer goods can be obtained from abroad.

2. The Chinese government directs the flow of exports, to assure that sufficient foreign exchange is generated to pay for needed imports. In this connection, the central government encourages provincial and collective enterprises to obtain export licenses.

3. The government controls foreign exchange to assure that it is utilized to pay for essential imports. This is done by setting the official exchange rate at an appropriate level, and regulating foreign exchange trading. Except for the free swaps centers used by foreign investors to flexibly manage their needs, foreign exchange has not been traded freely.

Import policy conforms to the following requirements. First, China does not import items that can be produced domestically. An active policy of import substitution operated throughout the decade of the 1980s.[6] Second, imports of technology and equipment needed for upgrading existing industries are organized in a manner that accomplishes the planned upgrading efficiently. Third, imports of equipment needed for expanding energy production, communications and transportation facilities are given high priority along with imports of equipment to upgrade technology.

The Chinese government has sought to expand exports and has enjoyed impressive results. In the 15 years since the opening, China's share of world exports has more than doubled. The following actions have been taken to promote exports:[7]

1. Exports have been decentralized. A number of commodities now are exported under the control of ministries other than the Ministry of Foreign Trade. Some commodities can be exported by trading companies newly established by provincial governments.

2. Export trading companies have been organized. This has been in cooperation with manufacturing enterprises producing goods mainly for export.

3. Exporting companies and export enterprises are given special treatment. This includes allowing partial retention of foreign exchange revenues, special loans in local currency, and capital expansion financing.

4. Several coastal provinces have established export processing zones (notably Guangdong and Fujian). Foreign investors can set up factories in these zones and receive a comprehensive program of

incentives (tax abatement, low cost loans, and favorable factory sites). No import duties are levied on materials processed for export.

Open Door Period

Two years after Mao's death, Deng Xiaoping gained control of government policy and moved quickly to implement his historic open door policy. During the 15 years that have elapsed since then, the country has persistently and gradually liberalized its foreign trade and investment regime. This has been accompanied by spectacular growth in foreign trade and GDP. For example, during 1980–90 GDP grew annually by 9.5 per cent, and in the same period exports grew at an annual rate of 11 per cent, more than twice as fast as world trade.[8] In 1992–93 GDP growth exceeded 13 per cent and annual growth of exports and imports advanced to 13 per cent and 27 per cent, respectively.

How was China able to achieve this dramatic growth, and what lessons can be learned for other economies in transition? A quick answer is that China followed a complementary policy of promoting new and competitive enterprises. Many of these were owned collectively by local governments in urban areas, townships, or villages. These enterprises enjoy a high degree of autonomy in their operations.

China's authorities have promoted an export culture. Part of this involved geographical targeting, creating the so-called Special Economic Zones (SEZs) and open coastal cities within which economic activity takes place in a more liberal environment than is available in the nation at large. The SEZs serve as focal points for investment, that facilitate links with the world market, assisted by the entrepreneurial activities of Hong Kong and Taiwanese businessmen.

SEZs enjoy considerable administrative autonomy in investment, pricing, taxation, housing, labor management, and land utilization. Also, the SEZs offer many economic incentives to investors, not available in the inland provinces. For example, the corporate income tax rate is 15 per cent for enterprises in the SEZs, compared with 33 per cent for foreign-funded enterprises and 55 per cent for state enterprises. Imported inputs used in exports are free of import duty and other indirect taxes. Also, tax holidays are more generous in the SEZs. The SEZs and open cities grew rapidly, and have become transformed into modern cities. In 1990 they accounted for 52 per cent of realized investment, and more than half of exports. In the period 1985–90 industrial output in Guandong and Fujian grew at annual rates of 16–17 per cent, compared with 6 per cent in the rest of the economy.[9]

China has targeted certain sectors for exports, especially light industrial products, textiles, machinery, and electronic goods. To achieve selected targets, China has used production networks for exports (PNEs), which aim at stimulating the exports of advanced enterprises, and substantial foreign exchange retention rights.

China's successful export performance can be related to the large foreign direct investment inflows, attracted by (1) policies designed to facilitate foreign investment, (2) flexible policies for joint venture pricing, employment, and wages, and (3) generous incentives for joint ventures in the SEZs and open cities. These incentives include:

1. exemption from state subsidies paid to employees;
2. priority in receiving Bank of China loans;
3. tax exemption on profits remitted abroad;
4. long holidays from corporate income tax;
5. tax benefits on property reinvested in export-oriented or technologically advanced projects;
6. reduced land use fees and priority in obtaining utilities; transport, and communication facilities.

As a result of these and other developments, China's trade with technologically advanced countries increased rapidly. The rapid expansion of China's trade created several problems. First, China's trade deficits increased rapidly. By 1985 the overall trade deficit was in excess of $15 billion (Table 9.2). The large trade deficit persisted, and in July 1986 Chen Muhua, State Counselor and Governor of the People's Bank of China announced a 15.8 per cent devaluation of the currency. While it is believed that this devaluation contributed to the improved trade balance of China in 1986–7, it is not possible to be specific in this area. The Chinese economy is operated according to the socialist model, with prices of many goods set by the government. Moreover, government policies play an important role in resource allocation, and many categories of productive inputs are not as mobile as they would be in a capitalist economic system. Therefore, demand and supply elasticities of China's exports and imports cannot be estimated very easily. Without these elasticities it is not possible to estimate the effect of devaluation on China's trade balance with a high degree of confidence.[10] Between 1986 and 1987 China's overall trade balance improved (Table 9.2). In 1988–9 China experienced a reversal in its trade balance, with the deficit increasing to $7.8 billion in 1988, and holding to $6.6 billion in 1989. The 1988 increase in trade deficit can be associated with an increase in the marginal propensity to import

Table 9.2　China's Overall Trade Position, 1985–93

Year	Exports	Imports	Trade Balance
1985	$27.5	$42.9	–15.4
1986	31.4	43.4	–12.0
1987	39.4	43.2	–3.8
1988	47.6	55.3	–7.7
1989	52.9	59.1	–6.2
1990	62.8	53.9	8.9
1991	71.9	63.8	8.1
1992	85.5	81.8	3.7
1993	91.6	103.5	–11.9

Note: Amounts in billions of US dollars.
Source: International Monetary Fund, *Direction of Trade*.

(Table 9.3), from .075 in 1987 to .161 in 1988. In 1990–1 China enjoyed a substantial trade surplus, exceeding $8 billion each year (Table 9.2), while simultaneously experiencing an upward trend in these years in the marginal propensity to import (Table 9.3). In 1992–3 the trade surplus narrowed, and moved into deficit.

Table 9.3　China's Imports, Income, and Propensity to Import (billions of yuan)

Year	GNP	Increase in GNP	Imports	Increase in Imports	APM	MPM
1985	856	–	126	–	0.146	–
1986	970	114	150	24	0.154	0.211
1987	1130	160	162	12	0.143	0.075
1988	1402	272	206	44	0.147	0.161
1989	1592	190	220	14	0.139	0.074
1990	1769	177	251	31	0.142	0.176
1991	1976	207	333	82	0.168	0.396

Note: First four columns expressed in billions of yuan. The APM represents average propensity to import and is derived by dividing imports by GNP. The MPM represents marginal propensity to import and is derived by dividing increase in imports by increase in GNP.
Source: International Monetary Fund, *International Financial Statistics*.

China has instituted an elaborate system of duty exemptions on imported inputs used in manufacturing exports. The schemes introduced in 1984 and later years seem to have played an important role in expanding China's exports.[11]

Hong Kong's Role

The Hong Kong connection has been a key element in China's export success. During the 1980s Hong Kong manufacturers began shifting production facilities to China. This brought much needed capital and new technology, as well as modern management practices to neighboring Guangdong Province. Currently, Hong Kong handles over half of China's exports, and accounts for close to 70 per cent of investment into China. A large part of Guangdong's export production is supervised by firms in Hong Kong.

China's economic system has become more decentralized, with policy implementation in part under provincial control. Provincial and local officials have become deeply involved in industrial development and export promotion. In some provinces, there is an elaborate export quota system. Under this system foreign trade companies (FTCs) benefit from their single buyer power, obtaining goods at prices below prevailing levels. This enhances their world competitive position.

Operating within central government guidelines, provincial and city governments decide the allocation of imported raw materials, sharing locally retained foreign exchange earnings among enterprises, collectives, and town and village enterprises in different sectors.[12] Provinces and cities indirectly subsidize exports by providing critical inputs, including electric power. Other incentives include bonuses for managers and workers, based on export performance. Finally, local authorities establish joint ventures between FTCs and enterprises to promote exports. In the Seventh Five Year Plan, Wuxi City alone established 160 of these ventures, and another 200 such ventures are planned for the Eighth Five Year Plan.

SPECIAL ROLE OF TRADE

Earlier in this chapter reference was made to the special role of trade in advancing China's economic development. On the import side, trade provides industrial inputs required to achieve and maintain high growth in production, as well as modern technology embodied in these industrial inputs. On the export side, trade provides a source of foreign exchange with which to purchase technology and imported industrial equipment, and to service a growing external debt. High export growth reflects competitive advantage in world markets, which should help to attract foreign investment inflows.

Trade and Foreign Exchange

The role of trade as a source of foreign exchange can be seen if we examine China's bilateral trade with the US (Table 9.4). Over the period 1985–93 China enjoyed a continuing trade surplus in its trade with the US. This surplus expanded steadily. In 1990–1 it was 10 times as large as in 1985–6, and in 1992–3 it was nearly twice as large as in 1990–1.

Similarly, the rapid growth of China's exports to the United States in the period 1985–93 (Table 9.4) provided a crucially important part of China's rapidly growing current account earnings.

Between 1985 and 1991 China's current account in the balance of payments turned from a deficit ($11.7 billion in 1985) to a surplus ($13.0 billion in 1991). In large part this was facilitated by the rapid growth of exports to the US. Table 9.5 brings these variables together in the form of a comparison of China's exports to the US and China's current

Table 9.4　China's Bilateral Trade with the US

Year	China's Exports to the US	China's Imports from the US	Bilateral Trade Balance of China
1985	$4.2	$3.8	0.4
1986	5.2	3.1	2.1
1987	6.9	3.5	3.4
1988	9.2	5.0	4.2
1989	12.9	5.8	7.1
1990	16.3	4.8	11.5
1991	20.3	6.2	14.1
1992	27.4	7.5	19.9
1993	33.7	8.7	25.0

Note: Data in billions of US dollars. The trade statistics issued by the US government and PRC give quite different pictures of the bilateral relationship. The data in this table reflect data provided by the US government. Data issued by the PRC indicate a less favorable balance for the PRC in its trade with the United States.
Source: International Monetary Fund, *Direction of Trade*.

Table 9.5   China's Exports to the US, as a Source of Current
Account Credits, 1986–92

Period	China's Exports to the US	Current Account Credits	Exports as % Credits
1986–7	$12.1	$70.8	17.1%
1988–9	22.1	97.1	22.6
1990–1	36.6	130.4	28.1
1992	27.4	84.2	32.5

Note: Amounts in billions of US dollars.
Source: International Monetary Fund, *Balance of Payments Yearbook* and
Direction of Trade.

account receipts over the period 1986–92. As can be noted, exports to the
US increased sharply, from 17.1 per cent of current account receipts in
1986–7, to 28.1 per cent of current account receipts in 1990–1 and to 32.5
per cent in 1992.

It can be argued that without this tripling of exports to the US in this
relatively short period of time, China's foreign exchange budget position
would have been under much more serious constraint, making it difficult
to build up official reserves, attract larger investment flows, and purchase
high tech industrial equipment.

Trade and Development

Trade and foreign investment can play an important role in promoting
economic development. In large part this works through the ability of
foreign trade and investment to dissolve major constraints that limit
growth. In the earliest stages of economic development the most severe
constraint limiting growth is lack of domestic savings. At a subsequent
growth stage, when higher domestic savings rates have been attained, it is
likely that a foreign exchange constraint may be most critical. At this stage
the developing economy will have incurred substantial foreign debt, and
the transfer required for servicing foreign investment (outward remittances) will absorb a significant portion of foreign exchange earnings. At
this stage trade can generate foreign exchange required to support outward
remittances related to debt service.

Four Constraints and Trade

Writing in 1987 Tsao points to four major bottlenecks or constraints, limiting China's growth:[13]

1. low productivity in agriculture;
2. lack of capital;
3. poor management skills;
4. shortage of energy.

China's agricultural sector suffers from lower productivity than in the industrial sector. In 1991 with a labor force approximately one-third as large as in the agriculture sector, the industrial sector produced 1 1/2 times as much value of output.[14] In 1980–91 agricultural output increased at a rate of 5.7 per cent per year, while industrial output advanced at 11.0 per cent per year. Probably the singly most important problem facing the agriculture sector is a shortage of arable land. Industrial projects and the creation of new satellite towns are bringing about a gradual shrinkage in arable land area reserved for use in agriculture.

A second constraint, lack of capital, is being dealt with aggressively. China has been increasing the supply of capital from different sources, including borrowing from overseas, allowing securities market development, and increasing exports to obtain foreign exchange. China is a substantial borrower at the World Bank, and also is a member of the Asian Development Bank.

China has long suffered from a shortage of management skills. This, coupled with bureaucratic management in government agencies, constitutes a formidable constraint to growth. The economic opening has ameliorated this problem to some extent, by exposing more and more Chinese to modern managerial techniques and sophisticated approaches to organizational behavior.

Finally, China faces severe energy shortages. Fortunately, China possesses substantial coal and oil reserves. What is required is greater exploitation and utilization of these reserves. In recent years China has given greater emphasis to offshore oil exploration.[15] Also, China is investing in a larger electric power generating capacity, and planning to build large hydroelectric stations such as the Three Gorges Dam.

Increased foreign trade provides some relief from each of these four constraints. Over the period 1970–91 imports of fuels increased as a per centage of total imports (Table 9.6). Similarly imports of machinery and

Table 9.6 Structure of China's Merchandise Imports (%)

	1970	1991
Food	7	6
Fuels	1	3
Other primary products	10	9
Machinery and transport equipment	39	41
Other manufacturers	43	41
Total	100	100

Source: World Bank, *World Development Report,* 1993, Table 15.

transport equipment required to expand the productive capital base has long represented close to 40 per cent of total imports (Table 9.6).

The structure of China's exports over the period 1970–91 reflects an increased ability to export higher value manufactured goods (Table 9.7). In 1991 manufactured goods exports represented 76 per cent of total exports. China has cultivated closer economic ties with the US and other important market countries for its exports. As a result, China's ability to generate current account foreign exchange earnings has been strengthened.

Finally, China has sought to use its growing trading relationships with leading industrial countries as a catalyst for attracting inward foreign investment. This business investment brings to China needed management skills. Foreign investors adopt the strategy of using China as an export

Table 9.7 Structure of China's Merchandise Exports (%)

	1970	1991
Fuels, minerals and metals	11	9
Other primary commodities	19	15
Machinery and transport equipment	15	19
Other manufacturers	55	57
Textiles and clothing	29	28
Total	100	100

Source: World Bank, *World Development Report,* 1993, Table 16.

platform. This aspect of China's trade *cum* investment strategy is discussed in detail in the following chapter.

Three Triangles Strategy

What should China's trade strategy be to achieve high economic growth? Huang Fanzhang, deputy director of the State Planning Commission's Economic Research Center, believes that triangular trade patterns are most appropriate to analysis of the future needs of the PRC. He espouses a future trade strategy based on three triangles.[16]

The largest triangle is composed of China, Japan, and the US. There exists economic friction within this triangle since the US and Japan want to play a leadership role in the Asia-Pacific region, while China advocates independent economic and trade relations. Prospects for trade and technology cooperation between China and Japan are most promising. However, there are potential obstacles to cooperation between the US and China, based on America's insistence on China conforming to certain political and economic behavior patterns. When economic relations between China and one of the other two members of this large triangle deteriorate, opportunities arise for improved relations with the third member.

During the early 1990s the US expressed growing concern over its trade deficit with China. In 1994 the US reported a trade deficit with China of $30 billion, second only to its $66 billion deficit with Japan. The US projects its trade deficit with China to reach $38 billion in 1995, and $45–50 billion in 1996. Beijing in turn has accused the US of exaggerating its trade deficit, and declared the deficit to be only $7.4 billion in 1994. In reply, the US has affirmed the statistics it issues, and attributed the large trade deficit to protectionism in China, and violation of intellectual property rights.[17]

The medium-sized triangle includes China, the four 'Little Dragons,' (Singapore, Hong Kong, Taiwan, and Korea) and the Association of Southeast Asian Nations (ASEAN).[18] China, the Little Dragons, and ASEAN are economically interdependent and compete with each other. The mainland is in a position to absorb advanced industries and technology from the Little Dragons, and transfer industry and technology to the ASEAN countries. In this case China is mid-positioned between the higher technology Little Dragons and lower technology ASEAN countries.

The small triangle includes China's mainland, Taiwan, and Hong Kong (Greater China). Economic relations within the smaller triangle have improved rapidly in the decade 1983–92. The three areas in the small triangle have taken on a high interdependency in connection with trade and investment flows. The mainland needs Hong Kong money, access to capital, and trade links. In addition, the mainland has found Taiwan's own capital, technology, and management experience highly useful. Alternatively, Taiwan and Hong Kong industries have found mainland-based manufacturing with its low-cost labor an important means of improving competitiveness. As world competition grows, labor-intensive industries will continue to move from Taiwan and Hong Kong to the Mainland.

CHINA'S IMPACT IN WORLD TRADE

China's economy could become one of the largest in the world in the first quarter of the 21st century. Between 1991 and 2010 China's share of world exports is expected to increase from 2.1 per cent to 6.2 per cent. Greater China's share (including Hong Kong and Taiwan) could increase from 7.2 per cent to 16.6 per cent (Table 9.8). This compares with the US share of world exports increasing by 10.9 per cent of the world total between 1870 and 1990, and Japan's share increasing by 7.8 per cent between 1950 and 1980.[19]

Developing countries will find themselves competing with China for markets in labor-intensive products and for foreign investment capital. Developing countries that export labor-intensive manufactures and low-income exporters of commodities will suffer the most intense competition from China. China enjoys a strong comparative advantage in such products. World Bank studies find that as China has adopted market reforms, it has moved in the direction of its natural comparative advantage and its exports have become more labor-intensive.[20] This competitive advantage should persist into the 21st century, especially as the large inland provinces, which lag behind the coastal provinces in development, begin to catch up and become more outward-looking.

According to one analyst close to local conditions, Greater China (China, Hong Kong, and Taiwan) could account for over one-sixth of world output and 10.3 per cent of manufactured exports by 2010. This analyst further cited a World Bank estimate that the China Economic Area (CEA) would be bigger in purchasing power parity than the US by 2002. The World Bank forecast that the CEA would account for 17.1 per cent of world output and 10.3 per cent of world manufactured exports by 2010.[21]

China's export performance and per capita income levels vary considerably from region to region (Table 9.9). The open coastal strategy adopted in the early 1980s encouraged participation in international trade. Nearly

Table 9.8 Export Growth, China, Greater China, and G5 Countries, 1991–2010

	World Total	China	Hong Kong	Taiwan	Greater China	US	UK	G5 Germany	France	Japan
1991	3412	73	98	76	247	398	185	402	212	315
as per cent	100.0	2.1	2.9	2.2	7.2	11.7	5.4	11.8	6.2	9.2
2001	5050	189	211	164	564	648	249	595	314	466
2010	7188	446	423	328	1197	1005	324	847	447	663
as per cent	100.0	6.2	5.9	4.5	16.6	13.9	4.5	11.8	6.2	9.2

Note: Exports are in billions of US dollars.

Table 9.9 Comparative Economic Performance in China
Economic Area, Data as of 1991

	Population (millions)	GNP per capita (US dollars)	Exports per capita (US dollars)
Shanghai	13.4	1 202.06	428.4
Guangdong	64.4	519.5	212.6
Other coastal provinces[a]	388.1	363.0	61.2
Western China[b]	263.6	226.5	13.0
Other inland provinces	424.1	273.2	21.8
Hong Kong	5.7	13 430.0	5 234.4
Taiwan	20.6	8 815.0	3 705.8

Notes: a. Includes Fujian, Guangxi, Hainan, Hebei, Jiangsu, Liaoning, Shandong, Tianjing, and Zhejiang.

  b. Includes Gansu, Guizhou, Ningxia, Quinghai, Shaanxi, Sichuan, Tibet, Yunnan, and Xinjiang.

Source: Uri Dadush and Dong He, 'China: A New Power in World Trade,' *Finance & Development,* June 1995, p. 37.

80 per cent of China's exports originate from 11 coastal provinces with 40 per cent of the nation's population. In 1991 exports from Shanghai were $428 per capita. This compares with per capita exports of $13 for western China (Table 9.9). As can be seen in the table, per capita incomes also vary widely on a regional basis. In general, regional variations in per capita exports and GNP appear to be closely correlated. If incomes in China's western provinces grow at the projected national average of 8.5 per cent yearly, they could attain Shanghai's current per capita income in two decades.

These relationships carry interesting implications for China's trade position.

1. Exports will not shift away from labor-intensive products very rapidly.
2. Large, less developed regions with large population will produce an increasing share of China's exports and labor-intensive exports will continue to grow at a healthy pace.
3. Regional disparities are significant and should enhance the potential for interregional trade within China.

Exports from China seem to be making inroads in OECD markets, partly at the expense of other Asian exporters (Hong Kong, South Korea, Taiwan). There are comparative advantage differences between China's more advanced (coastal) provinces and interior provinces. This suggests a dual pattern of comparative advantage in future, with the more developed coastal regions competing directly against the newly industrialized countries (in mid-technology products such as vehicles, ships, and consumer durables). At the same time, China's inland regions will compete effectively in world markets, selling lower technology, labor-intensive goods.

Beneficiaries of China's growth as a trading power will include principally high income countries, including Asian manufacturers (South Korea, Taiwan). These countries are becoming large importers of labor-intensive manufactures and leading exporters of sophisticated capital goods. Therefore, they are China's natural trading partners over the coming two decades.

CHINA'S SEAPORTS

Expansion of Port System

The development of China's foreign trade has required substantial investment in supporting infrastructure, taking the form of seaports, river and harbor facilities, airports, and road and highway construction. In this section we focus on China's seaport development.

China has lagged in developing seaport facilities. As late as 1949 there were only six major coastal ports in China, with a total of 119 deepwater berths. Since 1949 China's development of seaports has evolved through three distinct stages.[22]

1. Reconstruction (1949–72). Following many years of war and neglect, existing facilities were reclaimed and improved. Modest increases in the number of deepwater berths took place.
2. Expansion of trade and accelerated construction (1973–80). Major seaports became overburdened from the expansion in trade. China built 50 deepwater berths in this period. At Dalian and Qingdao facilities were established to handle bulk oil carriers.
3. Open Door Policy (1981–93). The Sixth Five Year Plan emphasized harbor construction, as well as redevelopment and expansion of existing ports. In this period work was initiated on 132 deepwater berths.

By 1988 there were 212 such berths and others were under construction.

Over the period 1949–85 coastal deepwater berths expanded in number from 119 to 3017. By the year 1987 the 23 main seaports had 587 berths. In Table 9.10 data are presented concerning ten of the most important ports by number of berths and tonnage throughput. Several coal, oil, and mineral deepwater berths have been completed during the 1980s equipped with modern loading equipment. Construction of container berths proved to be an important innovation. By year-end 1987 China had 23 ports capable of international container shipping.

Problems and Future Development

The expansion in handling capacity has not kept pace with demand. Between 1978 and 1987 cargo tonnage handled at the 23 seaports more than doubled. In the same period there were only modest increases in capacity in these 23 ports. Equally important, there exists a spatial maldistribution of seaports along China's coastline. Most of the larger ports are located north of Shanghai, and there exists a corresponding scarcity of good seaports and handling capacity along China's coastline south of Shanghai. In 1987 Shanghai handled one-third of the cargo passing

Table 9.10 Ten Major Mainland China Seaports

Port	No. Berths	Total Throughput
Shangahi	102	128.3 m tonnes
Guangzhou	87	6.9 m tonnes
Dalian	52	46.1 m tonnes
Tianjin	46	17.3 m tonnes
Xiamen	37	4.3 m tonnes
Qingdao	31	30.3 m tonnes
Huangpu	30	26.2 m tonnes
Ningbo	28	19.4 m tonnes
Zinhuangdao	18	53.8 m tonnes
Zhanziang	18	14.2 m tonnes

Source: Shen Wei-Cheng, 'Development and Problems of China's Seaports,' in G. Linke and D. Forbes, *China's Spatial Economy,* Oxford University Press, Hong Kong, 1990, p. 98.

through the 23 main seaports, requiring wasteful transfer of large tonnage for further transport to other cities and regions.

China faces a shortage of specialized ports and berthing facilities. This is particularly the case for coal, oil, cement, and containers. Lack of such facilities prevents efficient movement of energy inputs (coal) and imposes high real costs on the economy.

Future improvement of seaports requires development of a system for rational use of ports and efficient materials handling. Utilization of seaports should be based in part on port groupings. In this way it will be possible to minimize the extent of under-used and over-used seaport facilities. Construction of urban infrastructure must be synchronized with expansion of port facilities. Finally, a more coordinated management is required relative to China's foreign trade, land transport, and seaport development and use.

CONCLUDING ANALYSIS

What are the future prospects for China using trade strategy to achieve its growth and development objectives? In large part, this question can be answered with another question. What are the growth prospects for China's exports?

In Table 9.8 are presented comparison statistics for China and Japan for 1991 and projections for the year 2010. In 1991 mainland China's exports were $73 billion, representing 2 per cent of the world total. If we add exports from Hong Kong and Taiwan to this amount, Greater China originates over 7 per cent of world exports. This compares with Japan's share of world exports of over 9 per cent, and the US share of nearly 12 per cent. Projections to 2010 indicate a far more important role for mainland China (and Greater China) in world trade. By year 2010 mainland exports should be close to $450 billion, and exports from Greater China $1197 billion (Table 9.8). This represents 6.2 per cent and 16.6 per cent of world exports, respectively. Comparing these amounts with projected exports from the US and Japan of $1005 billion and $663 billion, respectively, it is clear that China will come to assume a major role in world trade, and a dominant role in trade in the Asia-Pacific region.

The projections in Table 9.8 are based upon expected high rates of growth in exports from mainland China, and Hong Kong and Taiwan. All three exporters are growing into an interdependent trading triangle, in which the competitive advantages of each support the trading positions of the other two.

There are strong reasons to expect high export growth on the part of China, Hong Kong, and Taiwan. First, output growth in China is expected to continue at an impressive rate, leading to substantial economies of scale in production. Second, Greater China currently enjoys a comparative advantage in many industrial production categories, witness the rapid growth in trade since 1985. Third, regional competitive relationships reflect considerably lower wage costs in China as compared with Taiwan, South Korea, Malaysia, and Thailand. At the same time countries like South Korea are suffering from intense labor disputes likely to increase the wage cost advantage of China.[23]

Another factor is the steady rise in income in Asia, creating a sequence of new demands for one consumer good after another.[24] For example, a rise of 10 per cent in average incomes in one Asian country will suddenly produce a sevenfold rise in the number of households with incomes above the threshold required for buying a given consumer good (bicycles, motorcycles, television sets), and lead to an explosion in demand.

A final factor is the strong likelihood that China will usurp Japan's position as leading manufacturer-exporter in the region. Japanese companies already have demonstrated a strong inclination to shift key parts of their production bases to mainland China and other Asian countries. This has been necessary to remain cost-competitive in regional and world markets that are becoming intensively more competitive. This trend is becoming an irreversible force in favor of China's economy.

10 Foreign Investment Strategy

Prior to 1979 China's economic policy was based on the principle of self-reliance. Foreign trade and investment played a very small role. The reforms from 1978 onward led to greater openness, more decentralized authority over economic policy, and a growing foreign trade system. The 1979 Law on Joint Ventures and subsequent legislation reinforced the trend toward an improving foreign investment climate in China.

The People's Republic of China has played the foreign investment strategy with high success. One by one it has broken the barriers to capital inflows by bank lenders, governments, international organizations, direct business investors, bond investors, and even stock market investors. In 1992–4 annual investment inflows ranged between 4 and 6 per cent of GNP, and may be expected to remain at that level in future.

Several strategies are becoming evident in China's treatment of foreign investment. First, the PRC has attracted sufficient amounts of foreign capital to help sustain a remarkably high economic growth rate. It is doubtful that this growth rate would be possible without these large amounts of foreign capital, and the management expertise and technology that accompanies these inflows. Second, increased two-way foreign investment flows between China and Hong Kong, and China and Taiwan, are creating a new business environment in this region. As a result economic and financial interdependence is increasing rapidly. In fact, the increased interdependence between Taiwan and China has brought forth a debate within Taiwan regarding appropriate policy toward outward investment, and increased economic links with the mainland.

Third, China is moving toward 'center of the stage' with regard to investment flows in the Asia-Pacific region. Over the period 1980–90 China ranked second, only behind Singapore as a recipient of foreign direct investment flows into developing countries. China has become the leading recipient of direct investment and loan capital provided by Japan. And the financial ties with Hong Kong and Taiwan indicate a growing triangular relationship, likely to become a dominant aspect of Asia-Pacific regional financial flows.

Based on the trends described above, we can expect that by the 21st century China will have become a dominant player in both regional and world investment flows. With continued success in implementing strategies appropriate to its resource base and needs, China will be able to demonstrate unequivocably its superpower status in regional and global foreign investment.

OVERVIEW OF FOREIGN INVESTMENT FLOWS TO THE PEOPLE'S REPUBLIC

Foreign investment inflows play a vital role in furthering the growth process in developing countries. This fact has been emphasized repeatedly in the economics literature. The economic development process is slow, and often several decades are required before any dramatic economic development gains can be seen. For this reason, foreign investment inflows must expand continuously to have any lasting effect on growth and be relatively free from disruption.

Different Flows for Different Purposes

China has been able to attract foreign investment taking many different forms. Bilateral flows refer to investment from other countries, and multilateral flows refer to loans and investments from international organizations such as the World Bank and Asian Development Bank. These institutions finance large investment projects in China (electric power, railroad extension, and agricultural development).

Official flows are made by governments of OECD countries (US, Japan, Germany, United Kingdom, France). Often these official flows finance purchase of capital goods exported by the lending country (telecommunications equipment, jet aircraft, trucks and construction equipment). Direct investment is carried out by foreign business firms that intend to produce and distribute their products in China, or use China as a low-cost production base from which to export. Portfolio investment includes foreign purchase of bonds and stocks issued by Chinese governments and enterprises.

Foreign Investment Flows to the PRC

We examine data originally provided by the Organization for Economic Cooperation and Development (OECD) showing financial flows to the People's Republic of China.[1] In this case financial flows are net flows (Table 10.1). The data in Table 10.1 reflect broad trends in the global

Table 10.1 Financial Flows to the People's Republic of China, 1979–89 ($ million)

	1979	1980	1981	1982	1983	1984	1985	1986	1987	1988	1989
Bilateral versus Multilateral											
A. Bilateral	116	286	1469	617	607	623	1604	2708	3571	3941	4417
Japan	40	291	890	128	384	596	1182	2086	2438	2456	2402
United States	12	105	56	-4	34	-189	169	292	234	-93	120
Europe	65	-107	523	488	145	154	167	225	695	1414	1626
OPEC	-	-	-	-	36	49	30	23	11	9	2
Others	0	-2	0	6	44	62	86	82	193	156	267
B. Multilateral	13	37	420	61	141	315	693	771	792	1326	1264
ADB	-	-7	-5	-4	-4	-4	-5	-5	-5	6	56
IBRD	-	-	-	-	4	73	354	324	206	514	542
IDA	0	0	0	1	67	124	218	282	394	552	505
United Nations	-	-	-	-	-	-	-	127	141	154	81
Others	13	44	425	65	74	123	127	43	56	100	80
Official versus Private											
C. Total Official (Net)	17	509	474	547	808	1077	1388	1663	784	2955	3522
ODA Grants	17	55	88	126	169	214	244	341	489	633	561
ODA Loans	-	11	389	398	500	584	696	793	973	1356	1596
Other Official Flows	-	443	-3	23	138	279	448	529	-678	966	1365
D. Net Private Flows	112	-186	1415	131	-60	-139	909	1816	3579	2312	2160
Direct Investments	0	24	26	42	-3	66	224	202	1271	-34	360
Portfolio Investments	64	55	-47	110	139	72	921	1699	1879	1282	694
Export Credits	48	-264	1436	-21	-196	-277	-236	-85	429	1064	1106
Total Receipts (Net)[a]	**129**	**324**	**1888**	**678**	**748**	**938**	**2297**	**3479**	**4363**	**5267**	**5681**

Notes: – = Not available.

a. Total receipts are divided into bilateral flows and multilateral flows. Therefore, the sum of items A and B is equal to total receipts. Total receipts are also classified into official and private flows. Therefore, the sum of items C and D is equal to total receipts.

Source: Organization for Economic Co-operation and Development, *Geographical Distribution of Financial Flows to Developing Countries* (various issues).

economy, as well as developments specific to the recipient country (the PRC). The global economy has witnessed an increase in the role of Japan as a source of capital funds, a relative decline in the importance of the US as a provider of investment funds, a temporary fall-off in global investment totals in 1982 due to the international debt crisis, a surge in foreign direct investment since 1985, and an interruption in the relative importance of bank loan funds as commercial banks react to the losses incurred following the international debt crisis.

These trends manifest themselves in part in the data included in Table 10.1. Japan plays a dominant role as a source of bilateral investment flows to the PRC, and Europe ranks second in this category. Financial flows to the PRC can exhibit high volatility. For example, in 1982 financial flows to the PRC were only 36 per cent as large as in 1982, reflecting a sharp decline in private flows to China in that period.

The aggregate financial flows to China shown in Table 10.1 also reflect special conditions and developments in that country. Bilateral flows dominate throughout the period 1979–89, accounting for 70–90 per cent of the total. Multilateral flows only gain importance after China gained membership in the IMF and World Bank. By 1988–9 multilateral flows from the World Bank-IDA exceed 20 per cent of total inflows. Loans from the Asian Development Bank lagged behind other financial flows to China in the years following the economic opening.

Official flows to China follow an erratic pattern, due in part to loan repayments in some years. Official grants appear to have peaked in the later 1980s, but loans continue to grow. Net private flows follow an even more erratic pattern than official flows, with large repayments of export credits in some years. In the period 1979–89 direct business investment into China exhibited instability, but grew rapidly in importance. Portfolio investment is much larger than direct investment in this period, reflecting (1) high risks and operating difficulties in direct investment as perceived by business investors, (2) government policy to limit foreign control over industry, and (3) more favorable terms available to the country when loans are utilized on a selective basis. Since 1989 there has been a rapid increase in direct investment flows into China. Between 1990 and 1993 actual direct investment inflows grew from $4 billion to approximately $25 billion. Contracted (planned) direct investment was considerably higher than these amounts. In 1994 direct investment inflows exceeded $33 billion.

INVESTMENT INFLOWS FOLLOWING CHINA'S OPENING

Foreign investment in China has grown rapidly. This growth has been impressive with respect to both official and private capital. In 1988–9 official flows to China averaged $3.2 billion, or 60 per cent of total inflows. In the same period private flows to China averaged $2.2 billion, or 40 per cent of total inflows (Table 10.1).

Borrowing From International Organizations

From 1979 the World Bank, International Monetary Fund, and Japan assumed the role of major lenders.[2] In the period 1979–83 a considerable part of the capital inflow went to key projects such as the Baoshan Steel Works, oil field equipment, and port improvements in Shanghai and Tianzin. In this period the government focused on modernization and technology improvement. Western bankers were stymied, both by the inefficiency and poor financial practices of Chinese enterprises, and the government emphasis on big projects and infrastructure where commercial feasibility could be questionable. By 1992–3 China was the heaviest borrower from the World Bank, obtaining $2.16 billion from that institution and $1.02 billion from its soft loan affiliate the International Development Association (IDA).[3] According to the World Bank *Annual Report 1993,* the three largest recipient sectors of this lending were transportation, rural development, and energy. At midyear 1993, World Bank loans to the PRC represented 4.1 per cent of total loans outstanding.[4]

In fiscal year 1993 the World Bank financed 28 projects in China, worth $3.2 billion. Some of the largest projects were railway modernization, highway construction, water resources, bulk grain handling, hydroelectric, and industrial sector restructuring. World Bank lending aims at supporting general economic development goals, widening further China's open door to direct investment, and assisting in establishing a new mechanism for operation of state enterprises.[5]

Lending to China by the Asian Development Bank is approximately as large as IDA lending to China. In fiscal year 1992 nine loans were approved by ADB, worth a total of $903 million. In 1992 China ranked third in dollar amount of loans from the ADB. These loans financed projects related to crop development, energy conservation, modernization of iron and steel production, bridge and highway construction, and rail network expansion.

The ADB operational strategy in China emphasizes improved efficiency, natural resource conservation, reduction of poverty, and environmental protection. The ADB seeks to ease sectoral capacity constraints in energy, transport, and communications. Another priority is improvement in technology in state and private sector enterprises.

Cumulative ADB lending to China at December 1992 was $1.9 billion (Table 10.2). Over a quarter of lending was in the industrial sector. The finance sector accounted for 22 per cent of loans provided by the ADB, and the energy sector 13 per cent of loans. Loans to agriculture represented a little over 8 per cent of ADB loans.

National Development Assistance

China receives official development assistance from industrial countries via long term concessionary loans at low interest. In 1980–1 the amount of this lending was modest, a few hundred million dollars annually. These loans reached the billion dollar level in 1988 and continued to increase in amount into the early 1990s. There was an interruption of this lending following the 1989 Tiananmen Square incident, but in 1991–2 lending recovered to former levels.

Japan was the first country to offer a program of official bilateral assistance to China. This assistance flows through several channels, including the official development agency (Japanese Overseas Economic Cooperation Fund – OECF), the Japanese Export–Import Bank, and others. The OECF is the most important source, financing projects in port and railway construction, infrastructure projects, and chemical plants. Aggregate Japanese bilateral lending to China over the period 1985–91

Table 10.2   Asian Development Bank Cumulative Lending to the People's Republic of China, December 1992

Sector	Loans	($ million)	Per cent
Industry and non-fuel minerals	5	478.30	25.10
Finance	4	420.00	22.04
Energy	4	251.30	13.20
Agriculture and agro-industry	3	154.60	8.11
Total	23	1905.20	100.00

Source: Asian Development Bank, *Annual Report 1992*, p. 72.

averaged $1.1 billion yearly. Japan has supplied close to three-quarters of all official development loans to China.[6]

Bond Issuance and Commercial Credits

China's entry into the World Bank and Asian Development Bank paved the way for concessionary loans, and also made it easier for China to carry out increasing amounts of commercial borrowing. China obtains funds from the international capital markets via syndicated loans, and the sale of stocks and bonds. In the period 1982–5 China's annual commercial borrowing averaged $450 million. This increased steadily in the following four-year period, averaging $2.2 billion per annum, and has held close to that level in the years following 1989. Over the period 1982–5 export credits received by China averaged $150 million per year, but in the following four-year period averaged $550 million per year.

Beginning in the early 1980s China tapped international banks for medium-term funds. Japanese bankers have led in providing such funds. At March 1993 the combined balance of Japanese bank lending to China and Hong Kong exceeded $29 billion ($9.4 billion to China). By contrast US and European bank lending to China was $700 million and $1400 million, respectively. In 1993 bank lenders were reported to be taking a more cautious view about extending new loans to China and Hong Kong.[7]

In addition to commercial borrowing and trade credits, China has sold bond issues on the international capital markets. Its first such bond issue was a ¥10 billion private placement by China International Trust and Investment Company (CITIC) in 1982. This was followed by several other yen denominated bond offerings in Tokyo in 1983–4. From 1985 the pace of China's international bond sales increased, with nine public offerings that year. By 1988 China had issued over $4 billion equivalent in bonds on international markets (Tokyo, Hong Kong, Frankfurt, Singapore, Luxembourg, London). China's international bond market activities came to a temporary halt in 1989–90 after the violence of Tiananmen Square and the downgrading of Chinese bonds by leading rating agencies.

China re-entered the international bond markets in mid-1991 when the Bank of China sold a ¥20 billion issue in the Tokyo market. For the next several years there was a virtual flood of issues by leading banking and financial institutions, including CITIC, People's Construction Bank, the Bank of Communications, Guangdong International Trust and Investment Corp., and the Bank of China. The first US (Yankee) bond issue took place at midyear 1993 when CITIC sold a 10-year $250 million bond issue in New York.[8] Later in 1993 Moody's Investors Service upgraded China's sovereign debt to A-3.[9] In October the government floated a $300 million issue of 10-year bonds in Asia (Dragon bond market). Early in 1994 the government sold a record $1 billion of 10-year global Eurobonds, and a month later the Bank of China announced a $500 million Yankee bond issue, the largest such issue.

Since 1989 a number of important changes have taken place in China's ability to issue bonds on the international capital markets. First, the average size issue is quite large, and small issues are no longer utilized. Second, the increase in the volume of bond sales has made China an important borrower in the international bond market. In the early 1990s China has become one of the ten largest country bond issuers among developing countries. Third, the sources of financing via bonds is very diversified, and Japanese dominance as a supplier of bond financing no longer exists. Along with this change, lead underwriters in China's bond issuance are more diversified according to their countries of origin (CS First Boston, Merrill Lynch, Morgan Stanley, Lehman). Fourth, risk premiums appear to be narrower, suggesting that the fears related to the Tiananmen Square incident have been dissipated. Despite these improvements, early in 1995 bond rating agencies downgraded the debt issues of large Chinese banks (discussed in Chapter 7).

Sale of Equities

China is raising increasing amounts of funds through the sale of equities to foreigners. Beginning in 1992 the Chinese have raised funds by selling B shares in selected companies listed on the two national stock exchanges. These are paid for by foreign investors with hard currency. In addition, sales of equities on international markets have been carried out. Chinese domestic firms, such as China Brilliance Automotive based in Bermuda was the first Chinese company listed for trading on the New York Stock Exchange. China Brilliance controls Jinbei Automobile Company in Shenyang, northeast China. The following year (1993) China Tire was listed on the New York Stock Exchange (NYSE). Subsequently, EK Chor Motorcycle Company and Shanghai Petrochemical Co. Ltd were listed on the NYSE. Since 1993 several additional Chinese companies have had their shares listed on the NYSE, including Shandong Huaneng Power, and Huaneng.

In situations where Chinese companies are unable or unwilling to meet the somewhat higher disclosure requirements of the NYSE, the Hong Kong Stock Exchange provides a suitable alternative. By year-end 1993 six of nine companies intended for Hong Kong listing had been introduced to the market. In 1994 the Chinese Securities Regulatory Commission approved an additional 22 companies for listing on international stock markets.

Another channel through which China obtains equity capital is for Chinese-controlled foreign corporations to sell shares abroad. For example, the Beijing-based China International Trust and Investment Company (CITIC) owns CITIC Hong Kong, which in turn owns 49 per cent of CITIC Pacific Ltd, which is listed on the Hong Kong Stock Exchange. CITIC Pacific has issued shares on the Hong Kong market.

CITIC was organized in 1979, and is owned by the Chinese government. CITIC is under the control and supervision of the State Council, the highest executive authority in China. CITIC operates as an external borrowing entity, and is authorized to borrow local currency and foreign currency funds.

CITIC is engaged in equity investment, financing joint ventures, banking and financial services, trading, and real estate. Its wholly owned subsidiaries are organized to specialize in certain businesses (banking, investment, real estate, technology). At December 1992 the equity investments of CITIC and its domestic subsidiaries in China were approximately RMB 2659 million ($462 million), and the equity investments of CITIC and its domestic subsidiaries in joint ventures and projects overseas were approximately RMB 1388 million (US$241 million). At the same point in time CITIC and its domestic subsidiaries had made loans and guarantees to joint ventures and other projects in China of approximately RMB 24 151 million ($4199 million).[10]

GROWTH OF FOREIGN DIRECT INVESTMENT

Since 1979 China has encouraged direct foreign investment inflows. Initially this encouragement took the form of the Joint Venture Law (1979). Subsequently the government adopted further measures to encourage direct investment, including a new constitution (1982), new implementing regulations in 1983, liberalization of foreign exchange provisions for foreign joint ventures (1986), provisions for the Encouragement of Foreign Investment (1986) which provided increased incentives for joint ventures, and the Law on Enterprises Operated Only with Foreign Capital (1986).[11] These provisions progressively improved the status of foreign direct investors and encouraged direct investment. Prior to these legislative changes, direct investment into China had lagged, especially when considering the greater importance of this investment in other developing countries.[12] The new regulations paved the way for a mini-boom in foreign business investment that carried through 1994.

Amount and Type of FDI

Foreign investment in China is predominantly in equity joint ventures and cooperative operations. These forms account for nine-tenths of total FDI. From 1986 when China enacted provisions for wholly foreign owned investment, this type of inflow began to displace cooperative operations, and continued to do so.

Direct investment into China faces several practical constraints, including foreign exchange risk, high operating costs, difficult domestic marketing channels, and bureaucratic interference. Nevertheless, direct investment has increased impressively. In the period 1980–90 the PRC ranked fourth among developing countries in the annual dollar amount of direct investment inflows, with $1.7 billion.[13] Hong Kong accounts for over 60 per cent of the annual direct investment entering the PRC. The US and Japan are the next two important sources of direct investment into China. Also, Hong Kong provides a conduit for investment from other countries (especially Taiwan), and overseas Chinese (diaspora) located in neighboring Southeast Asian countries. In 1993–4 actual FDI inflows to China exceeded $57 billion (Table 10.3). Since 1984 contracted FDI has exceeded actual FDI inflows by a ratio of over 3:1.

Initially, foreign investment was concentrated on labor-intensive industries. Later, significant diversification led to investment in high-technology and capital-intensive industries, construction, and hotels. With the rapid development of China's stock markets, foreign funds also are being invested in the financial markets.[14]

A considerable amount of direct investment in China is based on the activities of building construction in large projects. South Korean construction companies view China as a lucrative market. These companies were bidding for work on the $10 billion Hong Kong–Beijing motorway in 1993, but the project collapsed.[15] Dong-Ah, a Korean construction firm, signed a letter of intent with the Beijing municipality to build motorways and a subway. At the same time, Hyundai Engineering and Construction was bidding for a $3 billion dam project on the Yellow River. Leading Hong Kong companies also are pursuing large construction projects. In 1993 Hutchison Whampoa was a 50 per cent participant in a Yn 500 billion container port development project at Yantian in Shenzhen. Consolidated Electric Power Asia, a unit of Hopewell Holdings (Hong

Table 10.3 Inward Foreign Direct Investment, 1984–94 (US$ bn)

	Actual Investment	Contracted Investment
1984	$1.4	$2
1985	1.9	6
1986	2.2	3
1987	2.6	4
1988	3.7	6
1989	3.8	6
1990	3.7	6
1991	4.7	12
1992	11.3	58
1993	25.7	110
1994	33.0	–

Sources: Chinese government documents, *Financial Times*, *South China Morning Post*, *Wall Street Journal*.

Kong) was completing work on a thermal power station in Guangdong in 1993.

Who Invests in the People's Republic?

While several dozen countries have made direct investments in China, three-quarters of the inflow has come from countries closely neighboring the PRC. Hong Kong accounts for over 60 per cent of FDI into China. Japan ranks second in importance with 10–12 per cent of FDI. The US is close behind Japan with close to 10 per cent of FDI in China. Taiwan also is an important investor, followed by Britain, France, and Italy.

The PRC is becoming more important as a focus for business and investment among Asian countries, especially the newly industrializing countries. These countries (and Japan) have invested in China to secure lower labor and land costs, due to environmental concerns at home, and to secure market access. Among Asian countries, Hong Kong and Taiwan have the greatest relative concentrations of direct investment in the PRC (Table 10.4). At year-end 1989 it was reported that 77 per cent of cumulative direct investment of Hong Kong was in the PRC.[16] The Hong Kong economy is undergoing a metamorphosis in which much manufacturing is shifting to mainland China while Hong Kong intensifies its focus on services and business communications. It is difficult to obtain official government published data concerning Taiwan's direct investment into China.

Table 10.4   Degree of Concentration of Direct Foreign Investment
in Mainland China, Selected Countries (per cent of total DFI)

Hong Kong	77 %
Taiwan	42
Singapore	1.6
Japan	1.0
Korea	0.9

Sources: Chia Siow Yue, *Asian Development Review,* 1993, Vol. II,
No. 1, p. 84; and author's estimates.

Taiwan business firms have utilized Hong Kong as a conduit for their
investment on the mainland. One source indicates $3.4 billion of foreign
direct investment in China by Taiwanese companies to year-end 1991.[17]
This represents approximately 42 per cent of cumulative direct investment
of Taiwan. According to Segal, in 1992 Taiwanese investment in China
was $5.5 billion, over and above the $3.4 billion cumulative investment in
the previous decade.[18] Singapore's direct investment in China accounted
for 1.6 per cent of its total in 1989, but is growing in relative importance.
Finally, both Japan and Korea have approximately 1 per cent of cumulative direct investment in China.

Evolution of FDI into China

Since 1979 FDI inflows have responded to successive initiatives of the
government to improve the foreign investment climate. This is evident in
the numerous foreign investment laws and regulations put in place, the
regional incentives taking the form of Special Economic Zones and
financial incentives (taxation and financing). In the following we discuss
early investment by overseas Chinese, strategic investment, and investment in infrastructure.

   In the very earliest years following 1978, China benefited from the
wealth and talent of its diaspora, the vast numbers of overseas Chinese.
The Chinese diaspora is an economy without borders. It is estimated the
overseas Chinese generate annual economic output of over $500 billion,
exceeding the GNP of the People's Republic.[19]

   Ethnic Chinese control Hong Kong, Taiwan, and Singapore, and dominate business and finance in Thailand, Indonesia, and the Philippines. In
this world of overseas Chinese, the family enterprise is the basic economic
unit, and the company is controlled by the heads of family. Over recent
decades the center of overseas Chinese in Asia has been Hong Kong,

based on low taxes, a free currency, and anonymity available to foreign investors. Overseas Chinese businessmen raise capital in Hong Kong, use Hong Kong as an administrative and communications headquarters, and make use of this center as a special window into the PRC.

From 1979 on, many overseas Chinese have been shifting more of their business activities into coastal China, especially Guangdong. Some of the leading names in this regard include Gordon Wu, a major holder in Hopewell Holdings, who has built superhighway links between Hong Kong and Guangzhou and also has invested heavily in electric power projects in the PRC. An even more wealthy investor is Li Ka-Shing, whose flagship company, Cheung Kong, owns a controlling interest in Hutchison Whampoa. Li Ka-Shing has participated in port projects in Guangdong. Robert Kuok is one of the earliest investors in China, whose World Trade Center in Beijing cost over $480 million. Finally, we should mention Peter Woo, chairman of Wheelock Group in Hong Kong, who has shifted one-fifth of his assets into Chinese breweries, office buildings, and commercial projects.[20]

Strategic Investment

Many foreign business investors in China regard their commitment as strategic. This is based on the size of the potential market in China, expected high economic and market growth over the next few decades, and low labor production costs. An early American investor, Coca-Cola, has found China one of its fastest-growing markets overseas. The company expects annual sales growth to the year 2000 of 30–5 per cent.[21] Coca-Cola's strategy is to take 12.5 per cent shares in joint ventures with local Chinese entities. The company has been so successful, legislators of the National People's Congress have raised protectionist cries over foreign domination of the local soft drink market.

NEC, the Japanese electronics maker, undertook a joint venture in 1995 to manufacture personal computers and related products in Shanghai. NEC owns 60 per cent, with production scheduled at 150 000 units in year 2000. NEC is considering exporting output to other Asian markets.[22] The output of PCs in China (800 000 yearly) is expected to grow 20 per cent annually.

UK Companies, including Cadbury and Bass, have undertaken investment in China. In 1993 Cadbury set up a joint venture to produce 5000 tons of chocolate per year. This significantly increases production in the PRC. Products sold in China carry the Cadbury name.[23] Bass, the large UK brewer, has committed $40 million to a new joint venture with the Ginsbei Beer Group, with a 55 per cent stake. China is the world's second largest beer market, growing at 20 per cent a year. Consumption of beer in China is one-eighth the level in Europe.

In 1995 two US industrial companies, Whirlpool and Owens-Corning, announced joint venture investments in China. Whirlpool formed four joint ventures involving production of refrigerators, washing machines, and microwave ovens, with the intent of adding air conditioners to its production in China.[24] Owens-Corning has initiated construction of a fiberglass insulation plant in Guangzhou and signed a joint venture agreement to build a similar plant in Shanghai at a cost of $25 million each. With 80 per cent or larger stakes in each project, the company hopes to earn back its initial investment two years after startup.[25]

Retailing also offers opportunities for strategic investment. Yaohan International, a Japanese-owned corporation traded on the Hong Kong Stock Exchange, operates department stores and other retail outlets in Hong Kong. The company views China as a market positioned where Japan was 30 years ago. Yaohan has built up connections with substantial Chinese corporations. Yaohan plans to operate 1000 supermarkets in China by year 2010.[26] Yaohan has formed a joint venture with China's largest department store operator, Shanghai Number One to construct what will be Asia's largest department store. Yaohan plans to build 'International Merchandise Marts' which will circumvent China's inefficient wholesale system by acting as a distributor center for Yaohan franchise stores. Similarly, China's big state-owned retail stores are forming joint ventures with foreign firms. These companies are trading land use rights in exchange for design and merchandising know-how. Foreign partners include Jusco of Japan, Wal-Mart and Walt Disney of the US, and Giordano Holdings Ltd.[27]

Vehicle Production

Probably the most important sector attracting strategic investment is motor vehicles. This is based on the impact growth and development in this sector have exerted on overall economic expansion in countries such as the US, Germany, and Japan.

When in 1994 China's Ministry for Machinery Building asked for ideas for a 'people's car', most large international car manufacturers were quick to respond. In 1996 China is expected to produce 575 000 cars, up from only 147 000 in 1992 (Table 10.5). In 1994 China had fewer than 2 million cars in use, fewer than 5 per cent privately owned. China's government forecast car ownership of 22 million by 2010, with China producing 3.5 million cars a year, two-thirds sold privately.[28] These forecasts are based on potential demand in a huge urban population (now 300 million).

Table 10.5   China's Motor Car Industry, 1995 and 2010

	Number of Cars Owned	Domestic Car Production
1995	2.0	0.305
2010	22.0	3.500

Note: All figures are in million units.
Source: *Financial Times*, 'Foreigners Make Inroads Into China,' June 5, 1993, p. 14.

Foreign participation is sought by the government to rationalize a highly fragmented motor industry.

Consolidation is badly needed if the motor vehicle sector is to benefit from economies of scale. Foreign companies are competing for China's go-ahead, which may be forthcoming in 1996. At stake is the right to build a low-cost, fuel-efficient car for the Chinese family, with sales running into the millions. This would provide a solid platform for growth in a market with enormous potential. Auto industry forecasts, slightly different from those in Table 10.5, indicate sales and production in the year 2000 of 2.5–2.6 million units, of which 60 per cent would constitute commercial vehicles and the remaining 40 per cent passenger cars.

Volkswagen (VW) is especially well positioned in the Chinese market. The ubiquitous Santana model gives VW half of domestic output (1994), and 40 per cent of the total market including imports.[29] VW was among the first big foreign producers in China, in a joint venture in Shanghai in 1985. VW's great leap forward in production (1994–8) will more than double local output. VW has built the largest local supply network of any foreign manufacturer, with 180 suppliers. China plays an important part in VW's global rationalization plan, in which costly overlaps in production will be eliminated, the number of chassis types will be reduced, and production of identical vehicles will be concentrated.[30]

Other large foreign producers focusing on the Chinese market include GM, which produces a light pickup truck with Jinbei, Peugeot a French producer, Chrysler of the US, Daihatsu of Japan, and Citroën of France.[31]

Infrastructure Investment

Adequate infrastructure allows a country to expand production, diversify international trade, serve a growing population, and reduce poverty. In China infrastructure must expand rapidly enough to support national income growth across many regions that cover a wide geographic area.[32] Globally, infrastructure has been experiencing change. This change includes realization that government ownership, finance, and management of infrastructure may lead to less efficiency and greater financing burden. Currently there is increased emphasis on commercial development, innovative financing, and more efficient management.

High economic growth in China has magnified demand pressures for infrastructure services. Rapid expansion of industry in the coastal provinces and SEZs has led to repeated rumors of a possible energy crisis.[33] While China produces five times as much electric power as South Korea, the PRC has 25 times as many consumers.

China has been trying to bring its capacity to provide infrastructure services in better balance with growing demand. In 1990 there were two telephone mainlines per 1000 persons in China, compared with 10 for the Philippines, 89 for Malaysia, and 441 for Japan. Only 72 per cent of the population has access to safe water, compared with 81 per cent in the Philippines and 96 per cent in Japan.

Like other Asian countries, China is now engaged in an effort to bring its infrastructure capacity close to the levels enjoyed in modern industrial countries. This calls for massive investment. Peregrine Brokerage in Hong Kong estimated China will spend $233 billion to modernize its transport, power, and telecommunications systems in the period 1994–2000.[34] Almost half of this is needed in the transport sector. Another published report suggests the PRC will require over $1 trillion to catch up with needed infrastructure services.[35] The bulk of this will be spent in transportation (Table 10.6). A description of typical projects is provided in Table 10.7. The largest in this table covers construction of a new Hong Kong airport. The revamping of Shanghai is estimated to carry an aggregate price tag of $100 billion.[36]

Table 10.6   Required Infrastructure Investment Spending, to year 2000

	US$ bn
Transportation	968
Electric power	54
Telecommunications	25
Total	1047

Source: *Business Week*, 'Building the New Asia,' November 28, 1994, p. 66.

Table 10.7   Selected Large Infrastructure Projects in the People's Republic of China

Type Facility	Description	Cost
Super highway	Six-lane highway from Hong Kong border to Guangzhou, built by Hopewell Holdings.	$1.1 billion
Pudong district	Development of Shanghai's new commercial and industrial area, including roads, ports, and telecom links.	$6.0 billion
Nuclear plant	Daya Bay second nuclear plant in southern China, France's Framatone lead company.	$5.0 billion
Railway	Beijing–Kowloon Railway. 1500-mile project.	$3.0 billion
Hydroelectric plant	Three Gorges Dam.	$44.2 billion
Airport	Hong Kong's new airport, including access roads, bridges, tunnel.	$20.3 billion
Fiber-optic telephone network	Wharf Holdings in Hong Kong is prime developer.	$0.6 billion

Financing and construction needs have attracted western bankers and industrial corporations. Merrill Lynch, Morgan Stanley, and others are bringing Chinese power plant financings to the New York Stock Exchange. Similarly, General Electric, Westinghouse, Asea Brown Boveri, Siemens, and Toshiba are battling to manage construction and operation of electric power plants.

Many problems exist in the financing and installation of infrastructure facilities. China does not favor foreign investor control or exclusive operation of such projects. In 1994 the Ministry of Power Industry published provisions stating that except for build-operate-transfer (BOT) projects, a foreign investor generally is not permitted to take more than a 30 per cent equity interest in a power plant.[37] Further, the Chinese have sought to cap profits at 12–15 per cent of investment on infrastructure projects. Also, different type projects have time limits for foreign ownership and management. As with any China project, foreign exchange problems can arise. Infrastructure projects often have no foreign exchange generating capability. Also the renminbi (RMB) currency may devalue against the investor's currency. Tight credit in China has compelled a larger share of 'hard currency' financing, which exacerbates the currency problem. With these problems, infrastructure development in China requires strength of character for the foreign investor.

CHINA'S OVERSEAS INVESTMENT

The opening of China brought about a renewed interest in the People's Republic in overseas investment. This investment has been multi-directioned, reflecting a growing awareness among government leaders that China can benefit from developing various types of financial and investment relationships with the rest of the world. China's overseas investment activity focuses on (1) the developing countries, (2) the industrial countries, and (3) Hong Kong during the transition to 1997.

Developing Countries

Mainland China has long exhibited a strong interest in developing close ties with less developed countries around the world. In the period 1954–76 economic and military aid from China averaged over $130 million a year, aggregating $2.9 billion. Since the late 1970s two changes have taken place in this aid: first, it has expanded steadily; second, its composition has shifted, from mainly economic aid to predominately military aid. Woetzel interprets this change as indicating that China has decided to embark on a more active foreign policy. China has sent many thousands of economic technicians to the developing countries. Moreover, commercial relationships tie in with this overseas aid program. Since 1979 technicians from China have been commissioned to participate in contract labor or engineering service projects. In the period 1979–84 China signed 1950 such contracts worth $3.9 billion, generating almost as much foreign exchange from contract labor abroad as was derived from all direct investment into China in the same period.[38]

Industrial Countries and Hong Kong

Since the opening China has initiated numerous investments in the industrial countries. These investments appear to be related to two different type objectives, access to natural resources and acquisition of advanced technologies. CITIC has been a major instrument for overseas equity investment by the PRC. At year-end 1992 CITIC and its subsidiaries had aggregate overseas investments of RMB 1087 million ($US 189 million). These were distributed as follows: Hong Kong – US$85 million, United States – US$58 million, Canada – US$21 million, Australia – US$20 million, Germany – US$5 million, and Japan – US$1 million.[39] CITIC has purchased several lumber mills in the US and a mining venture in Australia. In addition, China has invested in more than 100 joint venture enterprises, gaining access through these investments to more advanced technologies.

In 1990 China held third rank in the aggregate amount of foreign investment in Hong Kong's manufacturing sector. China's investments in Hong Kong appear to be based on several sets of motives. First, Beijing has taken a more active role in Hong Kong financial activities, probably in an effort to minimize fears over the transition in 1997. For example, China Merchants, one of the largest Beijing-controlled conglomerates in Hong Kong, increased its ownership interest in Hong Kong Chinese Bank (HKCB) to 50 per cent in July 1993. HKCB is also owned by HKCB Bank Holding, controlled by Lippo, an Indonesian finance and property group listed on the Hong Kong exchange.[40]

Chinese state-owned companies are becoming the biggest foreign investors in Hong Kong.[41] Shougang, the mainland Chinese steel group, has made a number of investments in Hong Kong including Tung Wing Steel, Kader Investment, and Eastern Century. Eastern Century is a metal trading company, and Shougang's stake increased from 23 per cent to 60 per cent.

CITIC Pacific has been on an aggressive buying spree in Hong Kong, reflecting Beijing's growing political and economic importance as the colony approaches 1997. CITIC holds stakes in Hong Kong's two airlines, Cathay Pacific and Dragonair, and earlier took a 12 per cent stake in Hong Kong Telecommunications from its Beijing parent company, which retained 8 per cent. CITIC also purchased a 20 per cent stake in the Chase Manhattan's Bank Hong Kong credit card business, which will be expanding into the booming but at present tightly regulated China market.

A second aspect of China's strategy in Hong Kong is to control the centers of power in the colony, directly or indirectly. The news media is one part of this center of power. Sale of the *South China Morning Post* to Chinese interests may lead to a more conciliatory attitude toward mainland China and its policies. Beijing has made great efforts to win the support of newspaper proprietors in Hong Kong.

Finally, Hong Kong's importance to China cannot be overstated. Two-thirds of aggregate foreign investment in China comes from Hong Kong investors. In neighboring Guangdong Province, over 25 000 Hong Kong-backed factories employ well over 3 million workers. Forty per cent of China's trade passes through Hong Kong. Investment by mainland China increases economic ties with Hong Kong, supports the liquidity of Hong Kong's financial system, and demonstrates confidence and commitment to the stability and viability of the colony.

FOREIGN INVESTOR RISK

Foreign investors must consider conditions and prospective changes in government policy, to be able to properly evaluate investment projects. This evaluation is especially difficult with respect to China, for several reasons. First, information flow to the rest of the world is closely monitored and controlled by the authorities. Second, China is a very large economic and political unit. Trends and conditions in one region may differ from those in other regions. Third, the very size of the country gives rise to problems in statistical processing of information, and many data inaccuracies and inconsistencies manifest themselves. Finally, the rapidity of change can quickly make information and data obsolete or even misleading.

For these reasons, investors must exercise great caution and prudence in utilizing information concerning the People's Republic. The following two sections consider two areas of concern for investors, namely changing ground rules (government policy) and the growing external debt overhang.

Changing Ground Rules

In discussions and commentaries on doing business in China, experts on the People's Republic have noted that it is not productive to pose the question: Is China headed for capitalism?[42] The most that one can expect is a variant of market socialism, with producers getting some signals from the market, but with the government continuing to exercise whatever degree of control it decides is necessary. China is not a free market. Local authorities and the central government are continuously struggling to retain power, within a framework of gradual decentralization of political and economic control. Overlapping these uncertainties is a process of economic reform, unpredictable in its implementation and impact.

An equally important aspect of uncertainty in China is the state-owned industrial sector which accounts for 40 per cent of China's non-farm economy. In some years the combined operating deficits of the SOEs amount to 4–6 per cent of national income, attributable in part to the 25 million or more redundant workers on their payrolls. The Bank of East Asia estimated that if SOEs released all redundant workers in 1995, the urban unemployment rate would jump from 2.9 per cent to 14.3 per cent. The number of urban unemployed would rise from 4.8 million to 27 million.[43] Therefore, economic reforms must be guided carefully, around the SOEs, to avoid further weakening their already shaky foundations. The government does not wish to risk the angry reactions of millions of Chinese workers who until now have enjoyed guaranteed lifetime employment in the so-called iron rice bowl. The problems of operating losses in SOEs poses serious problems in the areas of social stability (unemployment), fiscal management (loss of tax revenues and financial support of enterprises), and viability of the banking sector (bank loans to SOEs).

Western enterprises operating in China must work within a system plagued by official favoritism, inside deals, often involving the relatives of Communist Party officials, and outright bribery. Since China's opening, enormous power has accrued to the gatekeepers, officials with the power to facilitate or obstruct access to the Chinese economy.

As foreign investors learn how to cope with these problems, there remains considerable and growing uncertainty about operating in post-Deng China. It is likely that a new wave of restructuring in China after Deng would contain a strong mercantilist cast. This mercantilist approach has given the government the initiative in formulating priorities, rather than allowing market forces to operate uninterrupted in allocating capital for investment. For example, in 1995 the Ministry of Foreign Trade and Economic Cooperation indicated its intent to issue guidelines classifying industries as encouraged, restricted, or prohibited. This represents Beijing's intent to encourage investment in certain sectors (high technology), while discouraging it in areas such as luxury real estate.[44] While these guidelines are described as intended to further open China's markets to foreign investors, they threaten to add another bureaucratic layer to an already complex government regulatory apparatus. More important, they leave considerable room for ambiguity, and even favoritism. If a foreign company decides to invest in an industry classified as encouraged, it would still need to deal with China's sometimes capricious regulators. In addition, not all industries will be explicitly addressed.

For example, it is stated that projects in several restricted areas, such as medicine, machinery production, and light industry, could still gain official approval. The government plans to encourage certain industries, including agriculture, infrastructure, and high technology with tax breaks and easy approval procedures.

One advantage seen in the revised investment incentives is that companies may be allowed to sell up to 100 per cent of their products in the domestic market.[45] The government also plans to provide incentives for investment in the deprived central and western parts of China, but only if such projects are in line with overall industrial policy.

Debt Overhang

China has a large appetite for foreign capital, and must steer a carefully balanced course between borrowing externally to feed economic growth and restraining its borrowing to maintain an acceptable credit standing. At year-end 1993 China's foreign debt was $83.8 billion, and probably reached $100 billion at yearend 1994.[46] The Chinese agency responsible for monitoring foreign debt has urged restraint among borrowers, and an official at the State Administration for Foreign Exchange Control under the People's Bank of China commented in 1994 that foreign debt had expanded a bit too fast.

China's reputation for meeting debt commitments was not helped in 1994 by a dispute between CITIC and the London Metals Exchange involving an alleged default over payments of $30–50 million lost in futures trading. This case was settled early in 1995. However other cases raise questions concerning legal protection available to foreign companies in China, notably the case of Revpower. Revpower is the Hong Kong subsidiary of a US company, which entered into a joint venture in China to manufacture industrial batteries in Shanghai. The joint venture failed, allegedly due to improper actions of the Chinese partners. Revpower sought and obtained from the Stockholm Chamber of Commerce an arbitration award worth $8 million. The Chinese partners refused to pay the award, and Chinese courts refused to adjudicate a suit brought by Revpower. At April 1995 the Chinese government rejected requests to comply with legal obligations. The significance of the Revpower case lies in the actions of the Chinese government, which constitute a clear and knowing violation of China's international treaty obligations under the New York Arbitral Convention.[47] Most foreign companies operating in China utilize arbitral clauses in their contracts, in the expectation that impartial foreign arbitral tribunals will fairly adjudicate any dispute.

China's debt overhang is large, growing, and likely to increase rapidly as it struggles to achieve satisfactory levels of investment. A 1993 analysis of China's foreign debt position came to a mixed answer regarding the debt overhang.[48] Covering China's experience to 1991, Platte details favorable and unfavorable factors. On the favorable side are (1) strong administrative control over external borrowing, (2) low debt relative to size of country, (3) productive use of borrowed funds, (4) ability to keep debt ratio below critical level, (5) long-term maturity of external debt, (6) ability to obtain funds on concessional terms, and (7) favorable trade performance. On the unfavorable side are (1) the gradual shift toward more decentralized borrowing, (2) high rate of growth in external debt, (3) and the concentration of debt mainly in two currencies (US dollar and Japanese yen).

Taking a more recent time period, we can continue our analysis of China's debt overhang. Over the past decade China has grown in prominence as a borrower and mobilizer of global capital. Between 1980 and 1993 external debt increased from $4.5 billion to $83.8 billion. In the same period debt service as a per cent of exports advanced from 4.3 per cent to 11.1 per cent, a period in which China's total trade and exports were growing consistently at double-digit rates (Table 10–8). In 1993 and 1994 China's external debt increased by over 40 per cent above the 1992 level. This debt overhang could prove to be a problem. However, in the 1990s China has skillfully prevented a debt overhang by (a) exercising strong control over foreign exchange resources, (b) following a trade policy that generates export growth and a favorable current account balance in external payments, and (c) pursuing policies that sustain a diversified and growing inflow of capital.

Table 10.8 provides comparisons between China's external debt position and several other large Asian borrowers. Key points emerge from this comparison. First, China's debt appears to be low relative to GDP, far lower than that of India, Indonesia, Pakistan, and the Philippines. Second, China's ratio of debt service and interest payments relative to exports is by far the lowest among the five countries in the table. Finally, the terms of borrowing extended to China (interest rate, maturity, and grace period) appear to be the least satisfactory. There are several reasons for this, including the relative newcomer status of China as an international borrower, and the relatively smaller amount of loan capital provided China from multilateral lenders on a concessional basis as compared with the Philippines, India, Indonesia, and Pakistan.

EVALUATION

Over the past decade, foreign investment inflows to the PRC have grown in amount and importance. In the early 1990s these investment inflows were in excess of 4–5 per cent of annual GNP, providing high positive leverage effects on national economic growth. Based on the level of success achieved in attracting various forms of foreign capital, China is rapidly moving toward superpower status.

The People's Republic of China enjoys many benefits from the large inflow of foreign investment:

Table 10.8   External Debt, Debt Ratios, and Terms of Borrowing, 1993

	Total External Debt[a]	Debt as % GDP	Debt Service as per cent Exports	Interest Payment as % Exports	Average Interest Rate (%)	Average Maturity (years)	Grace Period (years)
China	83.8	20	11.1	3.7	5.5	14	4
India	91.7	41	28.0	14.8	5.4	26	13
Indonesia	89.5	62	31.8	11.0	5.2	19	5
Pakistan	26.1	56	24.7	10.6	3.5	21	6
Philippines	35.2	62	24.9	10.5	5.5	17	6

Note: a. In billions of US dollars.
Source: World Bank, World Development Report 1995.

1. Higher level of domestic investment is made possible, adding to the nation's growth rate.
2. Additional capital is available for investment in interior regions, permitting more balanced growth levels on a regional basis.
3. Foreign capital provides better access to more advanced technology, with which to raise efficiency in lagging sectors.
4. Foreign capital can be invested in new industrial sectors, formerly not represented by local producers.
5. Large state enterprises can be reorganized more quickly and brought to higher efficiency levels as foreign shareholders are brought into the ownership structure.
6. Production efficiency improvements facilitate an improved trade performance on both the export and import sides.
7. Foreign exchange made available through foreign investment funds can be allocated in part to acquisitions of overseas enterprises, assuring better access to resources and technology.

In the not distant future the PRC will play a more important role as a global user and supplier of investment funds. This growing importance already is visible. As it increases, China will need the institutional mechanisms and channels that support its role as a world mobilizer of capital.

11 China and the World

It is important to anticipate how China will manage its relationships with the rest of the world over the next several decades. This will fundamentally affect China's ability to benefit from international relations, and more easily attain its domestic and foreign objectives. China's role in world events as an active and regular participant in trade, investment, and foreign relations is of relatively recent vintage. This makes it difficult to anticipate and project the behavior of the PRC in years to come.

CHANGING WORLD RELATIONSHIPS

Each period of history yields its own pattern of relations among the leading nations of the world. During the 1990s the world order is emerging as an interplay between three or four major powers. The 1990s has been characterized by shifting patterns of alliances as the old Soviet Union has broken apart, Western Europe seeks closer unity and China displays economic success. The bipolar struggle between the US and Soviet Union ended in 1990, to be replaced by a less certain or predictable multi-polar world.

Four powers dominate the new world order, the US, China, Russia, and Europe. While at mid-decade the economic and geopolitical weight of the US appears to stand ahead, the combined purchasing power of the European entity matches that of the US. As a high-tech military power the US is in a category of its own.[1] America's relative advantage may grow for another decade or more.

While the US appears to be enjoying a clearly increasing geopolitical advantage, Europe sits in a distinctly back-seat position. The Europeans have not gotten control of rising social costs which weaken their global competitive position. They show no inclination to spend the additional 2 per cent of GDP each year required to bring their armed forces up to the US's computerized satellite efficiency. Even the long anticipated single European state appears to be well beyond reach.

Compared to Europe, Russia looks better off, with lower labor costs and greater natural resource endowments. But Russia's downward economic plunge persisted longer than many thought possible, and overall its economic performance ranks a distant fourth among the four power regions of

189

the world. Russia lacks inward political consensus. Russia's desire to remain a force in the world order seems to be moving further and further from its grasp.

Taking the four main powers, China is probably the most upwardly mobile. This is based on the high rate of economic expansion, the increasing ability to develop a modern army, navy, and air force to an existing nuclear weapons base, and the ability to increasingly counter US diplomatic initiatives in the Asian spheres.[2]

China's emergence in world affairs should have a dramatic effect on the pattern of power. China wants to be the top power in Asia, and has large outstanding territorial claims against neighboring countries, including Russia. China will find it difficult to agree with the policies of America and Europe, even in matters far beyond the Asian sphere. China could become the party that turns off the music at the periodical world anniversary balls.

While in future we can anticipate many bases for lack of agreement among the four major powers, the country likely to face the greatest problems and issues due to its economic size and wealth status is Japan. Japan is a small, vulnerable island nation. Japan is caught between two powers, who do not wish to see it develop military strength. China does not want military competition in Asia, and the US thus far has indicated a desire to remain the chief military power in the world. Even in Japan, there is little support to rearmament.

Given the present world order of four major powers plus Japan, what role might China play over the next decade or two? One possibility is that China will use its rapidly growing economic base to project military strength and that an authoritarian government will seek to place China in a preeminent position in Asian and world affairs. This will cause alarm in Russia, which shares a long land border with the PRC and which occupies territory taken from China many decades ago. The Russians will seek, and probably obtain, a loose three-power alliance with America and Europe, aimed at containing the China dragon. This interpretation of world order relationships already is shared by senior members of China's military and political establishment. They assert that the US is actively conspiring to undermine China politically, economically, and militarily. To military officers the US is a wily and deceitful enemy which revealed its true nature when it approved the visit of the President of Taiwan to the US in 1995. According to one observer, David Shambaugh of the University of London, the emerging hard-line view in China hangs on four points: the US is trying to divide China territorially, subvert it politically, contain it strategically, and frustrate it economically.[3]

It can be hoped that over time China will take an unassertive role, posing no threat to Russia and its Asian neighbors. This will leave Russia free to focus on its long uphill fight to rebuild its economy. A mild China and a progressive Russia would allow Europe and the US to work cooperatively to share the responsibilities of world power for two or more decades.

NEED FOR INTERNAL STABILITY

It is generally accepted that there are few active dissidents in China. Nevertheless, the authorities take them seriously enough to follow them, infiltrate their groups, bug their telephones, and even arrest them.[4] In the Tiananmen Square incident of 1989 protesters were students and university-educated professionals. There was little interest in stirring up workers or other large groups in the population. Five years after it could be asserted that dissident organizations are run by educated people, with a strategy of mobilizing workers in factories and peasants in rural areas. The Communist Party is concerned, in part because it came to power itself through a strategy now employed by dissidents.

One dissident following this approach is, Wei Jingsheng, who stated, 'Of course the government is afraid of workers and peasants. It would be good for the government to make friends with them, but it just cannot do it, so it has to take the path of crushing them.'[5] Mr Wei formed the Labour Alliance, which models itself on Poland's trade union Solidarity. As small as this organization is (300 members), it is reportedly the biggest underground organization in China.

Given the relatively small number of dissidents and their organizations, one might ask why China is so concerned about them, and so obsessed with preserving internal stability. China's rulers command a vast security apparatus that cannot tolerate any challenge to Communist Party authority.[6] Frequent arrests of dissidents reflects mounting tension in China as democracy campaigners stir from the dormancy that followed Tiananmen. The economic boom has unleashed new demands for political reform. Even in a world giving greater emphasis to human rights, the security forces that keep the Communist Party in power are enforcing a totalitarian sense of public order, even when it injures China's foreign relations. This guiding philosophy comes from Paramount Leader Deng Xiaoping, who admonishes the younger generation of leaders that democracy leads to chaos, that they must never fear cracking down on dissidents, and that China should never worry about what the outside world thinks of it.

With the economy enjoying high prosperity in the early 1990s, the Communist Party leadership fears the eroding influence of inflation, labor unrest, and claims of political corruption. State industries are operating in the red, and workers' basic pay cannot be guaranteed. Many citizens are angered by persistent reports of factory managers taking kickbacks from suppliers, of bankers accepting bribes in exchange for each credit, and of local party officials fixing legal cases.[7]

There are many explanations for the Communist Party fear of dissidents and a pro-democracy movement. The following provide a summary statement concerning these explanations.

First, the question of succession of leadership after Deng raises questions of maintaining Communist Party control while preserving political stability. In 1994 Jiang Zemin was given the title of 'third generation paramount leader,' however, there could be a challenge from those he replaced or succeeded.[8] Second, China's leadership has been subject to several purges. Deng himself was purged twice during the Cultural Revolution. Nevertheless, preservation of party control at any price has been one of Mr Deng's cardinal principles.[9] Third, it is believed inside and outside China that free markets themselves will set forth a sequence of events leading to democracy. One American financier has noted that China's move from a state-controlled to a largely free market economy has changed the nation socially and politically.[10] Provincial government leaders are well informed about what is happening in Europe and America, and over 100 million Chinese now have access to satellite television. When asked, people in all walks of life invariably will agree that political liberty is on the rise. Fourth, current leaders fear the generational and ideological differences, and believe they must find more sophisticated ways to suppress the people.[11] Fifth, economic pressures are increasing, including the need for inefficient state enterprises to lay off workers at a time when jobless rates in some cities exceed 20 per cent.[12] This represents a large body of the population just ripe for revolution. Sixth, more and more people are willing to speak openly of the 'mistakes' made during the golden age of Mao. It is widely accepted that Mao was a successful wartime leader, but made many serious mistakes in peacetime.[13] Finally, a growing labor movement is feared as the potential core of a more widely popular dissident group.[14]

The implications following from China's high priority to internal stability are many and varied. First, political repression is likely to continue and increase. Asia Watch, an international human rights group, has accused China of increasing political repression, especially in Tibet.[15] According to Asia Watch, Chinese standards of justice remain abysmally low by international standards. Torture is reportedly practiced both to secure confessions and to maintain control in the extensive prison and labor camp system. The International Committee of the Red Cross is denied regular access to work for better treatment of those in detention. In response to these criticisms China's leaders repeatedly assert that international pressure on China over human rights amounts to interference in China's internal affairs.[16]

Second, analysis of PRC economic policy will require more complex study. For example, rising inflation in 1994 resulted in government authorities redoubling their efforts to contain the economic upswing via credit restrictions and investment cutbacks. The intensity of anti-inflation policy is likely to be a function of how officials perceive the degree of social unrest likely to follow from pressures on the cost of living.[17]

A third implication is a growing interest in 'preserving culture,' and the impact this may have on attitudes toward anything foreign. In the past China has striven to preserve the purity of its culture from 'barbarian influences.' These influences often are seen as a foreign assault on the sanctity of the Chinese language. Officials in the State Language Commission have warned that the adulteration of the Chinese language reveals a 'blind faith in things foreign.' Like France which has legislated to protect the French language, China is proposing to do the same with a draft bill that would seek to prevent further adulteration of the written and spoken word. One official has stated that 'foreign words should be banned from government reports, text books, government sponsored newspapers, and children's books.'[18]

Fourth, fear of unrest has led to endless postponements of plans to overhaul moribund state industries. Thousands of these companies are propped up by government loans, which drain the budget and fuel inflation. Rationalization of state enterprises is desperately needed to bring about a balanced economic progress.

Finally, concerns over internal stability lead to unexpected shifts in policy regarding the centralization–decentralization of economic decisions. In 1994 the Central Committee of the Communist Party approved a plan to strengthen the Party and its grassroots organization. In this case China's leaders have called for a reinvigoration of central authority, containment of regional authority, and limitation of provincial initiatives.[19]

In effect, China is pursuing two difficult to reconcile goals simultaneously. First, a stronger relationship with the US to protect the huge export market that is the engine of growth. Second, the preservation of stability at all costs, even if it means confronting Washington over a human rights policy that some Chinese assert will undermine communist rule.[20]

EXTERNAL RELATIONS

In the following we focus on China's relations with the US, and to a lesser extent with the former Soviet Union. These two nations pose a range of issues and questions relating to China's use of diplomacy to achieve a harmonious and stable external environment conducive to successful modernization.

Sino–US Relations

Relations between China and the US have moved through several distinct phases since 1978. After the death of Mao Zedong in 1976 and the election of Jimmy Carter as president of the US a year later Sino–US relations stagnated. The new Carter administration had to weigh the importance of the China relation vis-à-vis other pressing issues such as peace in the Middle East and the future status of the Panama Canal. Both governments needed to explore the prospects for improving relations with the Soviet Union, at that time still a nuclear superpower.

Normalization

After Deng established his dominance in China, there was a brief interlude in which China and the US both viewed the Soviet Union as a common threat.[21] A normalization of relations developed during the Carter years, despite continuing controversy over US relations with Taiwan.

Increased American willingness to engage in strategic cooperation with China took several directions. The US government issued public statements supporting Chinese security interests. Also, the US relaxed restrictions on export of advanced technology to China. This included more liberal treatment for geological survey equipment, increased scientific and technological exchanges, and sale of a nuclear reactor.[22] Finally, while the ban on American arms sales remained in effect, the US suggested it was prepared to engage in security cooperation taking the form of sharing military intelligence.

With the Soviet invasion of Afghanistan in late 1979, more highly visible security ties were manifested between China and the US. These included regular exchanges of military personnel, more active intelligence sharing, and liberalization of technology transfer.

Normalization included increased economic and cultural ties. In 1980 the Carter administration decided to sign a trade agreement with China extending most favored nation treatment (MFN). At that time very high tariff rates applied against Chinese export sales to America. However, MFN status under the terms of the Jackson–Vanik amendment was subject to annual renewal and conditional on PRC emigration policies. Moreover, at the time China was not eligible for lower American tariffs under the Generalized System of Preferences (GSP), since it was not a member of the General Agreement on Tariffs and Trade (GATT). Despite these obstacles normalization did give China MFN access to America's markets, and a steady stream of diplomatic and cultural exchanges reinforced this and other aspects of the closer relationship. Bilateral trade increased rapidly, and academic and cultural exchanges developed even more rapidly.

Growing apart

By the early 1980s a slowdown took place in Sino–US relations. The Reagan administration came into office, with the stated objective of strengthening the security and economic ties with Taiwan. Moreover, Reagan had indicated a desire to take a firm stand against Soviet expansionism, by upgrading the US military and nuclear arsenal. But the increased military capability would be multi-faceted and applicable against any aggressor. Finally, Sino–US cultural and scientific exchanges were experiencing growing pains. There were limits to US willingness to give technology and security-related information to the People's Republic.

Over the period 1980–2 the question of American arms sales to Taiwan generated considerable diplomatic heat between Washington and Beijing. An August 1982 communiqué focused on the points of agreement between the US and China regarding the US's relationship with Taiwan and the arms sales issue. However, the chill in Sino–US relations continued.

From 1981 China began to pursue a more independent path in its external relations. In that year, when Secretary of State Haig visited China, suggesting the US might liberalize arms exports to China, the Beijing government was not enthusiastic.[23] The continuing dispute over US arms sales to Taiwan was one factor causing the PRC to maintain an aloof attitude toward US arms sales. At that time the Chinese also perceived that Moscow's global ambitions were not being realized under an aging and tiring Brezhnev government. The strategic balance in the mid-1980s appeared to be tilting away from Moscow and toward Washington.

An independent foreign policy gave China the benefits of opposing superpower hegemony, so gaining the support of many smaller Third World countries. Also, China could more openly criticize US ambitions in Central

America and the Middle East as a threat to the interests of developing countries. Finally, closer ties with the Soviet Union would give America concern, and perhaps reduce the options available to the US in its diplomatic efforts.

From trade to euphoria

In 1983 the US signaled new efforts to achieve better relations with China. These overtures were welcome since the PRC was embarking on an ambitious economic development program. In May 1983 on an Asian trip Commerce Secretary Baldridge advised Chinese leaders of a major liberalization of export controls, which would open up opportunities for China in its trade with the US. This would facilitate sale of advanced technology to the PRC, place China in a friendly nation category, and lead to increased sales of Chinese exports in North America.

The mid-1980s was a period of economic restructuring in China, including urban economic reform, relaxation of central planning, an increased role of market forces in production and resource allocation, and decontrol of prices. State ownership also was liberalized, in agriculture and industry. The structural changes further opened China to the outside world.

These changes were a welcome contrast to China watchers in the US. Changes in US foreign policy reinforced the effects of China's restructuring, leading to a strong increase in American trade and investment with the PRC. The flow of tourists and other visitors to China also increased dramatically. Private American institutions provided financial support to China, and aided research on changes taking place in Chinese society. American foundations and exchange organizations began to establish a physical presence in China.

Sino–US exchanges again began to focus on strategic relationships. China referred more openly to a comprehensive security relationship with the US. In part, the Chinese motives were pragmatic. Placement of Soviet SS-20 missiles in the Far East placed much of China in range of Soviet nuclear attack.

By the late 1980s there was near-euphoric enthusiasm in the US toward China. Not only were economic relations with China improved, but also the PRC was transforming itself into a democracy with a capitalist economic system.

Tiananmen Square and the End of the Cold War

US investment in China grew rapidly throughout the 1980s. But in the later 1980s problems appeared to US investors, including operating losses, difficult foreign exchange constraint, unexpected changes in government policies, and differential treatment of investors by central government, provincial authorities, and municipal governments.[24]

Rapid growth of China's trade surplus with the US fueled criticism of China's imposition of obstacles on sales of American goods. China became increasingly criticized for high tariffs and regulatory taxes, restrictive quotas, and inadequate protection of American intellectual property.

Tibet became part of the US policy conflict with China when in 1987 Chinese troops and police suppressed demonstrators in Lhasa. At that time the Dalai Lama was visiting Washington where he presented an informal plan to US legislators for the withdrawal of Chinese military forces in return for Tibet acknowledging Chinese sovereignty. Congress passed several joint resolutions expressing concern about the situation in Tibet, including an amendment to the State Department Authorization Act (December 1987) urging the White House to make the treatment of Tibetan people an important factor in the conduct of its relations with China.

During the 1980s China's economic reforms far outpaced changes in political structure. By 1989 the moderate relaxation of political control over society had produced escalation in crime, including rape and murder. Social income inequality was another by-product of the many changes in China during the 1980s.

Public dissatisfaction with these negative consequences of reform and economic growth was becoming more apparent. Sporadic demonstrations, strikes, and calls for greater democracy took place in the years 1986–9. In the spring of 1989 the situation became particularly serious. This was related to signs of division among the central government leadership. Free market enthusiasts such as General Secretary Zhao Zyang were promoting more radical economic reforms. A second group headed by Premier Li Peng favored maintaining mandatory planning, and opposed growth of the private sector. At this time inflation was approaching 30 per cent in major cities, generating serious shortages of goods. In April 1989 former General Secretary Hu Yaobang died in Beijing following a heart attack. Hu Yaobang suddenly became the martyr of the democratic reform movement. Wreaths were placed on campuses and at the memorial to revolutionary martyrs at Tiananmen Square.

An acceleration of demonstrations led to martial law. The demonstrations continued, and regular soldiers untrained in the niceties of controlling urban protests faced the task of clearing the square. Many were killed by these soldiers.

Repercussions of the Tiananmen incident extended throughout all levels of China's government. The Party Central Committee announced the purge of Zhao Zyang from his leadership positions in the Party. There were many reshufflings of military commanders, government officials, and provincial leaders.

Following Tiananmen the Bush administration imposed a series of sanctions against China, including a warning against travel to China, suspension of military sales, postponement of all lending to China by international financial institutions, suspension of investment guarantees by the Overseas Private Investment Corp. (OPIC), and other actions. During this period the Bush administration attempted to maintain close dialogue, directly and indirectly with the Chinese government.

Conservative Chinese leaders, who had remained suspicious of US intentions toward China, argued that US sanctions proved the US had never given up hope of undermining communist rule in China.[25] They claimed US was involved in the political events leading to the protests in Tiananmen Square. These conservative leaders called for a reorientation of foreign policy away from the West. A second group of Chinese espoused continuity in policy, despite the western sanctions. They perceived a relative decline in the power of both the US and Soviet Union continuing, with less tension likely around the world. The outcome of this debate over foreign policy was closer to continuity with past policy than a break with the West.

Post-Tiananmen

The Tiananmen crisis has exercised a lasting impact on Sino–US relations. First, there developed a sense of outrage and horror over the human rights violations and killing of civilians by the military. Second, it produced a split in American attitudes, with one group maintaining the US should try to maintain a working relation with China, and another holding that sanctions must be kept in place until China reforms. Third, human rights groups have become more openly critical of China. Fourth, deep division prevails in the US government concerning China policy.

The deep division on China policy is reflected in the Clinton administration approach toward China's trade status each year. Initially, the Clinton administration insisted on using human rights criteria in assessing China's access to MFN treatment. However, after two years of applying this criterion, the Clinton administration has delinked the issues of trade and human rights.

Soviet breakup

The collapse of the communist regimes in Eastern Europe in 1989–90 had profound consequences for Sino–US relations. Americans previously had seen China as leading the reform of the communist countries in a transition to freer and more open systems. Now they see China lagging behind the entire communist world. At the same time, many leaders in China see the breakdown of communism in Europe as evidence that political liberalism carries its own seeds of destruction. Finally, the Chinese conservatives visualized the US as ready to focus on China, as the last stronghold to be toppled of reactionary communism.

The end of the cold war between the US and Soviet Union implied that the US no longer needed China as a strategic counterweight. But progress in Sino–Soviet relations in 1990–1 reduced China's need for assistance in balancing a formerly hostile neighbor to the north.

Regional Relations

To understand China's relations with its neighbors in Asia we must consider country size differences, the past history of conflicts over territory, the emphasis in the region given to growth through exporting, and China's growing appetite for energy sources. In some respects China can be compared with the man who could not see the rest of the world because his eyes focused inward. By focusing on the external world the man suddenly perceives opportunities and challenges that must be faced with strength and determination.

Territorial question

Perhaps the most significant territorial problem facing China and its neighbors is the conflict over the South China Sea and the islands in that region. The South China Sea is bordered on the east by the Philippines, on the south by the Malaysian Archipelago and Indonesia, on the west by Vietnam, and on the north by China. The area is close to 1200 km wide (east to west), and twice that in length. It displaces a region at least equal in size to the nations of Burma, Thailand, Laos, Cambodia, and Vietnam. Strategically, it sits astride important trade routes linking Southeast Asia, mainland China, Australia, Singapore, and ports engaged in trans-Pacific shipping.

China has laid claim to the Spratly Islands and Paracel Islands, and has built a number of small bases on these islands to reinforce its territorial claims. In 1994 in a series of articles marking the 67th anniversary of the founding of the People's Liberation Army, the Chinese media made clear the army's intent to scale up its power projections.[26] These territorial claims are opposed by countries that border on the South China Sea. In 1994 China deployed two warships to blockade a Vietnamese oil rig at a site claimed by both countries.[27]

The Spratlys consist of over 400 islands and reefs extending over an area of more than 800 km from north to south. China, Taiwan, and Vietnam claim all of the islands, while the Philippines and Malaysia claim islands close to their shores. Arguments over sovereignty have been going on since the 1950s. Suggestions that the waters surrounding the islands contain deposits of oil and natural gas have given a new urgency to the issue. Vietnam and China had a brief naval encounter in the area in 1988, and the Philippines has blown up several Chinese structures, which it asserts were illegal.[28]

In 1995 countries of the Association of Southeast Asian Nations (ASEAN) claimed to have made progress on the issue of competing claims to the Spratly Islands. China agreed to refer the dispute to the UN Convention of the Sea and continue talks with ASEAN officials. Still, Beijing reiterated its indisputable sovereignty over the islands. While China has undertaken to respect the United Nations Convention on the Law of the Sea, it has not as yet ratified this treaty. China has insisted that such disputes be resolved bilaterally, but this approach does not meet with favor among neighboring countries. Vietnam has stated that as a member of ASEAN, China should deal with this group of countries as a whole.

Energy needs

China is the world's fifth largest oil producer, with over 143 million tons of production in 1994. Most of China's oilfields are mature, and production levels are maintained only at high cost. While China seeks to find and develop new oilfields, it must in the short run develop closer trading ties with large oil exporters like Saudi Arabia. In 1993 China became a net importer of crude, and its dependence on imports is likely to grow in future. Between 1994 and 2000 China is expected to reach an annual oil import level of 50–60 million tons to meet projected demand. Reports indicate cooperative production and refinery deals with Saudi Arabian suppliers and South Korean investors. Conclusion of such arrangements would assure the PRC of stable sources of supply in the long run.[29]

China has given large international oil companies concessions to explore and develop oilfields in offshore locations. In April 1994 a concession was awarded to a consortium led by America's Mobil, and many other oil firms have been bidding for these concessions.[30] The intense competition between China and its neighbors for oil rights in offshore waters may escalate, especially as discoveries of oil deposits suggest that these rights may carry a high value.

Gunboat Diplomacy or Piracy?

How much control does Beijing have over its military and naval forces? Are the Chinese 'official' vessels that stop cargo vessels rogue units seeking private booty, a subtle method by which China extends territorial jurisdiction over international waters, or simply piracy? On January 27, 1994 the Panamanian freighter *Alicia Star* was stopped by what looked like an official Chinese vessel in the Luzon Strait between Taiwan and the Philippines. According to the International Maritime Bureau (IMB) in Kuala Lumpur, the ship was forced into a Chinese port, detained for a week, and its cargo of cigarettes (worth $5 million) confiscated without compensation with a fine demanded for release of the vessel. The *Alicia Star* had been intercepted more than 500 km from the Chinese mainland. Was this a case of piracy on the high seas or deliberate exercise of extra-territorial sovereignty?[31] Piracy long has been endemic to the shipping lanes along the coastal waters of Southeast Asia.

IMB records show that in the period 1991–3 half of the world piracy incidents were concentrated in the South China and East China Seas. Figures for 1994 suggest the pattern of interruptions persists.

China's responses to complaints by IMB and countries whose registered vessels have been intercepted include its indisputable right of sovereignty over certain waterways, the possibility of rogue units operating illegally, need to safeguard Chinese fishermen, and the need to pursue smugglers.[32]

Japanese vessels have not escaped these interceptions. Japan counted 78 cases of Japanese and foreign vessels being boarded or shot at by Chinese ships over the period March 1991 to June 1993. Only three of these were acknowledged by China. Most of these incidents involved forced inspections rather than piracy. Japan issued many protests with little effect. In February 1993 Japan proposed that coastguard officials from the two countries should meet to discuss these problems. The situation changed after this proposal by the Japanese. A possible explanation for this change is that there have been numerous Chinese agencies patrolling coastal waters, not all well informed or well disciplined. Apparently, Chinese authorities have made an effort to prevent local Mafia from faking markings of vessels. Also, the Chinese have changed uniforms and ship markings so that the Mafia cannot imitate these markings.[33]

MILITARY BUILDUP AND ARMS TRADE

The modernization and strengthening of China's military forces causes serious problems and issues for the rest of the world. These relate to (a) the extent of arms buildup, (b) trade in weapons and the possible undermining of non-proliferation efforts, and (c) the status and role of the military in China's political and economic affairs.

Extent of Arms Buildup

The degree of China's arms buildup and weapons modernization depends on several factors:

1. The ability of PRC to improve quality and amount of production of military goods and services.
2. PRC foreign trade in arms and weapons systems.
3. Transfer of foreign weapons applicable technology into China.

Many constraints

There are many types of constraint on China's military production and weapons buildup. We discuss five of these in close detail. Perhaps the most systematic constraint is the economy. Economic constraints include fiscal and level of development. On the fiscal side the government budget is constantly under pressure, with so many competing needs for infrastructure investment, support to state enterprises, and administrative services of government. China is unable to meet these many needs. The need to allocate a large share of GDP (36 per cent) to fixed investment to accelerate economic development reinforces the belief that China may be facing a tough economic constraint on military spending.

A second constraint relates to the quality of production and technology. China is not using all of its capacity to produce. In part this is because SOEs are operating under difficulties, in many instances incurring operating losses. The quality of military production often is unsatisfactory. For example, Thai purchasers of Chinese weapons have complained of poor quality and low level of sophistication. Third, there are serious administrative and managerial constraints. Government procurement often is wasteful, and ideology often works at cross-purposes with economic efficiency. Efforts to maintain secrecy about the amount and composition of military spending prevents good management. In some cases China suffers from poor technology absorption.

A fourth constraint relates to domestic political conditions. The provinces want freedom to develop their own private sector industries, which adds to their power, provides tax revenues, and keeps workers employed and happy. The provinces and municipalities are not anxious to allow resources to be shifted toward defense production.

A final constraint is the limited foreign sources of supply. China is seeking to develop in-flight refueling for jet aircraft, but in 1995 this was considered to be 2–3 years from realization. Also, the PRC is anxious to develop an early air warning system. Installing such a system requires the uninterrupted cooperation of foreign suppliers. In the past Israeli suppliers have been important in providing higher tech military equipment and systems. China's critical shortage of technicians and engineers makes Russian and Israeli help critically important. But once foreign engineers come to China to work on such projects, they are lured away by the private sector.

Spending $140 billion?

In 1995 it was reported that China's annual military budget was $140 billion, several times higher than the Pentagon estimate. The figure is 20 times higher than Beijing's own official records on spending. Drawn up by the Rand Corporation, a California-based research institute, this report was expected to damage ties between the US and China, and end discussions of Sino–US military ties.[34] Another group, the London-based International Institute for Strategic Studies, (IISS) estimated the current defense budget of the PRC at $28–45 billion. This figure is based on purchasing power parity, rather than current exchange rates.[35] The IISS reckoned Beijing would spend up to $6 billion on strategic nuclear forces. China is estimated to rank fourth in the world in nuclear arms stockpiles (Table 11.1), and is defiant about conducting nuclear tests. Nevertheless, the gap between China and the superpower arsenals of Russia and the US is huge.[36] Western intelligence agencies fear that Russia and the Ukraine are assisting China, transferring technology from the advanced SS-25 mobile missile. It is further reported that China's objective is to develop a 'survivable second strike' capability.

China's conventional armed forces of 3 million is the world's largest.[37] But the armed forces are not the most modern vintage. Two shocks have changed China's military thinking in the past few years, showing the government that it was ill equipped to deal with domestic instability or exter-

Table 11.1   Nuclear Stockpiles

United States	14 000[a]
Russia	29 000
France	550
China	450
Britain	200

Note: a. Number of warheads (strategic and tactical)
Source: *New York Times,* October 26, 1994, p. A10.

nal threat. First, in 1989 at Tiananmen the government needed the army when the latter came close to revolt. Many army officers and soldiers refused to shoot the civilians around Tiananmen Square. Second, in 1991 the Gulf War demonstrated the inadequacy of Chinese-supplied weaponry used by the Iraquis.[38]

Currently the bonds between the Communist Party and the army are being strengthened. Soldiers are being co-opted into the Party's ruling body, and military men account for a quarter of the Central Committee's members. The army has won favors from the government: the army will not be used to quell civilian disturbances; sharp budget increases have been provided to win loyalty and upgrade the quality of the military establishment; further, China is trying to beef up its own arms industry. Increased defense spending is geared toward more sophisticated weapons, securing access to sea routes, oil in particular.

Trade in Weapons

China and the US have experienced a deterioration in their relations during the 1990s, and a major factor in the increasing tension has been weapons trade. There are several facets to the weapons trade issue. The US, along with many European nations, seeks to curb world trade in weapons, especially the proliferation of nuclear weapons and delivery systems. China has been accused by the US of violating the international arms control agreement that bars it from exporting missile technology. Specifically, in 1993 the US asserted China has sold M-11 missiles to Pakistan. Such transfers are barred by the Missile Technology Control Regime. While China did not sign this accord, it promised to live up to its provisions as part of a trade negotiating package with the US.[39] US law requires a ban on American companies doing business with the Chinese and Pakistan agencies involved in the sale. Evidence that China violated the agreement by delivering M-11 missile technology to Pakistan led the Bush administration to postpone the sale of a sophisticated supercomputer to China in December 1992.[40]

The Clinton administration has appeared to shift policy toward China on several occasions, by threatening to revoke most favored nation treatment based on China's arms exports and poor record on human rights. In 1994 the Clinton administration faced a difficult issue concerning U.S. sale of gas turbine engines. Whereas the Chinese claim they need these engines for jet aircraft, nuclear non-proliferation experts insist Beijing has more sinister plans for this equipment. Within the Defense Technology Security Administration specialists are worried that these engines are suited to powering a long-range cruise missile. CIA studies have warned that if the US company Allied Signal sells not just the engine but the technology to build it, China will gain high-quality military technology that could be used for a new generation of cruise missiles. This would put most of Asia within range of a Chinese nuclear attack.[41]

In 1994 the US agreed to allow the export of high-technology satellites to China that were frozen after the secret transfer of missile components and technology to Pakistan. In return, China pledged that with waiver of these sanctions, it will not sell or transfer sensitive missile technology. The agreement signed by Foreign Minister Qian Qichen of China and Secretary of State Warren Christopher commits the two sides to cooperate in promoting an end to the production of fissile material for nuclear weapons. Under the agreement, China for the first time accepted an internationally recognized definition of what constitutes a violation of the missile accord.[42]

People's Liberation Army

Since 1978 the People's Liberation Army (PLA) has gone into private business activities. China's military enterprises are growing, expanding into peacetime production of consumer goods and services. The large trading houses such as Poly Group and Xinxing may come to rival the big Japanese trading companies.

Military–industry complex

One of the most striking by-products of economic reform in China is the military's involvement in business. This transformation started in 1978. According to Mr Wu Zhao, chairman of the Association for the Peaceful

Use of Military Industrial Technology, formed in 1978 to spur defense conversion, 76 per cent of production in defense factories is now for civilian use.[43]

The decision to beat swords into ploughshares among China's over 650 defense factories has made them dominant in some consumer goods products such as motorcycles, washing machines, and electric fans. The six main defense industries (nuclear, space, aviation, ordinance, electronics, and shipbuilding) account for 20 per cent of machine industry output by value. China's military enterprises are pyramiding their successes, plowing profits into new and bigger commercial enterprises, including hotels, truck and shipping companies, and even discos.

Today, China's military runs a pharmaceutical industry with earnings of $1 billion a year. It produces television dishes and cellular phones, as well as food, clothing, boats, and contact lenses. In Shanghai the city's hottest disco, JJs, is a joint venture between the military and a Hong Kong investor.[44] The size and scope of the military – industry complex in China is vast. The Central Military Commission and State Council carry ultimate responsibility. China Poly's Group is perhaps one of the most influential of the 'corporations' that make up this complex. The president is Major-General He Ping, the son-in-law of Deng Xiaoping. The range of China Poly's business is vast, including Hainan port development, shipping, finance, property, electronics, and telecommunications.

Xinxing Corporation owns 100 factories throughout China making garments, shoes, electrical products and military supplies. It signed large contracts with foreign investors to finance an expansion of its production and commercial activities.

Profits for commerce

The proceeds of China's military enterprises are estimated at between $5 and 10 billion. In general, the proceeds from the vast business and commercial ventures of defense industries are not benefiting the military directly. Generally, profits from ventures are either being invested in new commercial activities or spent on the welfare of the military units that control businesses.

According to David Shambaugh, a China scholar at the University of London who completed a study of Chinese military spending, the Chinese are not plowing profits from commercial enterprises back into more bombs, ships, and guns.[45] Even the declining sales revenues from export of Silkworm missiles, and F-7 fighters appear to be financing science and technology research, not military procurement.

ENVIRONMENTAL ISSUES

China's economic successes have produced negative side-effects in the form of environmental damage. China and its population suffer the most from environmental degradation, but the pollution of air and water in the PRC contribute also to global climate change and ozone depletion. Over the long run the consequences of China's environmental practices for the world will dwarf all other issues.

At present China is the third largest contributor to global climate changes, after the US and Russia. By the year 2050 China will be the world's leading air polluter, emitting 40 per cent of the world's carbon dioxide. China is also a heavy user of chlorofluorocarbon aerosols, in 1986 consuming 18 per cent of the world total. China invests a mere 0.7 per cent of GNP for environmental protection, where expenditure of at least 2 per cent of GNP is needed.[46]

Japan has made environmental issues a priority in its dealings with Beijing. Any new thermal powerplant built with Japanese money must be equipped with desulfurization technology. In the US the Clinton administration has voiced opposition to the Three Gorges Dam project because of environmental and human rights concerns, and worries over protracted litigation that could tie up Export–Import Bank resources. This is the largest public works project in the world, expected to cost up to $30 billion. Opponents of the dam say it will flood 350 miles of river canyon, destroying the homes and livelihoods of 1.3 million people, as well as the beautiful Three Gorges.[47]

The Three Gorges project would not be completed before the year 2009, if it is fully implemented. Meanwhile, opponents fear that vast stretches of the Yangtze ecosystem will be irreversibly upset. Environmentalists assert that river blockage will endanger or wipe out the Chinese alligator, the finless porpoise, the white crane, the river dolphin, and the Chinese sturgeon (unique to the Yangtze). The reservoir waters will engulf 13 cities, hundreds of villages, 955 business enterprises and factory towns, and 115 000 acres of the richest land along the river basin. The government has pledged to spend $4.8 billion on resettlement and $3.2 billion for compensation to the refugees who will be wrenched from the land of their ancestors.[48]

Critics of the project cite engineering risks for so large a dam. The World Bank refused to help with funding, and Merrill Lynch and other potential investors have withdrawn because of the financial and political risks. Opponents of the project argue that the electric energy required could be obtained in a less harmful manner by building smaller power plants along sparsely populated tributaries of the river system.

CHINA IN A MULTI-POLAR WORLD

The past cyclical pattern of friendly and hostile relations between China and the US was mistakenly based on unrealistic expectations, exaggerated concerns, and a belief that there could be a special relationship between these two great powers. A better basis of understanding should be the realities of a multi-polar world. A future relationship must be based on understanding that the US and China will become relatively less important as other nations grow in economic, political, or military status.

In this multi-polar world China will not and should not be treated as a third or fourth corner of a strategic triangle or square. Even in Asia other powers will grow in importance, including India, Indonesia, and Korea. The legacy of central planning for all transitional economies seems to be a series of structural reforms which only partially solve problems.

Differing ideologies suggest the Sino–US relationship will become more complex, with competition and cooperation operating side by side. Hard bargaining will solve problems, only if all parties are willing to reach mutually acceptable but complicated solutions.

Realism will become the cornerstone of successful foreign relations for China and the US, and for other Chinese relationships in the future. China cannot expect the US to freely transfer advanced military technology and offer unlimited opportunities for China's exports. At the same time the US cannot expect China to create a democratic republic in only 2–3 years.

Finally, China must come to understand that all countries have faced the internal and external stability problems currently burdening the Communist Party leaders. For these reasons, China must not allow itself to retrogress, especially in its thinking and attitudes toward the outside world. The communist dialectics could be put to effective use. Let the fresh ideas of the outside world reformulate attitudes toward new solutions.

Notes

1 FROM DRAGON TO SUPERPOWER

1. *Business Week,* 'China: The Making of an Economic Giant,' May 17, 1993, p. 55. *China Today,* 'Is China An Economic Superpower?' Nov. 1993, pp. 12–14.
2. Pete Engardio, 'China Fever Strikes Again,' *Business Week,* March 29, 1993, p. 46.
3. According to *The Economist,* Japanese companies invested $64 billion in Asia in the year to March 1993 of which investment in China nearly doubled to $1.07 billion. June 12, 1993, p. 74.
4. Victor Mallet, 'Fears Over China's Drive to Modernization of Armed Forces,' *Financial Times,* July 23, 1993, p. 4.
5. Robert Thomason, 'Japanese Fear Shift of Output to China,' *Financial Times,* June 17, 1993, p. 3.
6. *The Economist,* 'China: In Deep Water,' September 25, 1993, p. 44.
7. Martin Wolf, 'The Sleeping Giant Awakes,' *Financial Times,* June 28, 1993, p. 13.
8. Ibid.
9. The use of PPP estimates in measuring country GDP is discussed later in this chapter.
10. Adrian Wood, of the Institute of Development Studies at Sussex University, argues that the cumulative effect (to 1990) of North–South trade in manufactures was to lower demand for unskilled labor in industrial countries by 6 per cent of the aggregate employment base, and by 12 per cent of the manufacturing employment base. Adrian Wood, 'The Factor Content of North–South Trade in Manufactures Reconsidered,' *Weltwirtschaftliches Archiv,* Vol. 127, No. 4, 1991, pp. 719–43.
11. Clyde V. Prestowitz, *Trading Places,* Basic Books, New York, 1988, Chapter 1 titled 'The End of the American Century.'
12. Ezra F. Vogel, *Japan as Number One,* Harper & Row, New York, 1979.
13. Carol Lee Hamrin, *China and the Challenge of the Future,* Westview Press, Boulder, 1990, pp. 30–9 and 64–76.
14. *Business Week,* 'China Fever Strikes Again,' March 29, 1993, p. 46; and *Business Week,* 'China: The Making of an Economic Giant,' May 17, 1993, p. 56.
15. 'The Making of an Economic Giant,' p. 56.
16. James V. Feinerman, 'Enter the Dragon: Chinese Investment in the United States,' *Law & Policy in International Business,* Vol. 22, No. 3, p. 547.
17. World Bank, *World Development Report,* 1984, pp. 86–9.
18. *International Herald Tribune,* 'China's Government Keeps Racing Ahead of Projections,' London, June 24, 1993, p. 15.

19. Dusty Lee, 'China Economy Runs Wild Despite Controls,' *South China Morning Post,* October 22, 1994, p. 1.
20. Simon Holberton, 'Chinese Expected to Pursue Annual Growth Rate of 8–9%,' *Financial Times,* September 26, 1995, p. 1.
21. Ian Brodie, 'IMF Frees its Assessments of World Economies from Shackles of Dollar,' *The Times* (London), May 21, 1993, p. 12.
22. *The Economist,* 'Chinese Puzzles,' May 15, 1993, p. 83.
23. China's GDP has been a source of controversy for years. Converting China's GDP in 1992 into dollars at the official exchange rate yields $440 billion, or $370 per capita. This low figure is hard to reconcile with China's high life expectancy, daily food consumption, and ownership of consumer durables (e.g. 70 per cent of Chinese urban households have color televisions).
24. Most economists agree the PPPs give a more accurate measure of the relative size of economies than market exchange rates. This still leaves a problem, that the original local currency data may themselves be unreliable. This is due to statistical deficiencies as well as to the existence of large 'informal' economies.
25. 'China Fever Strikes Again,' p. 46.
26. Pan Zhongming, 'DuPont Ready to Shift New Investment to Asia,' *China Daily* (Beijing), October 4, 1993, p. 2.
27. Wangj Yong, 'Hughes Set to Gear Up in China Operations,' *China Daily* (Beijing), October 4, 1993, p. 2.

2   POLITICAL OPENING AND ECONOMIC REFORM

1. Robert Kleinberg, *China's Opening to the Outside World,* Westview Press, Boulder, 1990, p. 7.
2. Robert Gilpin, *U.S. Power and the Multinational Corporation,* Basic Books, New York, 1975.
3. According to one report, in 1992 state-owned enterprises accumulated losses of $76 billion. Tony Walker, 'Long Slog to a Smooth Landing,' *Financial Times,* August 5, 1993, p. 9.
4. Rensselaer W. Lee III, 'Issues in Chinese Economic Reform', in *Economic Reform in Three Giants,* Overseas Development Council, Washington, DC, 1990, p. 75.
5. Alvin Rabushka, *The New China,* Pacific Research Institute for Public Policy, Westview Press Boulder, 1987, p. 59.
6. Robert Dernberger, 'The Chinese Search for the Path of Self-Sustained Growth in the 1980s: An Assessment,' *China Under the Four Modernizations,* Part I, Joint Economic Committee, US Congress, August 13, 1982, Washington, DC.
7. Lee, p. 75.
8. Rabushka, pp. 69–70.
9. Lee, p. 76.
10. David Phillips and Anthony G.O. Yeh, 'Special Economic Zones,' in David Goodman, *China's Regional Development,* Routledge, London, 1989, p. 123.

11. The provincial distribution of per capita industrial and agricultural output reflects these trends. According to one study the coefficient of variation of per capita industrial output declined from 1.72 in 1974 to 1.32 in 1984. Peter Ferdinand, 'The Economic and Financial Dimension,' in Goodman, *China's Regional Development,* pp. 53–4.

12. The central government commands less than half of tax revenues, the larger part accruing to the provinces.

13. Motohiko Kitahara, 'China Tries a Lighter Touch,' *Nikkei Weekly,* September 20, 1993, p. 28.

14. Walker, 'Long Slog to a Smooth Landing,' p. 9.

15. Lincoln Kaye, 'This Money Has Wings,' *Far Eastern Economic Review,* July 15, 1993, pp. 72–3.

16. *The Economist,* 'Third-World Finance,' September 25, 1993, p. 20.

17. Nicholas D. Kristof, 'Chinese Dissidents' Odyssey: In and Out of Prison, Now Trying to Flee Abroad,' *New York Times,* July 19, 1993, p. A9.

18. *Far Eastern Economic Review,* 'Get Off Our Backs,' July 15, 1993, pp. 68–9.

19. *Financial Times,* 'Beijing Executes Eight for Fraud,' September 28, 1993, p. 4.

20. Tony Walker, 'Beijing Party Boss Under Investigation,' *Financial Times,* July 9, 1995, p. 4.

3 REGIONAL DEVELOPMENT: SPECIAL ECONOMIC ZONES

1. Jonathan R. Woetzel, *China's Economic Opening to the Outside World,* Praeger, New York, 1989, p. 53.

2. Yue-Man Yeung and Yu-Wei Hu, 'China's Coastal Cities as Development and Modernization Agents: An Overview,' in *China's Coastal Cities: Catalysts for Modernization,* University of Hawaii Press, Honolulu, 1992, p. 1.

3. Ibid., p. 2.

4. Ibid., p. 4.

5. The 14 cities include Dalian, Qinhuingdao, Tianjin, Yantai, Qingdao, Lianyungang, Nantong, Shanghai, Ningbo, Wenzhou, Fuzhou, Guangzjou, Zhanjiang, Beihai.

6. Lawrence C. Reardon, 'The SEZs Come of Age,' *The China Business Review,* November–December 1991, p. 14.

7. Ka-Ju Fung, Zhong-Min Yan, and Yue-Min Ning, 'Shanghai: China's World City,' in *China's Coastal Cities,* p. 130.

8. Tony Walker, 'Quick March Down the Capitalist Road,' *Financial Times,* August 14, 1993, p. vii.

9. Norman P. Givant, 'Putting Pudong in Perspective,' *The China Business Review,* November–December 1991, p. 31.

10. This figure includes population in several adjacent cities. The central city population was 5.5 million. *China's Coastal Cities,* p. 42.

11. Ibid., p. 51.

12. Guangzhou ranks as sixth largest city in China; *ibid.,* p. 240.

13.   Ibid., p. 248.
14.   Harry Xiaoying Wu, 'Rural to Urban Migration in the People's Republic of China,' *The China Quarterly,* September 1994, p. 698.
15.   The population numbers at each government level are: township (15 000–30 000), village (1000–2000), and production team (30 households with 150 people). W.A. Byrd and Lin Qingsong, eds, *China's Rural Industry,* Oxford University Press for the World Bank, London, 1990, p. 3.
16.   TVP sector refers to the township, village and private enterprise sector, and its economic-production activities.
17.   Byrd and Qingsong, p. 11.

4   EMERGING SUPERPOWER

1.   In 1980 China was testing ICBMs with a range of 7000 nautical miles, covering all the USSR and parts of the US. Paul Kennedy, *The Rise and Fall of the Great Powers,* Random House, New York, 1987, p. 449.
2.   The top ten countries in GDP rank in 1991 were: US $5610 billion, Japan $3362 billion, Germany $1574 billion, France $1199 billion, Italy $1150 billion, UK $876 billion, Spain $527 billion, Canada $510 billion, Brazil $414 billion, and China $369 billion. *World Development Report,* 1993.
3.   W.W. Rostow, *Rich Countries and Poor Countries,* Westview Press, Boulder, 1987, p. 73.
4.   Martin Wolf, 'The Sleeping Giant Awakes,' *Financial Times,* June 28, 1993, p. 13.
5.   This brief account of the rise and decline of European nations is based on materials found in Kennedy, *The Rise and Fall of the Great Powers,* pp. 38–66.
6.   Francis Fukuyama, *The End of History and the Last Man,* Free Press, New York, 1992.
7.   Clyde Prestowitz refers to several crises in the status of the US as world leader, namely the high-tech crisis and crisis in Wall Street. Chapter 1 titled 'The End of the American Century,' in *Trading Places,* Basic Books, New York, 1988.
8.   Richard W. Mansback, 'The New Order in Northeast Asia: A Theoretical Overview,' *Asian Perspective,* Spring–Summer 1993, p. 7.
9.   Ibid., p. 6.
10.   Joseph S. Nye, *Bound to Lead: The Changing Nature of American Power,* Basic Books, New York, 1990.
11.   James R. Kurth, 'The Pacific Basin Versus the Atlantic Alliance,' *The Annals,* No. 303, 1989.
12.   James Sterngold, 'Japan Rethinking the Nuclear Pact,' *New York Times,* August 8, 1993, p. L7.
13.   Some Chinese economists react strongly against the notion that China can attain superpower status with in two decades. They assert that the large and growing population will continuously hold down per capita incomes. They assert that China will become a medium-developed country by the middle of

the 21st century. Bian Hui, 'Is China an Economic Superpower?' *China Today,* November 1993, pp. 12–14.

14. World Bank economists have estimated considerably higher GNP based on purchasing power parity (PPP) comparisons. The 1992 estimate based on PPP is four times higher than the estimate based on market exchange rates. Martin Wolf, 'China as Next Superpower?' *Financial Times,* November 7, 1994, p. 22.

15. *Business Week,* 'China: The Making of an Economic Giant,' May 17, 1993, pp. 54–69.

5   GROWTH: PAST, PRESENT, AND FUTURE

1. The high savings rate has been a product of a high propensity to save among households, and forced savings related to central planning, gradually replaced by a hybrid system of resource allocation.

2. International Monetary Fund, *Economic Reform in China: A New Phase,* Washington, DC, November 1994, p. 36.

3. IMF, p. 37.

4. Ibid., p. 38.

5. World Bank, *China: Internal Market Development and Regulation,* 1994, p. 44.

6. William H. Overholt, *The Rise of China,* W.W. Norton, New York, 1993, pp. 32–3.

7. Nicholas R. Lardy, *China in the World Economy,* Institute for International Economics, Washington, DC, April 1994, p. 31.

8. Patrick E. Tyler, 'China Migrants: Economic Engine, Social Burden,' *New York Times,* June 29, 1994, p. A3.

9. Tony Walker, 'Long Leash for a Runaway Economy,' *Financial Times,* February 2, 1994, p. 11.

10. David R. Phillips and Anthony G.O. Yeh, 'Special Economic Zones,' in David Goodman, ed., *China's Regional Development,* Routledge, London, 1989, pp. 117–18.

11. Lora Savin shows urban employment increasing from 91.2 million in 1977 to 156.3 million in 1992. 'New Bosses in the Worker's State: The Growth of Non-State Sector Employment in China,' *The China Quarterly,* December 1994, p. 946.

12. These estimates are conservatively based on various press reports of the number of farmers moving to urban centers such as Shanghai, Guangzhou, and Shenzhen. Also, they are based on the per capita output values provided by province, which are broadly indicative of differentials in worker productivity throughout China. In this case the low and high productivity output values were placed at $500 and $2000, respectively.

13. Tyler, 'China Migrants.'

14. Patrick E. Tyler, 'Nature and Economic Boom Devouring China's Farmland,' *New York Times,* March 27, 1994, pp. 1 and 8.

15. Tyler, 'Nature and Economic Boom.'

214 *Notes*

16. Philip Shenon, 'Good Earth is Squandered: Who'll Feed China?' *New York Times,* September 21, 1994, p. A4.
17. Uri Dadush and Dong He, 'China: A New Power in World Trade,' *Finance & Development,* International Monetary Fund, June 1995, pp. 36–7.

6 DEVELOPMENT OF INTERNAL MARKETS

1. World Bank, *China: Internal Market Development and Regulation,* Washington, DC, 1994, p. 12.
2. Ibid., p. 12.
3. Ibid., pp. 33 and 194. Over this period there was a general trend of price convergence for all product categories.
4. During the later 1980s commodity wars broke out between neighboring provinces, due to shortages of materials and export embargoes.
5. World Bank, 1994, p. 40.
6. The data in this analysis cover only state enterprises and rural cooperatives. Private trade flows, which appear to be excluded, are likely to have increased over this period. Nevertheless, it is apparent the state enterprise sector continues to dominate the distribution system.
7. World Bank, 1994, p. 51.
8. Wally Wo-Lap Lam, 'Party Under a Volcano of Peasant Workers,' *South China Morning Post,* August 31, 1994, p. 7.
9. Christopher Adam, 'Nation's Masses Driven From Regions by Dream to Make Money', *South China Morning Post,* May 21, 1994, p. 7.
10. Cheung Po-Ling, 'Project to Create Jobs Expanded Nationwide,' *South China Morning Post,* January 21, 1995, p. 6.
11. The UK level is 300 tons per capita, and the Japanese norm is 800 tons per capita.
12. These goods include soda ash, nitric acid, timber, caustic soda, coal, steel products, sulfuric acid, cement, pig iron, and coke.
13. For example, over the period 1985–91 state enterprises accounted for the same 40 per cent of retail sales, there being little change in this proportion. World Bank, pp. 71–72.
14. World Bank, 1994, p. 75.
15. Ibid., p. 89.
16. Patrick E. Tyler, 'On China's Overburdened Highway System, It's the Big Stall,' *New York Times International,* July 1, 1995.
17. Foo Choy Peng, 'Shake-up for China Transport,' *South China Morning Post,* May 21, 1994, p. B1.
18. *The Economist,* 'Lee Can Do', August 21, 1993, p. 52.
19. Allan S. Whitney, *China Eyes Japan,* University of California Press, Berkeley, 1989, pp. 86–8.
20. Christopher Howe, *China's Economy: A Basic Guide,* Basic Books, New York 1978, pp. 97–8.
21. Ibid., p. 117.

22. Lincoln Kaye, 'Labour Pains', *Far Eastern Economic Review,* June 16, 1994, pp. 32–3.

23. On May 15, 1992, China's State Council promulgated the Share System Enterprise Experimentation Procedures. This provides for the formation and regulation of public share companies. This has led to the listing of state enterprises on China's emerging stock markets in Shanghai and Shanghen. Listing of key state enterprises that have converted to enterprises limited by shares on security exchanges provides a new financing source for state enterprises.

24. Shanghai Petrochemical Company, Ltd, *Prospectus,* July 23, 1993, p. B-5.

25. Richard Pomfret, *Investing in China: Ten Years of the Open Door Policy,* Iowa State University Press, Iowa 1991, p. 24.

26. Ibid., p. 25.

27. Patrick E. Tyler, 'Awe-Struck U.S. Executive Survey the China Market,' *New York Times,* September 2, 1994, p. Di.

28. *Financial Times,* 'Knocking at the Door of Corporate Mainland China,' October 21, 1994, p. 22.

29. Tony Walker, 'Chinese Airlines Struck by Bruising Losses,' *Financial Times,* October 27, 1994, p. 6.

30. Kerry Wong, 'Foreign Threat Means Cloudy Skies Looming for Mainland Aviation,' *South China Morning Post,* November 12, 1994, p. B4.

31. *Financial Times,* 'Ericsson Rings the Bell in Chinese Market,' October 20, 1994, p. 4.

32. Louise Lucas and Simon Holberton, 'Fear of China Cap on Power Profits,' *Financial Times,* May 13, 1994, p. 6.

33. World Bank, p. 13.

34. This is measured in terms of coefficients of variation, discussed in other sections of the chapter.

35. World Bank, p. 15.

36. Non-concentrated is used almost synonymously as non-monopolistic.

37. World Bank, p. 136.

38. Ibid., p. 139.

39. The 1008 enterprise groups represent the type more likely to engender anti-competitive effects.

7   BANKING, MONEY, AND CREDIT

1. *Asian Wall Street Journal,* 'China to Boost Bank Activity With Bond Issue,' January 6–7, 1995, p. 9.

2. Gang Yi, *Money, Banking and Financial Markets in China,* Westview Press, Boulder, 1993, Chapter 1.

3. International Monetary Fund, *Economic Reform in China: A New Phase,* Washington, DC, November 1994, pp. 13-14.

4. *The Economist,* 'China's Pig of a Problem,' September 17, 1994, p. 35.

5. *South China Morning Post,* 'Foreign Financiers Tighten Their Belts,' April 8, 1995, p. B5.

6. Tony Walker, 'China's Leaders Struggle to Keep Rampant Inflation Under Control,' *Financial Times,* September 5, 1994, p. 4.

7. *IMF Survey,* 'Currency Management and Monetary Programming in China,' July 31, 1995, pp. 237–8.
8. T.L. O'Brien, 'Citicorp Names Key Cost Cutter, Steffen, to New Post as Fifth Vice Chairman,' *Wall Street Journal,* January 18, 1995, p. B5.
9. *Business Week,* 'Morgan Stanley's Chinese Coup,' November 7, 1994, pp. 50–1.
10. Cecil Dipchand, Zhang Yichun, and Ma Mingjia, *The Chinese Financial System,* Greenwood, 1994, pp. 176–7.
11. A shares are reserved for domestic investors, while B shares are purchased by foreign investors.
12. *The Banker,* 'Shanghai's Renaissance,' May 1994, pp. 35–7.
13. Tony Walker, 'China May Permit More Banks,' *Financial Times,* January 30, 1995, p. 17.
14. *The Economist,* 'Banker to the Bureaucrats,' September 10, 1994, p. 97.
15. *Financial Times,* 'China Prepares Banks for the 21st Century,' July 4, 1995, p. 6.
16. *South China Morning Post,* 'Reforms Sinking in a Sea of Debt,' April 15, 1995, p. B5.
17. Peter Montagnon, 'Chinese Banks Suffer 20% Bad Loans,' *Financial Times,* October 30, 1995, p.1.
18. Lincoln Kaye, 'Labour Pains,' *Far East Economic Review,* June 16, 1994, pp. 32–3.
19. Foo Choy Peng, 'Central Bank a Long Way Off,' *South China Morning Post,* April 15, 1995, p. B5.
20. *South China Morning Post,* 'Bad News is Good,' April 29, 1995, p. 10.
21. *South China Morning Post,* 'Ratings Drop Halts BOC Issue,' April 22, 1995, p. B1.
22. Dede Nickerson and Foo Choy Peng, 'Outcry Over Downgrading as Banks Defend Record,' *South China Morning Post,* April 22, 1995, p. B2.
23. Christine Chan and Renee Lai, 'CITIC May Face Rating Change,' *South China Morning Post,* April 22, 1995, p. B2.
24. Duncan Hughes, Sean Kennedy, and Foo Choy Peng, 'Top China Banks Hit by Credit Rate Drop,' *South China Morning Post,* April 22, 1995, p. 11.

8 CHINA'S EMERGING CAPITAL MARKET

1. *The Economist,* Survey of Asian Finance, November 12, 1994, p. 9.
2. Paul Schroeder, 'Rebuilding China's Securities Markets,' *The China Business Review,* May–June 1991, pp. 20–1.
3. International Monetary Fund, *International Capital Markets,* September 1994, p. 25.
4. Ibid., p. 26.
5. Mei Xia, Jian Hai Lin, and Philip Grub, *The Reemerging Securities Markets in China,* Quorum Books, 1992, pp. 167, 171.
6. IMF, p. 94.
7. *South China Morning Post,* 'Beijing Plans 15 Futures Markets,' October 15, 1994, p. B1.

8. The 15 exchanges are located in Beijing, Shenzhen, Changchun, Chengdu, Chongqing, Dalian, Shenyang, Suzhou, Tianzin, and Zhengzhou.

9. Geoffrey Crothall, 'China Bonds Set To Grow,' *South China Morning Post,* May 21, 1994, p. B4.

10. Schroeder, 'Rebuilding China's Securities Markets,' p. 20.

11. R. Ramamuriti, 'Why Do Developing Countries Privatize?' *Journal of International Business Studies,* 1992, pp. 225–49.

12. Tony Walker, 'Rough Riding Ahead in China,' *Financial Times,* February 21, 1994, p. 21.

13. IMF, p. 93.

14. China may be somewhat unique, since the shares reserved for foreign investors trade at a discount. *China Economic Review,* 'B-Shares – A Practical Guide,' March 1993, p. 12.

15. *China Business Review,* 'The Allure of B Shares,' January–February 1993, pp. 42–8. *Far Eastern Economic Review,* 'How Not to Profit,' December 1992, pp. 10–11.

16. Foo Choy Peng and Christine Chan, 'Shanghai Exchanges Hostilities', *South China Morning Post,* May 14, 1994, p. B4.

17. Preston M. Torbert, 'Broadening the Scope of Investment,' *The China Business Review,* May–June 1994, p. 48.

18. IMF, p. 132.

19. *Beijing Review,* 'CITIC Issues Bonds in the United States,' August 30–September 5, 1993, p. 25.

20. IMF, p. 98.

21. Nikki Tait, 'First Chinese Flotation on Australian Stock Market,' *Financial Times,* September 29, 1993.

9   STRATEGIC TRADE

1. James T.H. Tsao, *China's Development Strategies and Foreign Trade,* Lexington Books, Lexington, MA, 1987, p. 81.

2. Ibid, p. 86.

3. National income measurements for China must be used with caution. Like other communist countries China excludes services from national income, and this results in an understatement of Chinese per capita income.

4. In 1972 President Nixon made his famous visit to China, leading to the normalization of economic relations with the PRC.

5. Tsao, p. 92.

6. Gregory C. Chow, *The Chinese Economy,* Harper & Row, New York, 1985, p. 290.

7. Ibid., pp. 290–1.

8. A Panagariya, 'What Can We Learn From China's Export Strategy?' *Finance & Development,* June 1995, p. 32.

9. Ibid.

10. This point is emphasized by Tsao, p. 105.

11. Panagariya, p. 33.

12. Ibid., p. 35.

13. Tsao, pp. 64–7.
14. In 1991 agriculture contributed 27 per cent of gross domestic product, whereas industry contributed 42 per cent of gross domestic product.
15. Joshua Mills, 'East China Sea Opened to Oil Exploration,' *New York Times,* November 1, 1993, p. D1. Chevron, Texaco, and two non-US oil companies signed contracts with the Chinese government to undertake exploration in the East China Sea, opening another front in China's search for oil for its booming economy. China is the fifth largest oil producer in the world.
16. *China Daily,* 'Expert Maps Out New Trade Strategy for China,' July 15, 1993, p. 4.
17. *Financial Times,* 'U.S. Fears Growing China Deficit,' October 7, 1995, p. 3; Simon Holberton, 'Beijing Protests Over U.S. Claims of $30 bn Trade Deficit,' *Financial Times,* October 9, 1995, p. 3.
18. The Four Tigers include Singapore, South Korea, Hong Kong, and Taiwan. ASEAN includes Singapore, Thailand, Brunei, Indonesia, Malaysia, and Philippines.
19. Uri Dadush and Dong He, 'China: A New Power in World Trade,' *Finance & Development,* June 1995, p. 36.
20. Ibid.
21. Sean Kennedy, 'Region Set to Overtake U.S.,' *South China Morning Post,* May 6, 1995, p. B8.
22. Shen Wei-Cheng, 'Development and Problems of China's Seaports,' in G. Linke and D. Forbes, *China's Spatial Economy,* Oxford University Press, Hong Kong, 1990, pp. 96–8.
23. *The Economist,* 'An Oil-Fashioned Strike,' July 31, 1993, pp. 32–3.
24. *The Economist,* 'Murdoch's Asian Bet,' July 31, 1993, p. 13.

10   FOREIGN INVESTMENT STRATEGY

1. Two alternative but somewhat different sets of data on investment flows come from the International Monetary Fund (IMF) and World Bank. There are substantial differences between these sources of information due to different definitions of terms and inconsistencies in country coverage.
2. Jonathan R. Woetzel, *China's Economic Opening to the Outside World,* Praeger, New York, 1989, p. 99.
3. Peter Norman, 'World Bank to Raise Lending Commitments,' *Financial Times,* September 20, 1993, p. 4.
4. World Bank, *Annual Report 1993,* p. 194. This represents $9.1 billion, which places China fifth in rank among all borrowers.
5. Ibid., p. 116.
6. Nicholas R. Lardy, *China in the World Economy,* Institute for International Economics, Washington, DC, April 1994, p. 57.
7. *The Nikkei Weekly,* 'Lenders Turning Cautious Toward China, Hong Kong,' September 6, 1993, p. 17.
8. *Beijing Review,* 'CITIC Issues Bonds in the United States,' August 30–September 5, 1993, p. 25.

9. This upgrading was important in permitting sales of bonds to the European market. European fund managers generally require ratings of A-3 or higher. Jennifer Cody, 'China Gains Better Ratings from Moodys,' *Wall Street Journal,* September 13, 1993, p. 93.

10. *Prospectus,* 'China International Trust and Investment Corporation,' dated July 28, 1993, pp. 11–12.

11. Woetzel, pp. 100–2.

12. Woetzel (ibid., p. 102) notes that in 1984 the direct investment stock in Malaysia was 25 per cent of GNP, in Mexico 9 per cent, in Brazil 11 per cent, but in China only 0.8 per cent of gross social product.

13. Roy J. Ruffin, 'The Role of Foreign Investment in the Economic Growth of the Asian and Pacific Region,' *Asian Development Review,* 1993, Vol. II, No. 1, p. 14.

14. Edward K.Y. Chen, 'Foreign Direct Investment in East Asia,' *Asian Development Review,* 1993, Vol. II, No. 1, pp. 36 and 50–1.

15. *Financial Times,* 'Investors Wary About China,' November 26, 1993, p. 6.

16. Chia Siow Yue, 'Foreign Direct Investment in ASEAN Economies,' *Asian Development Review,* 1993, Vol. II, No. 1, p. 86.

17. Philip Kiu, 'Mixed Diagnosis for Mainland Fever,' *Free China Review,* September 1993, pp. 42–3.

18. Gerald Segal, 'Deconstructing Foreign Relations,' in D. Goodman and G. Segal, *China Deconstructs,* Routledge, London, 1994, p. 330.

19. *Fortune,* 'The Overseas Chinese,' October 31, 1994, pp. 91–5.

20. Andrew Tanzer, 'The Bamboo Network,' *Forbes,* July 18, 1994, pp. 137–40.

21. Tony Walker, 'Beijing Urged to Impose Curbs on Coca-Colonisers,' *Financial Times,* March 20, 1994, p. 4.

22. Michiyo Nahamoto, 'NEC to Produce Computers in China,' *Financial Times,* May 11, 1995, p. 5.

23. Michael Skapinker, 'Cadbury to Tempt China with Chocolate,' *Financial Times,* August 3, 1993, p. 15.

24. Bob Hagerty, 'Whirlpool Official Realizes Goal of Tapping into Chinese Market,' *Wall Street Journal,* April 7, 1995, p. B7C.

25. Craig S. Smith, *Wall Street Journal,* March 17, 1995, p. A5A.

26. Simon Davies, 'Japanese Retailer Takes a Surprise Gamble on China,' *Financial Times,* October 5, 1993, p. 22.

27. Sally D. Goll, 'China's Big State Owned Retail Stores Form New Ventures with Foreign Firms,' *Wall Street Journal,* March 13, 1995, p. A11C.

28. Tony Walker and Kevin Done, 'Chinese Roads Paved with Gold,' *Financial Times,* November 23, 1994, p. 21.

29. Haig Simonian, 'VW Defends its Supremacy in China,' *Financial Times,* May 2, 1995, p. 7.

30. Ibid.

31. Lynne Curry, 'Foreigners Make Inroads into China,' *Financial Times,* June 5, 1993, p. 14.

32. World Bank, *World Development Report 1994,* p. 2.

33. Frank Leeming, *The Changing Geography of China,* Blackwell, Oxford, 1993, p. 27.

34. Alexa C. Lam, 'Infrastructure Investment Tips,' *The China Business Review,* September–October 1994, p. 34.

35. *Business Week,* 'Building the New Asia,' November 28, 1994, p. 66.
36. Ibid., p. 68.
37. Lam, pp. 45–6.
38. Woetzel, p. 105.
39. *Prospectus,* 'China International Trust and Investment Corporation,' p. 13.
40. *Financial Times,* 'China Merchants Lifts HK Bank Stake,' July 17, 1993, p. 12.
41. Stanley Reed, 'Greater China Could be the Biggest Tiger of All,' *Business Week,* September 28, 1993, p. 58.
42. Remark attributed to A. Doak Barnett, professor emeritus at Johns Hopkins University. Dan Corditz and Richard Meyer, 'Inside China Today,' *Financial World,* December 8, 1992, pp. 36–7.
43. Dusty Clayton, 'Survey Shows Investors Remain Bullish Despite Skills Shortage,' *South China Morning Post,* June 10, 1995, p. B5.
44. Kathy Chen, 'China Aims to Steer Foreign Investment by Giving Certain Industries Priority,' *Wall Street Journal,* March 30, 1995, p. A10.
45. Tony Walker, 'China to Scrap Some Investment Incentives,' *Financial Times,* March 17, 1995, p. 5.
46. Tony Walker, 'Debt Fears Deter Investment in China,' *Financial Times,* November 23, 1994, p. 22.
47. Letter from Alberto J. Mora, 'Not a Good Sign of China's Legal Intent,' *Financial Times,* March 6, 1995, p. 14.
48. Erika Platte, 'China's Foreign Debt,' *Pacific Affairs,* Summer 1993, pp. 481–95.

11   CHINA AND THE WORLD

1. *The Economist,* 'Back to the Future,' January 8, 1994, p. 21.
2. In December 1993 China's prime minister stated that if the US called for economic sanctions to prevent North Korea acquiring nuclear weapons, China would block the use of sanctions. *The Economist,* p. 22.
3. Seth Faison, 'Beijing Sees U.S. Moves as Plot to Thwart China,' *New York Times,* August 1, 1995, p. A2.
4. *The Economist,* 'Seed of Subversion,' May 28, 1994, p. 32.
5. Nancy Dunne, 'China Must Move Further on Rights,' *Financial Times,* April 12, 1994, p. 5.
6. Patrick E. Tyler, 'Chinese Crack Down: Challenge is Still Prohibited,' *New York Times,* March 7, 1994, p. A8.
7. Patrick E. Tyler, 'Discontent Mounts in China, Shaking the Leaders,' *New York Times,* April 10, 1994, p. 3.
8. Patrick E. Tyler, 'In the Twilight of Deng, China's Rising Stars Jostle,' *New York Times,* August 21, 1994, p. 3.
9. Tony Walker, 'Great Reformer Near to His Meeting with Karl Marx,' *Financial Times,* August 22, 1994, p. 4.
10. Stephen Robert, 'In China Let Free Markets Aid Liberty,' *New York Times,* April 24, 1994, p. 11.

11. Patrick E. Tyler, 'A Dissident Finds the Political Prospects Bleak,' *New York Times,* April 16, 1994, p. 4.
12. Tony Walker, 'Air of Stability Belies Leader's Nervousness,' *Financial Times,* June 4, 1994, p. 3.
13. Tony Walker, 'Making Money Out of Mao,' *Financial Times,* December 24, 1993, p. 6.
14. Tony Walker, 'Dissidents Feel Lashes of Nervous Leadership,' *Financial Times,* April 11, 1994, p. 6.
15. Tony Walker, 'China Political Repression Increases,' *Financial Times,* February 21, 1994, p. 5.
16. Patrick E. Tyler, 'China Allows a Prominent Dissident to Leave,' *New York Times,* May 11, 1994, p. A12.
17. *The Economist,* 'Soldiering Pays,' July 9, 1994, p. 39.
18. Tony Walker and Shi Junbao, 'Barbarians at the Great Wall,' *Financial Times,* August 20, 1994, p. 9.
19. Tony Walker, 'Ruling Party Aims to Tighten Grip on China,' *Financial Times,* September 29, 1994, p. 16.
20. Patrick E. Tyler, 'In U.S. Demand, China Sees Risk to its Stability,' *New York Times,* May 19, 1994, p. 1.
21. This was based on Kremlin intervention in the Horn of Africa, support for Vietnam intrusion in Cambodia, and refusal to make deep cuts in strategic arms. Harry Harding, *The US and China Since 1972,* Brookings, Washington, 1992, p. 67.
22. Harding, p. 89.
23. Ibid., p. 120.
24. Problems of doing business in China were exemplified by the difficulties American Motors Corp. encountered with its investment in Beijing Jeep Corp. These were widely discussed in the American press in 1986 and later.
25. Harding, p. 235.
26. Willy Wo-Lap Lam, 'Army May Expand on Spratlys,' *South China Morning Post,* August 6, 1994, p. 7.
27. Philip Shenon, 'China Sends Warships to Vietnam Oil Site,' *New York Times,* July 21, 1994, p. A17.
28. Tony Walker, 'Hint of Progress on Spratlys,' *Financial Times,* July 31, 1995, p. 3.
29. Tony Walker, 'Saudis in Oil Supply Talks with China,' *Financial Times,* May 17, 1994, p. 8.
30. *The Economist,* 'Trouble on Oily Waters,' July 23, 1994, p. 33.
31. Michael Vatikiotis and Michael Westlake, 'Gunboat Diplomacy,' *Far Eastern Economic Review,* June 16, 1994, p. 28.
32. *Far Eastern Economic Review,* 'Hot Pursuit,' June 16, 1994, p. 26.
33. Charles Smith, 'Abrupt Change,' *Far Eastern Economic Review,* June 16, 1994, p. 28.
34. Simon Beck, 'Beijing Spends U.S. $140b. on Arms,' *South China Morning Post,* June 10, 1995, p. 1.
35. Simon Holberton, 'China May be Third in Defense Spending,' *Financial Times,* July 13, 1994, p. 6. *The Economist,* 'Soldiering Pays,' February 9, 1994, p. 39.

36. Patrick E. Tyler, 'As China Upgrades Its Nuclear Arsenal, it Debates Need for Guns vs Butter,' *New York Times,* October 26, 1994, p. A10.
37. Tony Walker, 'China Defiant After Second Nuclear Test,' *Financial Times,* October 8, 1994, p. 3.
38. *The Economist,* 'China's New Model Army,' June 11, 1994, p. 29.
39. Steven A. Holmes, 'China Denies Violating Pact by Selling Arms to Pakistan,' *New York Times,* July 26, 1993, p. A2.
40. Elaine Sciolino, 'U.S. May Threaten China with Sanctions for Reported Arms Sales,' *New York Times,* July 20, 1993, p. 3.
41. Kevin Fedarko, 'Confounded by the Chinese Puzzle,' *Time,* April 25, 1994, p. 39.
42. Elaine Sciolino, 'U.S. and Chinese Reach Agreement on Missile Export,' *New York Times,* October 5, 1994, p. A1.
43. Simon Holberton and Tony Walker, 'The Generals Big Business Offensive,' *Financial Times,* November 28, 1994, p. 13.
44. Patrick E. Tyler, 'Chinese Military's Business Empire Puts Profits into Commerce, Not Arms,' *New York Times,* May 24, 1994. p. A6.
45. *Financial Times,* 'PLA Seeks Cash for its Ploughshares,' July 9, 1993, p. 4.
46. Elizabeth Economy, 'China's Power to Harm the Planet,' *New York Times,* September 9, 1995, p. 19.
47. Paul Lewis, 'Export Agency Likely to Deny China Dam Aid,' *New York Times,* October 14, 1995, pp. 1 and 34.
48. Audrey R. Topping, 'Ecological Roulette: Damming the Yangtze,' *Foreign Affairs,* September–October 1995, pp. 139–40.

Index

223